LANGUAGE TEACHING: NEW INSIGHTS FOR THE LANGUAGE TEACHER

Edited by
Christopher Ward
and
Willy Renandya

Anthology Series 40
Published by
SEAMEO Regional Language Centre

Copyright © 1999
SEAMEO Regional Language Centre
30 Orange Grove Road
Singapore 258352
Republic of Singapore

ISBN   9971-74-065-6
ISSN   0129-8895

CONTENTS

Foreword   i

Introduction   ii

Section I: Focus on the Teacher

Preparing for Language Teaching: A Teacher Education Perspective   1
    S. Gopinathan

Teacher Supervision: The Key to Professional Development   13
    John Joseph Moran

Changing Teaching: Insights into Individual Development
in the Context of Schools   28
    Donald Freeman

Section II: Language Teaching and Learning

Teaching is at Most Hoping for the Best   48
    N.S. Prabhu

Perspectives on EAP Oral Communication Instruction:
Beliefs, Principles and Instructional Models   58
    Joan Morley

Grammar as a Metasemiotic Tool in Child Literacy Development   89
    Geoff Williams

Integrating Language and Content Teaching
through Collaborative Tasks   125
    Merrill Swain

Pragmatics and English Language Teaching   148
    Jenny Thomas

Pragmatics and Language Teaching Revisited:
Some Implications for the Teacher   180
   Asim Gunarwan

Teaching English as an International Language in Japan   197
   Nobuyuki Honna

Language Learning Strategies: A Malaysian Perspective   221
   Florence G. Kayad

Learner Autonomy and the Language Teacher   241
   David Crabbe

Text and Task: Authenticity in Language Learning   259
   Andrea H. Peñaflorida

Educational Innovations in the Thai National English Textbooks
for Primary Schools: "On the Springboard"   271
   Chaleosri Pibulchol

Section III: Computers and Language Learning

Computer-Assisted Language Learning:
What Teachers Need to Know   278
   Michael Levy

Computer-Imaginative Tools for the Design of Digital
Learning Environments   295
   Martin A. Siegel

FOREWORD

This anthology contains sixteen papers that were presented at the annual RELC Seminar on "*Language Teaching: New Insights For The Language Teacher*" held from 20 to 22 April 1998 and attended by more than 450 participants from 21 countries. A total of 120 papers and 17 workshops were presented in the Seminar. The papers in this collection have been selected to represent a wide range of insights from both theoretical and practical standpoints.

RELC takes pride in hosting our annual seminar, a forum where language teachers, teacher educators, administrators and researchers critically examine new developments in language education, explore emerging theories of language and language learning, and share new insights and practical classroom experiences. The papers in this anthology should be of great interest to language educators in the region and beyond. On behalf of RELC, it is my privilege to commend this anthology to those with a keen interest in how to make our language classrooms a better place for language learning.

"Dedication to Language Teacher Education"

Goh Chi Lan (Mrs)
Director
SEAMEO Regional Language Centre
Singapore
19 May 1999

INTRODUCTION

The sixteen papers in this anthology have been selected to represent a cross-section of both theory and practical insights from the 1998 RELC Regional Seminar on *"Language Teaching: New Insights For The Language Teacher"*. We felt that these papers have to a large extent reflected the main aims of the seminar, i.e., (1) to examine the changing role of teachers as they seek to prepare themselves for the challenges of a fast-changing world, and (2) to document current trends, innovations, projects, and research findings in language education that have a bearing on successful language teaching.

The papers in this anthology have been grouped into three sections. Section 1, *Focus on the Teacher*, deals with theoretical issues surrounding teacher preparation programmes and teacher development. Section 2, *Language Teaching and Learning*, represents a wide range of issues, both theoretical and practical, related to teaching and learning. Section 3, *Computers in Language Education,* examines key issues and practical considerations in the application of computers in language teaching and learning. Below are brief summaries of each paper.

Section 1: Focus on the Teacher

In his paper, **S. Gopinathan** begins by exploring the social, linguistic, educational and professional dimensions of language teaching and learning in Singapore. According to Gopinathan, Singapore can claim success in its national language policy. One indicator of this is that school leavers are effectively bilingual and biliterate: they are proficient users of their mother tongues and English. He cautions, however, that language educators should not be complacent. The era of globalisation calls greater attention to what have been called *critical literacy* and *cultural literacy*. These types of literacy need to be addressed in the language curriculum of tomorrow. To meet the challenges of developing critical and cultural literacy in the language learners, traditional teacher preparation programme need to be carefully reconceptualised and redefined.

ii

John J. Moran points out that despite the crucial role teacher supervision plays in the teacher preparation programme, it is an area that has not been given enough attention. He examines the nature of teacher supervision in detail, highlighting the complexity involved in supervision, and stressing the inextricable connection between teacher supervision and the teacher's professional development. For it to be carried out properly and effectively, Moran suggests that teacher supervision be given more prominence in pre- or in-service teacher development programmes.

Donald Freeman discusses the relationship between the processes of change and the socio-cultural environments. He argues that change is so intricately related to its environments that it is not productive to study change without examining the contexts in which it is situated. To illustrate how change is related to its environments, three images of the change process are discussed in the paper – change as substitution, change as integration, and change through infusion and transformation. It is the third type of change, also known as systemic change, which Freeman believes to be the most robust in education.

Section 2: Language Teaching and Learning

In his paper, **N.S. Prabhu** seeks to clarify the relationship between teaching and learning. Prabhu argues that teaching and learning are two separate entities. Teaching takes place after careful planning on the part of the teacher; learning, on the other hand, occurs without conscious effort on the part of the learner. In other words, teaching is intentional while learning is incidental. Because teaching and learning possess radically different characteristics, it is not surprising that what learners learn may not be the same as what teachers try to teach. Prabhu, however, is quick to point out that teaching can indeed result in learning, and that one form of teaching can produce more learning than another. He stresses that we need to explore different ways of organising teaching that allow greater learning to take place.

A good number of ESL learners suffer from poor intelligibility in speech patterns, which, more often than not, brings about grave disadvantages in a whole range of academic, vocational, and social contexts. One of the most important reasons for this lack of speech competence, according to **Joan Morley**, is that traditional language teaching programmes have typically placed greater emphasis on literacy skills than oral skills, often allocating limited time for the teaching of the latter. In addition, the traditional approach to speech instruction has been inadequate to address the oral communicative goals of the learners. In the paper, Morley discusses recent developments in speech instruction with the aim of identifying an instructional model that conforms to what is currently known about the nature of language and language learning, examines beliefs and principles about the teaching of oral skills, outlines concrete guidelines for programme development, and offers suggestions on the training of English teachers for the next millennium.

Grammar has always had a central role in language education. Different approaches to grammar instruction have been proposed, tried out, discarded, and later on reintroduced in language curricula. **Geoff Williams** points out that very often the decision to introduce a new model of grammar instruction has been based on community interest, rather than on an informed understanding of the nature of language and language learning. Drawing on the work of Halliday and Vygotsky, Williams describes his research study that examines the relationship between children's understanding of grammatical concepts and their ability to use these concepts in literacy work. Preliminary findings of his research indicate that this kind of inquiry holds a lot of promise for the articulation of a more principled approach to grammar instruction.

In language teaching, the notion of tasks refers to communicative activities in which learners' attention is primarily focused on meaning rather than on form. Meaning-focused tasks, **Merrill Swain** claims, are not sufficient to help learners develop native-like proficiency. Her extensive research in the French immersion classes in Canada has demonstrated quite clearly that while immersion students are capable of reaching quite a high degree of communicative competence, their speech is characterised by non-target-like features in syntax and discourse patterns. To address this issue, Swain suggests that teachers design tasks that aid learners focus their attention equally on meaning and form. One such task is known as dictogloss, a procedure which encourages learners to pay attention and reflect on their own language output. A large part of Swain's paper is devoted to describing her research on how dictogloss can be employed to enhance learners' syntactic development.

Pragmatics is a relatively young discipline within linguistics. It studies language use as it occurs in context. The next two papers by **Jenny Thomas** and **Asim Gunarwan** look at a number of topics covered by pragmatics with a view to identifying their relevance to language teaching. Two broad areas of pragmatics can be identified: pragmalinguistics and sociopragmatics. The former deals with how an utterance is formed and interpreted while the latter is concerned with the effect an utterance may have on the listener. Thomas and Gunarwan state that as most learners do not automatically acquire pragmatic rules of the target language and that failure to observe appropriate pragmatic norms can lead to serious social consequences, language teachers should consciously and systematically incorporate the teaching of pragmatic rules in their language class.

Although English is taught as a foreign language in Japan, its importance within the education system cannot be underestimated. Virtually all secondary school students are required to study English for six years, three years in junior high school and another three in senior high school. According to **Nobuyuki Honna**, one of the reasons for the lack of success in ELT in Japan is that the goal of the English language teaching in Japan is too idealistic – students are expected to acquire a native-like proficiency in English. Not only is this goal unrealistic, it also ignores the fact that English is now seen as an international language, a language that is widely used for multinational and multicultural communication. Honna suggests that the goal of ELT in Japan should be to help learners develop international intelligibility rather than native-like competence. One of the consequences of this view is that teachers and students should accept Japanese English as a legitimate variety.

Florence Kayad reports on a study which examines the relationship between ESL proficiency level and strategy use in the Malaysian context. Data for her study primarily come from her ESL learners' responses to a language learning survey questionnaire originally developed by Rebecca Oxford. Overall, the results show that strategy use does not seem to be related to L2 proficiency. In terms of amount and frequency of strategy use, there is only a small difference between the proficient and the less proficient learners. A more detailed analysis, however, indicates that the more proficient learners report using cognitive strategies more often than the less proficient students. On the other hand, the less proficient group report employing affective strategies more than the more proficient learners. Kayad concludes her paper by offering some possible implications of her findings for L2 teaching in Malaysia.

David Crabbe explores the notion of learner autonomy which in recent years has gained a lot of attention in language education. Three key questions that relate to the concept of learner autonomy to the changing roles of teachers are addressed in the paper. These are: (1) What is the relevance of learner autonomy to language teachers? (2) How can language curricula accommodate learner autonomy as one of their essential learning goals? What needs to be done to enhance the development of learner autonomy? (3) What is the role of the language teacher in fostering learner autonomy in the classroom.

Andrea H. Peñaflorida explores the notions of text and task, and how they relate to the notion of authenticity. Texts and tasks are important components in language learning; but in order for them to produce the most learning benefits, they have to be authentic. Authentic texts and tasks expose learners to the kind of language use that they will encounter in real life. This type of learning material tends to be more interesting and challenging, two crucial components which are often lacking in many language programme. In her paper, Peñaflorida describes how authentic texts and tasks can be designed to give learners varied opportunities to engage in language learning activities which are interactive, learner-friendly, and highly motivating.

Teaching materials are a key component in most language programme. Textbooks, in particular, play crucial roles in language teaching. They serve as a source of classroom activities, a source for organising and sequencing language teaching, and a support for less experienced teachers, etc. According to **Chaleosri Pibulchol**, the new English textbook for primary schools in Thailand "On The Springboard" was written to serve these purposes. The new textbook provides learners with language input and activities that will enable them to use English for communicative purposes. More importantly, it gives teachers clear guidelines on how to carry out the lessons using effective instructional techniques, and to take on a more learner-centred approach to teaching.

Section 3: Computers and Language Education

Computer-Assisted Language Learning (CALL) has been around for quite some time. Quite a number of language educators have embraced the idea of integrating computers in language education. In many developed countries, schools are aggressively adopting this new technology in a big way. **Michael Levy** claims that proponents of CALL often overlook the implications of the new technological options for language teachers. In order to obtain the maximum benefits of CALL, the needs of the teachers must be recognised and properly supported. Levy further argues that although technical knowledge is essential, language teachers need to develop an understanding of the theoretical framework within which CALL can operate successfully. A deeper understanding of CALL can result in better learning, and at the same time can significantly affect the way language teachers approach the task of teaching.

The last paper by **Martin Siegel** discusses a new breed of computer-based learning that makes heavy use of the capability of the internet. This new web-based instructional paradigm has been called the "Digital Learning Environment" (DLE), whose features are specifically designed to "facilitate big concept, multi-disciplinary learning, and the development of authentic, cooperative problem-solving strategies." Siegel maintains that DLE is a powerful learning tool whose potential is limited only by our imagination and creativity. Although work on DLE has focused mainly on content subject areas (e.g., history), the applicability of this instructional model for language education is worth exploring.

Section I : Focus on the Teacher

Preparing for Language Teaching: A Teacher Education Perspective
S. Gopinathan

Teacher Supervision: The Key to Professional Development
John Joseph Moran

**Changing Teaching: Insights into Individual Development
in the Context of Schools**
Donald Freeman

PREPARING FOR LANGUAGE TEACHING: A TEACHER EDUCATION PERSPECTIVE

S. Gopinathan

I wish to begin my paper with the observation that language learning, and therefore language teaching, does not occur in a vacuum; the larger context is the society within which the language or languages are to be learnt and used; the more restricted context is the school system – which even if we consider it the most important site for language learning, is but one of many sites – and indeed, since the school is embedded in the society which sustains it, it often mirrors the features, aims and tensions of the larger society.

How should we think of this context? It is commonplace to describe Singapore as a developing plural society – which puts us together with countries like Sri Lanka, Cyprus and Fiji. I would like to suggest however that we consider instead Switzerland as a more suitable comparison. With a per capita income of S$25,000, large surpluses, a world class urban infrastructure of schools, universities, hospitals, housing and transportation network, strong social and community organizations like the judiciary and the bureaucracy, we are a developed nation in all but name. It is true that this is not paradise – not yet anyway, that ethnic and religious faultlines do exist but even here government management is assured and consistent. In a context of ethnic pluralism we have ethnic and linguistic peace. Language issues are no longer as divisive as they once were, and the fundamentals of policy, of English-knowing bilingualism are settled. Over the last three decades literacy and biliteracy levels have arisen, and a bilingual, principally Chinese-English speaking elite has been created. These are extraordinary achievements in little over three decades.

Singapore has a stable and well-resourced education system, emphasising high academic achievement and one that is well regarded by parents. Recent reform changes announced by the government are intended to improve on the strong fundamentals, not rescue a discredited system.

An important point to bear in mind is that considerable effort and political acumen were needed to bring this about. Singapore, in the fifties

1

and sixties, was riven by political and linguistic tensions, had to cope with a divided school system, alienation and hostility on the part of the non-English educated. The *All-Party Report on Chinese Education* in 1956 proposed trilingualism as a way of dealing with language diversity. The Chinese-medium Nanyang University was founded the same year to provide tertiary education opportunities to the Chinese educated not available at the English-medium University of Malaya in Singapore. Eventually, the formulae of *One National Language, Four Official Languages* was settled upon and in 1965 schooling became compulsorily bilingual. English was to be studied for its economic utility and a second language, Mandarin Chinese, Malay, Tamil, to be studied for rooting individuals in their traditional cultures which were seen as sources of important core values. The government has also sought to change and influence home and community language environments through such campaigns as the *Speak Mandarin* campaign.

It is important to note that in the schools language examinations are high stakes examinations for performance in them determines positions in the various language streams that characterize primary and secondary schooling in Singapore. Yet another important facet of the school language learning environment is terminology – English is the first language, the others are second languages, even though they are to be regarded as carriers of core values. The government is committed not just to minimum standards in language, but to produce equilinguals where pupil ability warrants it. Finally, though language learning is a device to unify the ethnic groups, it is also the case that second language learning takes place in classrooms segregated by ethnicity; this, I believe, has very important consequences for the wider purposes of language learning, consequences which I believe have not been sufficiently addressed.

The goals of language teaching in Singapore then can be said to produce school leavers who are bilingual and biliterate, able to communicate in English in an internationally intelligible way, appreciate and treasure the values embedded in the mother tongue cultures and able to empathise with the languages and culture of Singapore's ethnic groups. These are challenges then that those involved in teacher preparation must face.

Let us now consider the issues in teacher preparation. Does one need to learn to teach in order to teach others? And, if so, how does one learn to teach? – upon that answer is built structures of teacher education. And if one looks at the variety of teacher education models available within countries and in different countries, the answer is obviously not simple; – indeed, there is probably greater consensus about how doctors or engineers should be trained than there is about teacher preparation. In part the complexity arises from how one understands the concept, *teaching*. At the risk of over-simplification, one could say that three principal approaches have been to regard it as:

1. residing in behaviour, which leads to a bias towards skill training,
2. cognition, which emphasises a more theory to practice approach or
3. an interpretative approach which emphasises the importance of a teacher having sufficient knowledge and skills to be able to understand how contexts call for different strategies, to be able to critically consider and improve upon practice.

If we take a historical view, training for teaching was not considered essential. We note that early teacher preparation models were based on the notion of teaching as a craft (thus learned through apprenticeship) and not requiring theoretical and evidence-based knowledge. Indeed, even subject mastery was not considered essential and today in some countries, some teachers have only 10-12 years of general education. In the UK, it is still possible for good Oxbridge graduates to land teaching jobs at elite private schools without undergoing teacher preparation. A variant of this view is that teaching younger pupils does not require rigorous academic preparation; what is needed, it is argued, is empathy, skills in motivating pupils and patience!

In the mid-sixties teacher education, especially in the UK, sought respectability within higher education and there was a brief blossoming of the education disciplines – psychology of education, history, philosophy, sociology of education; this was the period when teacher training became overly theoretical and abstract. This in turn gave way in the eighties in the UK and US to a profound scepticism that university based programmes were the best way to train teachers. Both Ronald Reagan in the US and Margaret Thatcher in the UK were severely critical of the teaching profession, blaming the failures of the school system on poor teaching. Their response took two forms. In the UK, preparation for teaching was made more school-based and governmental views became more prescriptive and in one sense, traditional i.e. a reemphasis on phonics in reading instruction. There was a turning away from understanding, of emphasis on the reforming power of education to an emphasis on basics. In the US, there has been traditionally less room for government involvement in education but a slew of independent commission reports detailed shortcomings in teacher preparation – one major strategy was the concept of the Professional Development Schools (PDS). More recently, in Canada much attention has been paid to how notions of empowerment and teacher professionalism can be realised in a context of major structural and curricular change in schooling. Fullan (1993) and Hargreaves (1994) have argued for a greater and more genuine partnership between campus based faculty and experienced practitioners; in my view it is the partnership model that holds most promise.

Typically, in developing programme structures in teacher education we consider *values and teacher attributes*, the *knowledge base*, *skills or competencies*, and *outcomes*. It is becoming increasingly clear that in a time of major socio-economic change such as Singapore is experiencing, it is important to be clear about the outcomes of schooling that teaching is intended to bring about. The Ministry of Education statement of the *Desired Outcomes of Education* well reflects this concern. However, even as we assert the importance of qualities those aspiring to teach should possess, i.e. dedication, empathy and patience, these attributes are given short shrift in a time of scarcity for recruits into teaching. Can teacher education programmes instill these qualities or can they only seek to awaken students to the need to examine their own views and conceptions about purposes and processes in teaching? There is strong evidence that beliefs held about teaching, rooted as they are in the trainee's own experience of schooling are hard to change; but it is not impossible, otherwise, teacher training will be a futile exercise. It is important to consider values as well. Language learning is empowering as knowledge and competence in language(s) enriches and extends innate ability. It seems

4

to me that this view is especially pertinent to language teaching for such teaching gives students' voice and the facility for expression.

The knowledge base of teaching can be thought of in terms of three categories, a) disciplinary or subject matter knowledge, b) pedagogic content knowledge and c) general pedagogic knowledge. Mastery of *disciplinary knowledge* is very important, especially as one seeks, in the best of teaching, to transform the subject matter in a way that will enable pupils to learn. This ability to transform is crucial when disciplinary knowledge needs to be represented to pupils. Increasingly, it has become evident that in the context of teacher preparation appropriate disciplinary knowledge is more important in teaching than general disciplinary knowledge. An emphasis on educational linguistics, for instance, would be crucial for those intending to teach. *Pedagogical content knowledge* is deep knowledge of subject syllabus and curriculum materials, knowledge of methods and strategies and their appropriate use, subject learning goals and assessment strategies. Linked to disciplinary knowledge, pedagogic content knowledge leads to an ability to represent the subject. Shulman (1991) called pedagogic content knowledge the missing paradigm (variable) in teacher education research. It is more broad-based and integrated than methods. Grossman (1990) has produced evidence to show that such knowledge builds capacity to transform subject knowledge in a way that facilitates student learning. *General pedagogic knowledge* is knowledge and beliefs about learner characteristics, education policies, classroom management strategies, examination structures, etc, much of which can be taught in school rather than campus contexts.

Within the skills category would come, for instance, competencies to prepare lesson plans, grouping and whole class teaching skills, questioning strategies, and use of AV media equipment. Even in this domain recent research (Richards, 1990) has indicated the importance of teacher understanding to enable judicious choice in the use of these skills – it is important not just to know how to ask questions but when, with what level of difficulty, to whom, how paced and so on.

What many models of teacher education lack, even those that emphasise an interpretative approach is explicit connections to *'communities of practice'* in the schools; teaching practice, for instance, does provide useful practice opportunities, but in practice, constraints of time and poor faculty-cooperating teacher links result in the practicum being less productive than it should be for teacher trainees. More significantly, what is needed is provision for systematic induction, by sympathetic mentors both during and after initial training. The wealth of context bound experiences that expert practitioners in the schools possess is valuable both during the practicum and the induction; no matter how sympathetic campus based faculty are to good classroom practice, they cannot be the mentors in such practice; the richness, the variety and the constraints, these only the experienced practitioner can share with the novice teacher. Campus based programmes need to tap into this expertise in a systematic and collaborative way; too often faculty have tended to see practitioners at best as conservative and at worst obstructionist. Such collaboration can benefit not only the trainee, the novice, but also help increase the professionalism of teachers for it provides an opportunity for practitioners to reflect, to codify their knowledge and *'grounded theory'* and to hone skills of explanation and demonstration. Such collaboration can also provide campus-based faculty with valuable insights about classroom and school processes. However, while mentoring is to be valued, not all master teachers can mentor, can represent and explain their skill and can both support and challenge their mentees in a way that promotes growth. Mentors, in addition, need to guard against replication of their practice and provide opportunities for the mentee to fashion his own style.

These aspects which constitute the building blocks of any teacher preparation programme can of course be organized in a number of ways. I shall take a number of aspects to illustrate the decisions to be made. What entry (academic qualifications) should trainees have? In most developed countries, teaching is an all graduate profession – in Singapore, the bulk of primary teachers are non-graduates, entering National Institute of Education programmes with twelve years of education. More recently, polytechnic graduates have entered teacher education programmes. It is possible to argue that teacher education should be considered a value-added profession, that training can overcome initial limitations. However, if teaching is about bringing about learning in others, it would be prudent to ensure that sufficient academic attainment is a vital part of entry qualifications.

Let me quote a paragraph from Shulman (1991).

It is one thing to know the subject matter in a flexible and eclectic way; it is yet another thing to develop the capacity to transform and represent those understandings for teaching purposes. The teacher should be someone who doesn't merely know one discipline; a teacher should know how to think about a discipline pedagogically, how to look at a text in a flexible, multiply-represented way. ...the more you know about the learning and teaching of particular content areas, the more you know about the most likely preconceptions and misconceptions and become capable of anticipating and forestalling them.

Related to years of general education is the adequacy of academic preparation. The less the number of years of general education the less likely that entrants have an adequate grasp of disciplinary knowledge; yet that is vital in making others learn the discipline. If teacher education institutions have to teach academic content, then it is important to decide how much relation such content should have with the content of school subjects. Related to this is the duration specified for the programme; sometimes in a two year programme too much is attempted, and this is often compounded by a lack of clarity about what knowledge and skills beginning teachers should possess.

Let me turn finally to what our present understandings about educational outcomes, particularly in the language classroom, and our understandings of the value and structure of teacher education, say to the issues confronting language teaching in Singapore's classrooms.

The first point that needs to be made is that, by most conventional measures of success in language learning, Singapore can claim success. There is a large measure of acceptance of the policy of bilingual education and literacy levels in English have arisen thus enabling more Singaporeans to participate in the benefits from globalisation. Literacy levels have also risen in the mother tongues and there is certainly evidence of much wider use of Mandarin; media consumption in the two languages has risen and indeed there is some evidence of creative activity flourishing in all four official languages. That said it must also be noted that there is wide acceptance that the curricular costs of emphasising bilingual education is high, that those not endowed with linguistic ability struggle in school and are over-dosed with tuition and that standards, at least in English oral and written communication, have declined. Finally, we need to note that earlier rationalisations about the respective domains for English and the mother tongue have almost completely broken down. Very few will accept that English is a neutral language, that it can be learnt purely as a tool, that it has no cultural relevance to us and that the mother tongues have only cultural not economic relevance. Globalisation is both a cultural as well as an economic phenomenon, we are citizens of a more and more English dominant world and the language is a carrier of culture, norms and ideals. If East Asia recovers, Mandarin Chinese will have greater cultural resonance but only because East Asia has economic strength.

In my view, two principal problems face us in the English language classroom. I see the present as a time of increased expectations in Singaporean's use of English due to globalisation and the economic opportunities it brings, a time of curricular upheaval which calls for a greater attention to what has been termed *'critical literacy'* and the ever important need to strengthen *'cultural literacy'* so that Singapore's multiethnic fabric can be strengthened.

Too much of language teaching in Singapore's classrooms is an exercise in content mastery. There is a proliferation of language learning materials, which overwhelms the teacher – and the parent. Evenings are spent with worksheets to be completed, spelling lists to be memorised, comprehension texts to be mastered, compositions to be written from picture sequences. Practice never seems to end. Some primary children are sent to creative writing classes, which produce yet more worksheets to be completed. Faced with a mass of work to be marked, teachers routinise their strategies and are less sensitive than they might be to emergent literacy's both critical and creative needs. What the curriculum reform promises is a taking apart of established practice – dare we *'Seize the Day'*?

The fundamental premise of the new curriculum is that Singapore's school leavers must become better *learners*, *creators* and *communicators*. True, the three must be built upon a fundamental mastery of the English language but equally important will be the school leavers' capacity to use English flexibly, creatively as a tool, and as a means to communicate effectively. To do that pupils must see English as invested with power to alter their lives, to extend and shape their dreams, to think with the language. To do this requires teachers to model appropriate language use and learning behaviours themselves and to create open and interactive classroom cultures. My concern is that we are not getting suitably qualified entrants into language teaching. As Shulman (1991) and Saravanan & Gupta (1997) have shown, those who have neither competence nor confidence in the subject cannot represent the subject in a way that invites learning and creative use. Innovative approaches like Pupil Experience which forces students to confront early on the difficulties learners face (Skuja, 1990), journal keeping, remedial grammar modules cannot be expected by themselves to solve the problems. What is now needed, I firmly believe, is greater use of practitioner expertise in post initial training situations to devise the new strategies required; a renewed in-service thrust is needed to make the schools the learning zones for the new literacy. That it is possible to change the language classroom for the better is found in accounts of how practice changed with the introduction of the Reading and English Acquisition Programme (REAP) in the mid-eighties (Cheah, 1997).

A second major issue is *'cultural literacy'*. It is somewhat paradoxical that we need to stress this in multi-ethnic Singapore, where multiculturalism is proclaimed a pillar of the state, where the very rationale for bilingual education is stated to be, through the mother tongue, to strengthen and enrich cultural roots. However, in the implementation of this policy, we have wandered into the dead-end, culturally speaking, of ethnically segregated classrooms and schools; even our teachers unions are language based. How are we to square the circle when with English as the main medium of instruction, we ignore the rich possibilities for cultural learning by insisting that it be learnt as a linguistic tool, for assessing economic not cultural resources? The reality is that English cannot and is not being so contained. What we have to do is explicitly acknowledge that in Cheah's (1996) words classrooms are sites for *"cultural border crossings"*, sites for culture creating and culture sharing. A view of curriculum as content has meant that even in history, geography, social studies we have taught cultural information neutrally. The English language teacher is in a unique position to access these resources for culturally meaningful language learning. I believe NIE has a greater responsibility in this regard; we need to share the insights we have of learning and teaching English with colleagues in the Chinese, Malay and Tamil units. We need to draw more explicitly upon the students' own experiences in learning and mastering two languages. We need to transform our own classrooms and be more adept ourselves at cultural negotiation and dialogue.

It is my belief that we stand on the threshold of many important changes in Singapore's education system and especially with regard to language teaching. The new curriculum innovations promise much about the remaking of practice. We know that classroom cultures can be changed for the better as happened when REAP was introduced. New globalisation pressures make creative and skilful use of language vital for individual and group mobility providing incentive and motivation for language learning. A robust teacher preparation programme allied to strong affiliations with experienced practitioners provides the best guarantee that the promise and challenges of both critical and cultural literacy can be successfully met.

References

Calderhead, J. (ed.) 1988. *Teachers Professional Learning*. London: The Falmer Press.

Cheah, Yin Mee. 1996. Language Learning or Culture Learning: English Literacy lessons in a Singapore Classroom. *The Language-Culture Connection*. ed. by J. E. James. Singapore: SEAMEO Regional Language Centre.

Cheah, Yin Mee. 1997. Shaping the Classrooms of Tomorrow: Lessons from the Past. *Education in Singapore: A Book of Readings*. ed. by Jason Tan, S. Gopinathan & Ho Wah Kam. Singapore: Prentice Hall.

Freeman, D. & Richards, J. C. (eds.) 1996. *Teacher Learning in Language Teaching*. Cambridge: Cambridge University Press.

Freeman, D. 1989. Teacher training, development and decision making. A model of teaching and related strategies for language teacher education. *TESOL Quarterly*. 23,1. 27-45.

Freeman, D. & Richards, J.C. 1993. Conceptions of teaching and the education of second language teachers. *TESOL Quarterly.* 17,2. 193-216.

Freeman, D. 1996. Renaming experience/reconstructing practice: Developing new understandings of practice. *Teacher Learning in Language Teaching.* ed. by D. Freeman & J.C. Richards. Cambridge: Cambridge University Press.

Fullan, M. 1993. *Change Forces: Probing the Depths of Educational Reform.* London: The Falmer Press.

Gebhard, J. G. 1990. Interaction in a teaching practicum. *Second Language Teacher Education.* ed. by J.C. Richards & D. Nunan. Cambridge: Cambridge University Press.

Gaudart, H. 1994. Merging Theory and Practice in Pre-Service Language Teacher Education. *Exploring Second Language Teacher Development.* ed. by David C. S. Li, D. Mahoney & J. C. Richards. Hong Kong: City Polytechnic of Hong Kong.

Gopinathan, S., Pakir, A., Saravanan, V. & Ho, Wah Kam (eds.) 1994. *Language, Education and Society.* Singapore: Times. & Academic Press.

Gopinathan, S. 1988. Bilingualism and Bilingual Education in Singapore. *International Handbook of Bilingualism and Bilingual Education.* ed. by C.B. Paulston. New York: Greenwood Press.

Gopinathan, S. 1994. Language Policy Changes 1979-1992: Politics and Pedagogy. *Language, Education and Society.* ed. by S. Gopinathan, A. Pakir, V. Saravanan & Ho Wah Kam. Singapore: Times. & Academic Press.

Grossman, P. L. 1990. *The Making of a Teacher: Teacher Knowledge and Teacher Education.* New York: Teachers College Press.

Hargreaves, D. 1994. The New Professionalism: The Synthesis of Professional and Institutional Development. *Teaching and Teacher Education.* 10,4. 423-438.

Li, David C. S., D. Mahoney & J. C. Richards. (eds.) 1994. *Exploring Second Language Teacher Development.* Hong Kong: City Polytechnic of Hong Kong.

Richards, J. C. & Nunan, D. (eds.) 1990. *Second Language Teacher Education.* Cambridge: Cambridge University Press.

Richards, J. C. 1990. The dilemma of teacher education in second language teaching. *Second Language Teacher Education.* ed. by J. C. Richards & D. Nunan. Cambridge: Cambridge University Press.

Saravanan, V. & Gupta, R. 1997. Teacher Inputs in Singapore English Classrooms. *RELC Journal.* 28,1. 144-160.

Shulman, L. 1990. *Pedagogical Ways of Knowing.* Keynote Address at the 1990 ICET World Assembly, Singapore.

Skuja R.V. 1990. Pupil Experience: A Hands on Approach to Micro-Teaching. *Singapore Journal of Education.* 11,1. 49-55.

TEACHER SUPERVISION: THE KEY TO PROFESSIONAL DEVELOPMENT

John Joseph Moran

Introduction

I would like to begin by encouraging you to ask yourselves an introspective question.

For those of you who have experienced supervision, either as teachers or supervisors, how successful was that supervision?

I imagine most of you would probably answer that the supervisory experience was of some value, but perhaps not always carried out to a high professional standard, or in the way you would like it to be. In other words, there is room for considerable improvement.

In my view, teacher supervision within language teaching, and indeed education as a whole, is greatly underestimated, and often given little attention. This in fact creates a ludicrous situation when you consider the nature of teacher supervision. Most, I am sure, would agree that the art of teaching is a complicated process involving skills that can take years to master. In comparison, teacher supervision is one of the most complex of human interactions: that of teaching teachers to teach effectively. In this respect, you might like to think of teacher supervision as "a highly specialised form of teaching". In this paper, I would like to explore the following four main themes which show how teacher supervision is inextricably linked to the teacher's professional growth and development:

1. The nature of supervision.
2. Supervision for promoting reflective teaching.
3. Constraints imposed within teacher supervision.
4. Innovations for enhancing professional development through teacher supervision.

The Nature of Supervision

First, I think it is important to make a distinction between two levels of supervision. One level of supervision, often referred to as "surface supervision", involves examination and development of the teacher's practical teaching skills: for example, improving questioning technique, written presentation on the whiteboard, or even the teacher's approach to developing their students' reading and writing skills. Such surface supervision often encompasses microteaching, which is commonly used within teacher pre-service education.

The second stratum of supervision lies at a deeper level, and is of particular significance, because it provides the underlying rationale for the teacher's professional growth and development. At this level, educators should be asking themselves questions like, "Why and how should teachers be supervised?" This underlying level of supervision is essential for experienced teachers at the in-service stage, because with the hindsight of their experience they are ideally placed to facilitate their own professional development.

I believe most people would probably support the notion that supervision of teachers is a necessary function, as it is generally used as a method to produce better teachers, which in turn improves the quality of both the teaching situation and the students' learning situation. The teacher's professional development therefore has to be a primary concern of teacher supervision, and must lie at the heart of the process if genuine long-term educational and pedagogical improvement are to occur. In a sense teacher supervision concerns synergistic co-operation between the teacher, the supervisor (or) supervisory medium, and the institution where the teacher works. A similar view is expressed by Glickman (1985) who refers to supervision as the "glue" of a successful school in terms of this intermix of interdependent relationships between the supervisor, teacher, the educational institution, and the teacher's professional growth.

Another useful distinction can be made in the type of supervisory approach adopted, which can be either directive or collaborative according to the teacher's particular needs. A directive approach would essentially impose authoritative instruction and direction, which many would argue is necessary for pre-service and novice teachers who require considerable guidance in the early stages of their teaching career. In contrast, the collaborative approach would involve the teacher and supervisor working together, making joint decisions. This approach clearly has many advantages, particularly for more experienced teachers, because it encourages individual reflection which in turn contributes to the teacher's professional development.

Teacher supervision is in fact quite a broad umbrella, and can take many forms according to a teacher's particular needs. This variation in teacher supervision is illustrated in the following list.

1. Individual supervision
2. Group supervision
3. Collaborative supervision between supervisors
4. Peer supervision
5. Self-supervision

Some of you might be asking the question, "Which form of supervision is preferable for professional development?" This is not an easy question to answer, and in much of the literature on the subject, there are considerable differences of opinion. In practice, probably all of them are necessary to some degree.

In a recent study, however, I asked this question of various English language teachers and supervisors in different parts of the world, and the majority reported that individual supervision between a supervisor and teacher, on a one-to-one basis, is by far the most beneficial and valuable form of supervision. This was because they perceived this form of supervision as a medium for providing more individual attention to the teacher in a private and non-threatening situation, and for passing on valuable experience. The second most useful form of supervision was reported to be peer supervision, as this was generally perceived to be a method for encouraging teachers to share ideas and learn from each other on equal terms.

In many educational and language teaching settings, a system, or format of "clinical supervision" is often employed. Clinical supervision was a term first coined in the 1950's by the American educationist, Cogan (1973), and over the years has proved to be an effective tried and tested

15

means of supervising teachers. Clinical supervision relates directly to the teaching situation in the classroom, and at some stage incorporates observation of the teacher. Different forms of clinical supervision may be applied by supervisors, and the following are typical examples.

1. **One stage only** – class observation
2. **Two stages** – class observation/post-observation conference (or) discussion with teacher
3. **Three stages** – pre-observation meeting with teacher/class observation/post observation conference (or) discussion with teacher.

Although undoubtedly a useful system for promoting professional development, some writers, such as Goldhammer et al (1980) and Abbott and Carter (1985), suggest that clinical supervision should in fact include five separate stages, as the three stages outlined previously do not go far enough for professional development purposes. They suggest that, after the classroom observation stage, there should be an analysis and strategy stage: at this point the supervisor would sit down and make a conscious effort to analyse the data collected during the class observation, and then determine how and in what order to treat the material in the forthcoming post-observation conference with the teacher. This may be a complex process, requiring the supervisor to evaluate the effectiveness of the lesson observed in the light of his/her own teaching experience. In addition, they recommend a fifth post-conference analysis stage, after the post-observation conference, as a means for monitoring the supervisor's performance. With this extension, supervisors would undoubtedly benefit professionally, by gaining valuable feedback into their own supervisory style, which could then be used as a basis for modifying and improving future supervisory practice.

Finally, in relation to this first theme on the nature of supervision, I would like to draw your attention to a useful model of clinical supervision presented by Gaies and Bowers (1990), which further emphasises the importance of careful consideration and analysis of the teacher's performance before the final feedback session. This model is referred to as H-O-R-A-C-E, which makes it easy to remember. This is shown below.

H – Hear   *(Listen to the teacher and what the teacher says about objectives, methods, content, procedures for evaluation.)*

O – Observe *(Watch the teacher in action, in as representative a set of classroom situations as possible.)*

R – Record *(Use a variety of techniques to record for subsequent discussion the events and skills observed.)*

A – Analyse *(Use a variety of techniques to make sense of the data collected.)*

C – Consider*(Think about the findings trying to justify all that has happened. Consider the intentions and limitations of the teacher, the objectives and constraints enforced by the system, and the recognised principles of good teaching.)*

E – Evaluate *(Only then reach a judgment of the teacher's performance. Give praise where due, and criticise areas where adjustment is not only desirable, but also feasible.)*

Supervision for promoting Reflective Teaching

Most educators would probably support the notion that an important aim of teacher supervision is to assist teachers to become more reflective about their teaching: this ability is generally perceived as a necessary prerequisite to ensure professional development. However, opinions are divided on this matter, because reflection is a difficult concept to define. Similarly, there remains some controversy about the processes teachers go through in becoming reflective. To shed some light on this concept, Ross (1989) provides a useful benchmark with the following definition:

At a general level, reflection is defined as a way of thinking about educational matters that involves the ability to make

17

rational choices and to assume responsibility for those choices.

One of the most comprehensive and insightful discussions concerning reflective practice is provided by Schon (1987). He argues that all professional practitioners involved in areas such as Teaching and Education, Medicine, Law, Architecture, and even professional sportsmen and women share a similar predicament in that their professional practice involves two distinct areas of operation. The first is "a technical rational area", where problems are solved by applying readily available technical knowledge pertaining to that professional area. Examples of this could be when a teacher uses a particular teaching methodology based on educational theoretical principles, or when a doctor prescribes a particular drug to a patient based on medical knowledge and research. It therefore becomes a process of "naming" and "framing" problems within the professional area of reference that technical problem solving becomes possible.

The second area of operation within the professions is referred to by Schon as the "indeterminate zone". It is far more nebulous to define as there are no readily available technical answers to assist the practitioner, who nevertheless is enabled to solve all kinds of complex problems through his own professional artistry or intuition. Examples of this might include a teacher using his/her intuition to deal successfully with a problem that suddenly arises in the classroom, such as an obstructive or deviant student. Alternatively, professional sports people frequently produce that special touch of flair at the right moment by utilising the same kind of knowledge. Such knowledge, which seemingly enables us to perform extremely well, is based on intuitive reflection. This form of reflection, therefore, should be widely encouraged within teacher supervision for promoting further professional development.

Reflective teaching can of course encompass other different forms of reflection. The following serve as typical examples:

1. **Reflection in Action** – reflecting on teaching during the teaching situation.
2. **Reflection on Reflection in Action** – reflecting on one's reflection of teaching

18

3. **Critical Reflection** – reflection on one's teaching with an intention to take action and change whatever is necessary.

As a point of interest, in my recent study, it emerged that most teachers perceived "critical reflection" to be the most valuable form of

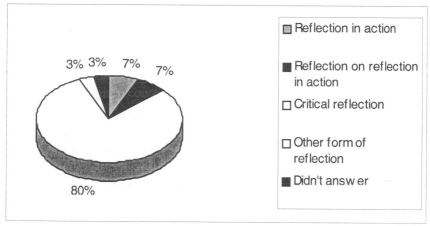

Figure 1: The most valuable form of reflection for professional development purposes selected by teachers

reflection for promoting professional development. This is shown in the following pie graph (Figure 1):

Versatile teachers are more likely to be reflective teachers, who do not teach merely according to prescribed practice but are prepared to adapt the teaching situation to the perceived needs of their students. This has been a common observation within educational practice over the years, and Dewey (1933) first drew attention to this fact by making a distinction between "reflective action" and "routine action". Dewey demonstrates this distinction with the following explanation:

> Reflective action involves active, persistent, and careful consideration of any belief or supposed form of knowledge in the light of the grounds that support it, and the further consequences to which it leads. Routine action, however, is simply guided by tradition and authority.

A similar view is put forward by Prabhu (1990) who points out that "a sense of plausibility" on the part of the teacher is essential to prevent teaching from becoming a set routine. Maintaining an active sense of plausibility, according to Prabhu, is extremely difficult for teachers to do alone, and there is a danger that in the absence of such teacher self-awareness teaching routines may become "frozen" or "ossified." Here, there is clearly an important message for experienced teachers who have been teaching for many years in the same repetitive routine. In such cases it is again incumbent on teacher supervision to break the ice, as it were, and to provide that stimulus for instigating developmental change.

Although reflective teaching is highly desirable, there are a few dilemmas arising from the process of developing reflective teachers that need to be considered within teacher supervision. Such dilemmas are discussed by Calderhead (1993) in terms of contradictory situations. For example, he points out that frequently "a conflict of values" occurs between reflective teachers interested in professional development and their educational institution, which may be interested in other priorities. In this case, the institution may attach greater value to unreflective action from the teacher. Similarly, a supervisor may find his/her role of assessor impedes the role of facilitator because if teachers feel they are primarily being assessed and scrutinized, they may be reluctant to confide in their supervisor and discuss their concerns openly. Therefore, in order to avoid a situation where the teacher's professional development is compromised by two opposing forces, it is again incumbent on teacher supervision to actively seek ways of resolving such dilemmas and, in so doing, discover more about the reflective process.

Constraints imposed within Teacher Supervision

Unfortunately, various constraints are commonplace within teacher supervision and these need to be clearly identified and removed in order to clear the path for professional development. Such constraints may be imposed by the educational institution, the curriculum, the supervisor or the teacher. For example, the educational institution may view teacher supervision as a form of control in order to preserve the status quo within the institution. In this scenario, teachers may find themselves shackled within an education system that restricts their pedagogical freedom and provides little opportunity for them to exercise their judgment as teachers.

Some educational institutions may even discourage or prevent teachers from coming together for professional development activities, such as professional discussion groups, workshops, or peer supervision. There may even be a total lack of inservice teacher supervision and professional development support within the institution.

In my own study of teacher supervision, the majority of teachers and supervisors reported that the school or educational institution acts as the most common form of constraint, which is also a view frequently expressed and supported in much of the literature. The supervisor was then reported to cause the next significant form of constraint. This does suggest that supervisors are not always skilled practitioners in their supervisory role, and that they need to devote more time and attention to the supervisory process. It would also seem that they would benefit from further professional training and guidance in supervising teachers.

Another very common form of constraint reported was a general lack of time devoted to teacher supervision: often supervisors have limited time to visit and spend with teachers. Similarly, teachers are often very busy dealing with the practicalities of teaching, and can afford little time to assist in supervision.

Another major constraint for many teachers concerns classroom observation, particularly if it is carried out for the wrong reasons. Indeed, teachers may find it an unpleasant experience to be observed, especially if they are convinced that the chief aim of the supervisor is to assess their teaching ability. Although assessment of a teacher's teaching ability is generally necessary, it should only play a small part of teacher supervision and not act as the major determinant. Supervisors, therefore, should not be controlled by an oppressive desire to assess through class observations, but rather should be prepared to open the right doors for teachers in order to present real opportunities for their professional development. In connection with this point, it is suggested by Allwright (1988) that classroom observations carried out by supervisors are in fact highly problematic because such observations often amount to little more than impressions which may not be accurate and which should not be used for final evaluations of professional ability.

A further constraint imposed by supervisors which may have a counter-productive effect on teachers' development and cause unnecessary anxiety concerns an overly prescriptive approach from the supervisor allowing the teacher little room for manoeuvre. This idea is discussed by Gower (1988) who reflects on the structure of the current RSA training courses for English language teachers: he points out they are dominated by procedures, techniques and activities that tend to have a manipulative effect on learning. According to Gower, what teachers really need from this type of training course are opportunities to develop insights into the strengths and weaknesses of their own teaching styles and approaches.

The last constraint that I wish to mention concerns feedback given to the teacher from a supervisor as this can be another major contributor to the teacher's professional growth. For some supervisors, giving feedback can almost become a routine. It may even be given in a ritualistic and non-committal manner, particularly in the case where the supervisor is responsible for supervising a large number of teachers. To avoid this scenario, supervisors need to develop ways of varying feedback sessions with different teachers, and at the same time demonstrate a vested interest and commitment to their overall professional development: such feedback must therefore, be genuine and relevant to the individual teacher. Furthermore, supervisors need to be aware of not giving "unconscious feedback" which may be pejorative. This idea is discussed by Rinvolucri (1994) who suggests that this form of feedback may include projections, fantasies, and hidden demands, and thus becomes parental by nature, with power on the side of the feedback provider. In my study, I asked teachers the question, "What kind of feedback from a supervisor do you find most useful?" In answer to this question, it was generally reported that it needs to be of a constructive nature and include practical suggestions and solutions to perceived problems. The following provide further common examples of such useful feedback given by these teachers:

- Feedback that builds confidence.
- Reinforcement about one's ideas, constructive critical comments and useful alternative suggestions.
- Frank and positive discussion on the aims, techniques, materials, management and outcome of the lesson.
- Feedback that encourages reflection on one's teaching.

- Objective feedback in relation to a set of criteria.
- Feedback that provides an accurate description of what transpired. For example, a supervisor recording a lesson on video would be useful.
- Verbal feedback as opposed to written so things can be clarified immediately.
- Personal discussion followed by a referenced written report.
- Suggestions on alternative approaches or ways of developing a lesson.
- New ways of doing routine things.
- Questions about teaching that force the teacher to focus and reflect on a particular aspect of the class that didn't 'work' as well as it could have.

Innovations for Enhancing Professional Development through Teacher Supervision

There is a great deal of work to be done within teacher supervision in terms of adopting a more professional and organized approach in order to enhance professional development. Perhaps the first step in this process would be to provide more openness about the nature of supervision that teachers receive. Teachers should, therefore, be encouraged to examine the underlying rationale for teacher supervision in relation to professional development, and to explore the many different forms of supervision available under the broad supervisory umbrella for assisting in their professional growth. For this to occur the supervisor has to adapt his / her role as a facilitator or helper to provide the conditions conducive for professional development. In addition, teachers have to play an active part in directing their own development as autonomous professionals.

Perhaps one of the most effective means for achieving this goal is by teachers conducting their own "Action Research" in the classroom as it provides a practical opportunity to reflect and evaluate the teaching situation. Action research thus enables teachers to learn directly from their own practice as opposed to learning from a theoretical external source which may have less impact on their development. This point is emphasised by Tsui (1993, 173) in the following way:

Action research is a very effective way of helping teachers to reflect on their teaching and to come up with their own alternatives to improve their practice. In asking them to record their own lessons, review them, and identify an area for improvement, we are helping them to distance themselves from the lesson and to focus on one problem at a time.

Similarly, other useful professional development activities for teachers might include regular professional discussion groups, group workshops, or even mentorship schemes, all of which can be instigated with relative ease through teacher supervision. In order to really empower teachers, and place them in a position where they become responsible for their own development, the supervisor has to have confidence in the teacher's ability to make the necessary changes in their practice. Counselling is another method that can achieve this aim, as it is based on an understanding approach where a counsellor attempts to see the other person's world through the other person's eyes, without reaching into it and changing it. In a counselling situation, a supervisor might use leading questions to direct the teacher's attention to the root of a particular problem, but would not tell the teacher directly how to solve it. This would be left to the individual teacher. However, it should also be borne in mind that counselling in a professional capacity imposes greater demands and responsibility on the supervisory role, for which the supervisor needs to be sufficiently prepared.

A variation of counselling that can be used within teacher supervision is "Co-operative Development", a term and concept discussed by Edge (1992). He suggests that Co-operative Development is essentially a mixture of awareness raising and disciplined co-operation between teaching colleagues for professional development purposes. He points out there are 3 important areas of learning:

1. Learning through our experience.
2. Learning through our intellect.
3. Learning through the formulation and expression of our ideas.

Co-operative Development in the main encompasses this third area by focussing on the power of learning through expression. In addition, he also suggests that three particular qualities must be present during the interaction between speaker and understander for Co-operative Development to take place. (In this scenario, 'the understander' refers to the more passive teacher partner who adopts the role of listening, observing and eliciting further information from his/her colleague. In contrast, the other partner acts as 'the speaker' who adopts a more active 'lead role' in expressing his/her ideas and opinions about the teaching experience in question.) The three qualities are as follows:

1. **Respect** – The understander has respect for the speaker's decisions and opinions, and must be non-judgmental.
2. **Empathy** – The understander attempts to see things through the speaker's eyes.
3. **Honesty** – The understander has genuine respect and empathy *(not pretending)* in order to help the speaker develop.

A further crucial innovation would be to gain support and approval for a coherent educational policy endorsing professional development within teacher supervision from the governing education authority. Such central support would further empower teachers by ensuring that educational institutions are committed to encouraging their teachers to share responsibility in the control, planning and organization of their supervision. In this way, as professional educators, helping to enhance its own professional development, the institute will benefit, and the quality of teacher supervision will improve.

The complex and varied nature of the supervisory role also demands that training of supervisors should in fact be a priority in order to prepare the supervisor adequately for the supervisory task ahead. At present throughout much of education supervisors rarely receive training at all. Such training would primarily need to focus on strategies for facilitating the teacher's professional growth. From this, the quality and depth of teacher supervision would undoubtedly improve as supervisors acquire specialised supervisory skills such as counselling, managerial skills, or learning how to deal with sensitive areas like giving criticism and feedback to teachers.

Teacher Supervision: The Key to Professional Development

In this paper I have stressed that teacher supervision is a highly specialised form of teaching, and as such, I would argue that sufficient quality time needs to be allocated to the process, so that it can be carried out properly and effectively. It is also equally important that it should not be regarded as purely judgmental for assessment and evaluative purposes: rather, supervision should be a means of fulfilling its main executive function of enhancing the teacher's professional growth.

References

Abbott, S. and Carter, R. 1985. Clinical Supervision and the Foreign Language Teacher.   *Foreign Language Annals* 18(1), 25-29.

Allwright, D. 1988. *Observation in the Language Classroom.* London: Longman.

Calderhead, J. 1993. Dilemmas in Developing Reflective Teaching. *Teacher Education Quarterly,* 93-99.

Cogan, M. 1973. *Clinical Supervision.* Boston: Houghton Mifflin.

Dewey, J. 1933. *How We Think.* Chicago: Henry Regnery.

Edge, J. 1992. *Co-operative Development.* London: Longman Group UK Limited.

Glickman, C. 1985. *Supervision of Instruction: A Developmental Approach.* Boston: Allyn and Bacon.

Goldhammer, R., Anderson, R. and Krajewski, R. 1980. *Clinical Supervision: Special Methods for the Supervision of Teachers.* New York: Holt, Rinehart and Winston.

Gower, R. 1988. Are Trainees Human? *Explorations in Teacher Training: Problems and Issues,* ed. by T. Duff, 21-25. London: Longman.

Moran, J. 1997. *Perceptions of Supervision within Teacher Education.* Unpublished MA Extended Study – Moray House Institute of Education, Heriot-Watt University, Edinburgh.

Prabhu, N. 1990. There is no best method: Why? *TESOL Quarterly,* 24, 161-176.

Rinvolucri, M. 1994. Key Concepts in ELT: Feedback. *ELT Journal,* 48(3), 287-289.

Ross, D. 1989. First Steps in Developing a Reflective Approach. *Journal of Teacher Education,* March, 22-30.

Tsui, A. 1993. Helping teachers to conduct action research in their classrooms. *New Ways in Teacher Education,* ed. by D. Freeman and S. Cornwell, 171-175. Alexandria, Virginia: TESOL Inc.

CHANGING TEACHING: INSIGHTS INTO INDIVIDUAL DEVELOPMENT IN THE CONTEXT OF SCHOOLS

Donald Freeman

The punch line: 'What you do is shaped by where you do it.'[1]

The point I want to make is actually a very simple one. My punch line is this: 'What you do is shaped by where you do it.' This statement probably sounds simple and even self-evident. I could expand on it by adding: 'How you do it, with whom, and for what reasons, are all also shaped by where you do it.' But a simple statement is not the same as a simplistic one. Although I am using rather straightforward words here, the idea itself is far from simplistic. My argument is that all the work we do as teachers is intimately bound up in the socio-cultural environment in which it occurs, which is simply a wordier version of the same basic idea. By 'socio-cultural environment', I mean the colleagues, students, administrators, and other people, the 'socio' dimension of the 'socio-cultural environment', as well as the ideas, values, beliefs, and assumptions about teaching, about English and the Anglophone world, about the role of teachers, about what learners are capable of, what they will and won't do, and so on, in other words the 'cultural' dimension. Thus 'socio' means the people with whom you work, and 'cultural' means the values and beliefs of the institution and setting in which the work is done.

When administrators, policy-makers, and researchers think about teaching and learning, they constantly overlook these socio-cultural environments. They tend to concentrate on the tangibles of curriculum, resources, and teaching methodology, for example. The point of entry is taken to be the actor and the actions rather than the context. But this assumption is perilous, for it is, in essence, an egotistical assumption that *what I am doing* matters most of all. It is easier to focus on the actor and the actions than on the context; on the doer and the doing rather than on where, how, with whom, and the reasons for which it is done. It is easier, but not necessarily effective. This blindness can apply equally to

---

[1] Because this paper was originally prepared for oral presentation, and the images around which it is built were introduced experientially, I have maintained its spoken style. Also, for that reason, there are few references throughout the text.

administrators who are trying to implement change, to researchers who are trying to understand classroom teaching and learning, to textbook writers who are creating new materials and curricula, to teacher educators who are training teachers. And, lest you think this is all about people other than you, I will say that I think the assumption of egotism applies directly to teachers. For most teachers teach lessons and not students.

In this paper, I will explore the connections between the processes of change and the socio-cultural environment. To do so, I will present three images of the change process, each of which illustrates, as a concrete metaphor, how change is related to its environment. I will then turn to what we are calling 'reflective teaching' as an example of a change in the status quo. Drawing from my experience as a classroom teacher to frame this case study of individual change, I will review the obstacles and benefits of adopting this stance towards my work, which has to do with recognizing the assumption of egotism that guides most teaching. What happens to teaching when we start to take learners seriously? In closing, I will put these pieces together to illustrate what we must try to avoid and what we must try to do when we change a conventional way of doing things in the classroom, like changing from teaching lessons to teaching learners. There is a basic riddle here: If 'what you do is shaped by where you do it,' then how do you do something in a different way while you are in the same place? This is the riddle of individual and systemic change, which I mean to unpack and try to better understand.

Change as Substitution: The Leggos

One way to think about change is as a set of Leggo blocks. Here you can simply substitute one block for another by taking one out and snapping another in its place. But look closely at this image as a metaphor: What makes this kind of change work? One attribute is that the Leggo blocks are the same scale, so one block can be exchanged for another without necessarily having to reorganize the whole. I will refer to this property as the 'commensurateness' of a change, which simply means that if the new is roughly equal to the old then you should be able to substitute one for the other. In our work lives as teachers, there are lots of examples of so-called commensurate changes.[2] There are commensurate changes in curriculum, for example, when one textbook series is changed for another. There are

---

[2] For an interesting discussion of this point in curriculum innovation, see Markee (1997).

commensurate changes in scheduling, when a teacher moves from teaching one class level to teaching the same level at a different hour or day of the week. There are commensurate changes in class composition, when a student is moved out of one class and into another. There are commensurate changes in staffing, when one teacher takes over a class from another, and so on. The problem is that this notion that two changes are commensurate – that A can be exchanged for B – makes some serious assumptions about the nature of the socio-cultural environment.

Another attribute that makes this Leggo kind of change work is that each block fits into the others in the same way. Each block has a top and a bottom, so they snap together in only one direction. This is a refinement on the notion of commensurateness, namely that pieces all fit together in the same way. In other words, the elements being changed are 'equivalent' to one another. I will call this combination of attributes 'equivalent and commensurate' change.

The following story illustrates this notion of 'equivalent and commensurate' change. Some years ago, I visited Harpers Ferry, West Virginia, a small town about two hours west of Washington D.C., with my family. Harpers Ferry sits at the confluence of the Potomac and Allegheny Rivers and is famous, as most American students know, as the site of John Brown's raid. In 1859, anti-slavery activist John Brown and his men attacked a government arsenal in Harpers Ferry and seized the weapons there. Many history texts mark John Brown's raid as the start of the American Civil War. While we were there, my family and I took a tour of the battlefield at Harpers Ferry because my older daughter was studying the Civil War. During the tour, the guide explained the raid, the seizing of the arsenal, and so on. As it turned out, the guide was a very good teacher. He noticed that as he talked, many of the younger people in the group were losing interest, so he took off his hat and he tossed in three cheap plastic ball-point pens which he had in his shirt pocket. He asked one boy to take the pens apart, which he did. Now the guide's hat was full of ballpoint pen parts – springs, caps, tubes, and assorted metal and plastic bits. He then mixed everything up and asked for another volunteer. To this girl, he said, "Can you make me a pen out of these parts?" She did so quickly; it was actually pretty easy, as you know if you've ever taken a cheap pen apart and reassembled it.

The guide then asked the girl, "How did you do it?" "The parts are all the same." she answered promptly. "All the same?" he looked at her quizzically. "But here's a spring, and here's a top, and I don't know what this is – a metal ring…" She thought for a couple of seconds and said, "Well, they're not exactly *all* the same. It's just that the *same parts are the same.*" "That's what we now call 'interchangeable parts'", he said. He went on to explain that the Civil War marked the beginning of widespread manufacturing using interchangeable parts, especially in arms and munitions. In fact John Brown's raid on the arsenal caused government concern not simply because of the 50 or so guns he took, but because of the parts and the fact that those guns could be disassembled and their parts used – interchangeably – to repair other guns. Thus rather than just having the 50 guns to use, the raiders had the potential to have 49 guns and use one to repair, say, 10 others with its parts.

Equivalent and commensurate change is really about interchangeable parts, and interchangeable parts gave the world industrial manufacturing as we know it. But more fundamentally, the notion gave us the perspective of breaking complex things, from guns, to computers to automobiles, into their component parts. When a new text is introduced at the Intermediate level, you have to make sure it fits, or 'articulates' to use the curricular term, with what comes before and after it in the course sequence. Just like the Leggo blocks, it needs to figuratively 'snap into place.' It is a powerful idea. When applied to education and supported by developmental psychology, the notion of interchangeable parts gave us age-grading in schools for example: the idea that children of the same age should learn and progress at the same pace. Applied to teaching and supported by economics, interchangeable parts gave us what has been called the 'factory model' of education, with teachers responsible for segmented subject-matters like math, science, geography, and English, working at their individual work stations, or classrooms, on semester or year-long shifts. That change, which began about 150 years ago in the 1850's, had a profound effect on education. Some would argue that it led to dehumanizing teaching and to focusing on lessons as products rather than on learners and the processes they are engaged in.

To make this type of change work across wide variations in context, proponents needed to establish standards. These standards function as agreed-upon measures that allow the parts to fit together in such a way that those from one locale will work with those from another. In manufacturing for instance, you want the computer chips made in Singapore to fit into the machines being assembled in Korea or Malaysia. Standardized sizing was, in fact, another innovation that came about in the United States around the time of the Civil War. Prior to that period, shoemaking, for example, was an individualized art. The cobbler fit the shoes he made to the customer's feet. With the advent of large military build-ups, however, suppliers began to realize that it would be useful to have standardized sizes, so that shoes and clothes could be made without a specific person in mind. Instead, they should fit an average or prototype sized person. In education, we are now in the midst of global standardization of learning outcomes.

On-demand, computer administered TOEFL tests is a case-in-point. This innovation allows students to measure their 'learning' against the metric of a standardized test. If they achieve a certain TOEFL score, for example 550 in the case of many US universities, then that amount of learned language should translate into a building block for further study in a subject area. A TOEFL score of 550 is thus taken as equivalent and commensurate to the English language proficiency of an entering student for whom English is the mother tongue. Whether the English was learned in the socio-cultural context of Brooklyn, New York, Chicago, Toronto, Johannesburg, Tokyo, Madrid, or Addis Ababa does not matter. The standard measure allows it to be interchangeable.

To summarize then, the idea of equivalent and commensurate change depends on the notion of substitution. It depends, as the girl told the guide, on 'the *same* parts being the *same*'. In terms of teaching and learning, it depends on teaching being a group of behaviors that can be exchanged one for another so that they still add up to the same whole, like the ball-point pen parts in the example. This view also depends on the assumption that students will learn material in more-or-less the same way, the way in which it is presented by the teacher, the book, and the curriculum. There is little room for individuality or difference, or the parts that do not fit. And there is little room for local contexts. Equivalent and commensurate change ignores the socio-cultural environment.

Change as Integration: Water into the glass

Let us turn now to the second image of change: pouring water into a full glass. How is this image a metaphor for change? First there is a similarity to the Leggo example: What is being added to the thing is the same substance as the thing itself. So it's Leggo to Leggo and water to water. The difference in this case is that nothing is being taken away. To put one Leggo in, we have to take one out, but when you add water to the glass, it displaces some of the water that is already there. The new water fits in with the old, just like the Leggos snapping together, except some water overflows and splashes out. Using the terms of analysis then, this change is *equivalent* but it is not *commensurate*. It is equivalent because the new water can replace the old without disrupting the whole; but it is not commensurate since some of the water overflows. So water isn't interchangeable (except on the molecular level) in the same way that Leggos are. In fact, adding and subtracting amounts of water – like many changes – is hardly ever entirely commensurate. If you were to remove some of the water in the glass before pouring in the new water, you might pour too much out, or spill some, or you might not pour enough and leave the glass less full than it was. Water is interchangeable because it is equivalent, but it is not usually commensurate. The new combines with the old quite readily, however, because it integrates so quickly and seamlessly into the system, it is hard to see what is different.

Consider the water that is splashed out of the full glass, when new water is poured in, which I'll call the 'splash-back effect'. There's no real way of knowing whether what is splashed out is some of the new water that was poured in or some of the old water that was already in the glass. This type of change is *displacement,* rather than the *replacement* seen in the Leggo example. Something is gone, we don't know what; and something new is there but we don't know what. This splash-back effect is instructive for two reasons. First, it shows that what is retained and what is rejected in a change may not be what those who instigate the change had intended. Second, the process is messy and difficult to predict or control, especially when compared to the neat 'snap-the-new-one-into-the-place-of-the-old-one' Leggo approach.

When we consider change in teaching, this second image is probably more apt than the Leggos, at least from the teacher's point of view. This image of change as integration captures the sense that as new ideas come in, they are integrated into what is there, and quickly become indistinguishable. In fact, it's hard to point to when such changes have happened. For instance, when did you change from *not* knowing how to handle an information gap activity to knowing how to do one? In the process, something old went away – the fact that you didn't know how to do information gaps – but that loss too is hard to pinpoint. So something new came in and something old went away, but the distinction and the timing of the process is hard to pinpoint.

In a way, this is the process that we often call 'learning from experience.' John Dewey, the American educational philosopher who pioneered the whole notion of reflective teaching in the early 1900's, talked about the process this way:

> What [an individual] has learned in the way of knowledge and skills in one situation becomes an instrument of understanding and dealing effectively with the situations which follow. The process goes on as long as life and learning continue.[3]

This image of change is an integrative one, at least from the perspective of the individual who is changing. It seems to fit with the way we experience the gradual constancy of things getting to be different – by becoming older, more experienced, and more skilled. In teaching, this image seems to capture the feeling of becoming more proficient at what you are doing over time. Like learning how to handle teenagers in our classes, or teach writing, or becoming comfortable with video. There are lots of small changes that somehow add up to doing things differently.

I want to mention 'seeming transparency' as another key aspect of this second image. If you look at this glass of water from a certain point of view or even from a certain distance, you can't tell whether the glass is full or empty. In fact, it may look empty, even though it is full. There is a parallel here that I think is worth making. Too often when changes are made in education, those who are making them assume that teachers are empty vessels – just like glasses without any water in them – and therefore that new ideas or innovations can be poured into the void. So when the splash-back effect happens, as it inevitably does, teachers are called 'resistant', 'stubborn', and 'unwilling' to change. That is because we don't recognize that there is already something there, in the glass, when the new water is added.

What is in the glass already is what I call 'status-quo explanations for teaching': the reasons you give to yourselves and your colleagues for why things are the way they are[4]. For instance, if I ask you which level you prefer to teach and you give me an answer, that is a status-quo explanation. Or if I ask you how you feel about teaching kids, that is a status-quo explanation. Or what makes your institution a good or not so good place to

---

[3] See Dewey (1938: 44)
[4] See Freeman (1998). Also Freeman (1996).

work, that is a status-quo explanation, and so on. These status-quo explanations are the psychosocial equivalent of the water in the glass. They are what the new water splashes against when it is poured in, some of them may get splashed out while others will stay in the glass. There are two important things to recognize in this process. First, these status-quo explanations are there even though they may be invisible; they already fill the mental space of reason and explanation that each of us has, and therefore, to change them something must be displaced. Something has to slosh over if something stays. Reasons for doing things cannot be neatly replaced, through a commensurate and equivalent change process, like the Leggos. The second point is that these status-quo explanations are not necessarily good or true just because we believe them. But we are usually blind to the fact that we are taking them for granted. They are invisible; transparent to us, like our water. This fact makes them tough to change.

These status-quo explanations come from many sources. In general they come from – or perhaps better put, they exist in – the socio-cultural environment, in the social fabric of peers and colleagues with whom you work and in the culture of this institution. Accepting these status-quo explanations is what makes you part of that place as a community of explanation. It's what makes you talk and think and act like teachers at that certain institution. Let me give an example. When I was first starting out as a high school French teacher in rural New England, I remember despairing about my French II class that was scheduled everyday at 12:30 just after lunch. To call the students 'energetic' would be putting it mildly. They were – to use the American idiom – 'off the wall'. I could barely get them to sit down or focus on the lesson, let alone use any French at all. One day, after a grueling class, I stumbled into the teachers room ready to quit teaching and find a new career. The only other person in the teachers room was a much older teacher, a guy named Len who taught chemistry and physics. He looked up from the newspaper he was reading when I came in. After a while, he said something like 'Glad it's Friday.' 'Yeah,' I answered, and, without intending to, I launched into the French II class and how I'd as soon quit as teach them. 'It's because they're after lunch,' Len said in a matter-of-fact way and went back to reading his paper.

Now Len had hardly solved my French II problem but he had given it a name. Now it wasn't 'my French II problem', with all that implied about my failures as a teacher; it was the 'after lunch' problem. Now I could talk about it with a bit of detachment, even say to other teachers, 'What do you do when you have those kids 'after lunch'?' Now I had a status-quo explanation for what was happening. It had a recognized reality and I had a way to talk about it. When I mentioned the 'after lunch' issue, other teachers pretty much knew what I meant. I was one of the group; I made sense to them. And by making sense, I belonged.

Clearly there were many other ways to talk about the French II situation. No one explanation is right. We could say, 'The class is too big.'; 'It has Ralph and Gary and Steve in it and they always cause trouble.'; or 'It is due to their phase of adolescent development' and so on. Or we could entertain explanations that implicate the teacher more directly like: 'The material isn't appropriate; it's too hard, too boring, out-dated etc.' My point is that these explanations exist like water; they run through our lives as teachers. They are difficult to see because they are transparent to us, because we accept them as making sense. In accepting them we belong where we are, doing what we do.

Changing status-quo explanations means undoing all of these connections. It means abandoning belonging to one group and gaining membership in another one. It means, in essence, making sense in a different way to a different group of people. It is like uprooting a plant from its spot in the garden in order to transplant it elsewhere. Again let me illustrate. In the teachers room I may report that my French II class is an 'after lunch problem' and perhaps another teacher will disagree. 'No,' she will tell me, 'it's their phase of adolescent development...' 'I don't know about development,' I say, 'but after they eat and hang out in the lunch room they come into class with their energy all over the place.' And maybe you may hear someone else kid her, saying: 'What happened? D'you go to some fancy in-service? Listen to that, 'adolescent development' ... These kids just need discipline. You got to make them toe the line' So we have the collision between different ways of explaining the same phenomenon. In this discussion, the collision is the competing reasoning of different groups.[5] Accepting the legitimate reasoning of the explanation means belonging to the group; it's like speaking their language. Changing the explanation means changing groups, and speaking a new language of explanation.

This analysis offers a different perspective on why the 'splash-back effect' exists. If a teacher accepts a new idea or way of doing something in his or her teaching, he or she can run a risk of getting out of synch with the

---

[5] See Freeman (1992).

socio-cultural environment, with the norms and values of the people with whom he or she works. It is one reason why change is hard, dislocating, and often feels painful.

Change through infusion and transformation: Ice cube in glass

The third image of change involves putting an ice cube into a full glass of water. As the ice cube is introduced, depending on how it is done, some water will splash out. Then the ice cube will float, gradually melting and being absorbed into the contents of the glass. This image combines key attributes of the first two. There is *commensurate* change and there is *displacement*. The ice cube replaces an amount of water – that is the commensurate aspect of the change – and in the process some of the old water splashes out of the glass – that is the displacement. However, unlike the 'splash back' effect, we know that it is the water in the glass that is displaced and the new water – frozen as the ice cube – stays put. But if you look closely you will note how this new input, the ice cube, stays put. It floats, partially above the surface of the water; it does so because it is frozen. Frozen water is the same substance that is in the glass, but in another form. As it melts, the liquid integrates into what is in the glass, or environment, and becomes part of what is there, while changing and transforming it.

These are the two key ideas to highlight in this image of change. When the change is introduced, as the ice cube in the image, it appears to take more space than the water it displaces. The new material introduced by the change is made out of what is already in the glass, but in a different form. As the ice cube melts, the new water infuses the old, mixing together but not overflowing. After the change is introduced, there is no further displacement; nothing more spills out. These two ideas redefine the idea of equivalence we saw in the Leggo metaphor. With the Leggos, one thing replaces another; something new is introduced and something old is removed. With the ice cube, the process is very different. The new idea, the change that is introduced, starts out as seemingly big, hard, and immutable, but gradually it melts, dissolving into the environment. As it melts, the frozen water – now liquid – becomes part of the water in the glass. This is how the big idea becomes small. I will call this type of change, infusion and transformation.

In the current literature on educational change, the term for infusion and transformation – for the ice cube melting – is 'systemic change.'[6] 'Systemic,' the adjective derived from 'system,' refers to change *to, in,* and *via* (or through) a system. Systems theorist Bela Benathy defines a system as "... a configuration of ... components connected ... together in a web of relationships. By this joining and integration, the relationships are creating emerging properties ... of the whole system rather than its parts."[7] Edward Clark, who develops curriculum from a system perspective, writes the implication is that "no single, discrete entity can be fully understood apart from the complex whole of which it is an integral part. The whole provides the context without which our knowledge of the part is necessarily limited."[8] Systemic change is change through and throughout the whole. While this may sound complicated, in truth we live systemic change all the time. Eating is systemic change; exercising is systemic change; so is getting sick or healing. And, so is education.

Let me give an example of what I mean by systemic change in education. In a study of innovation in curriculum development in Britain in the mid-1970's[9], researchers looked at what they called 'diffusion' of curricular innovation, in other words, the way in which the new curriculum 'melted' into the socio-cultural environment. The researchers were intrigued by when and to what degree teachers adopted new ideas in their teaching, which, in this case, was a new high-school biology curriculum. The chart reproduced on the next page shows the relationship between the intentions and the actual practices of 142 high school science teachers in connection with the new biology materials.

Across the top, from left to right are the teachers' statements of intention: what they said they would do with the new curriculum as they left the in-service training. Down the left hand side are what the teachers actually did with the new curriculum. The total figures are pretty normative, which means the teachers' intentions are pretty much equally distributed across all four categories. What actually happened reflects what you might expect, namely that most people clustered in the 'partial adoption' group.

---

[6] See, for instance, Fullan (1993). Also Kotter (1996).
[7] Banathy (1992: 10).
[8] Clark (1998).
[9] Kelly (1980).

38

Table 1: Intentions of 142 teachers towards adoption of the Nuffield A-level Biological Science project compared to what they did one year later

Intentions ... A year after...	To adopt early	To try out, then adopt	To try out	Considering trial	TOTALS
Adopted early	5	4	12	6	27
Adopted late	7	13	6	9	35
Partial adoption	19	19	5	8	51
Not adopted	11	2	7	9	29
TOTALS	42	38	30	32	*142*

In examining the interior figures in the table, an interesting and more complicated picture emerges. To read this table you must keep in mind that each interior number is part of the total of teachers' intentions, at the bottom of its column, as well as the total of their actual adoption, at the end of the row on the right. Thus each number is part of two wholes, which recalls Edward Clark's statement just above. If we exclude the 29 teachers who intended to adopt the new curriculum in some way but ended up not doing anything with it at all, which may have been for reasons beyond their control, we see that 62 out of 142 teachers integrated the innovation into their on-going teaching practice. (The above figures do not include the 51 teachers who took parts of the innovation on board in their practice.) To use the ice cube image, this means that, as the innovation melted, just under half of the teachers accepted it, while another almost one third took parts of the ideas. This number compares with 29 out of 142, or about 20%, of the participants who did not use the new curriculum at all.

These same proportions – about half who do and about one fifth who don't – are borne out in most socio-cultural environments into which new ways of teaching are introduced. There are a couple of ways to interpret this phenomenon. Perhaps the most common one in the public mind is to see teachers as inherently conservative and opposed to change. That is the 20% view, to use shorthand. Another way to interpret these figures is that teaching is so deeply embedded in its particular socio-cultural environment, so heavily influenced by social norms at the school and local community level, so deeply based on the individual teachers' beliefs and status-quo explanations for what works in their classrooms, that adopting any innovation will always be partial. This is the 50% view.

The 20% view ignores the realities of the socio-cultural environment. The 50% view takes them into account, accepting the premise that 'what you do is shaped by where you do it.' In the 20% view, a failed innovation is one that hasn't reached complete 100% adoption. But if you think about it, that would mean that there is no status-quo already in place, no reasoning – legitimate or not – for why things work as they do, no explanations for how current practices operate. It would mean an empty glass. Assuming 100% adoption would further imply that teachers themselves have no sense of purpose, no investment in what they do, and little recognition of the complexity of change. It would mean the glass would always be waiting to be filled. To look at it the other way, if added together, the 20% view and the 50% view suggest that 70% of the teachers in this case made some sort of change based on the new biology curriculum. In other words, 70% of the water in the glass was eventually infused by the melting ice-cube.

Change in education cannot proceed like the Leggos unless we ignore the socio-cultural environment. Educational reform efforts around the world are littered with examples of how the substitutive approach to change does not work. Further, change cannot be entirely integrative either, like pouring water into the full glass, unless we ignore the ways in which individuals are intimately connected in and through their socio-cultural environment by the power and belonging of what I have called status-quo explanations. To endure, any change in education – or more concretely in what you do in the classroom – must be understood as systemic change. Like the ice-cube melting into the glass of water, the new, immutable idea infuses itself into, even as it is transformed by, the socio-cultural environment.

Reflective teaching: A personal case study of change

These three images of change provide the big picture which frames ways of thinking about how individual changes in teaching operate within your workplace and professional community. I now want to shift the focus from the whole, or the system, to the individual who is changing. I want to examine one instance of individual change – reflective teaching – to describe it briefly from my own experience and then to link it back to these larger frames. My aim is not to describe what reflective teaching is or how it is done, because it is not a method or way of doing things, not a series of teaching behaviors, not some Leggos to be snapped into place. Reflective teaching is a way of approaching what you do both inside and outside the classroom. It boils down to the idea that, like it or not, learning is always right.

There are two corollaries to this basic principle. The first is that 'learning can tell you how to teach' and the second is that 'you can't teach anyone anything.' Both of them mean the same thing: You are wasting your time as a teacher if you concentrate on teaching, you need to concentrate on learning, what it is, how it works – and doesn't work – and how to get out of the way and let it happen. This is hardly an abdication of the teacher's role; rather it is the ultimate responsibility of teaching. Effective doctors know that they cannot heal their patients. The patients must do so themselves with the guidance, support, and necessary intervention of the doctor. Likewise, effective architects or engineers know that they can't build the building, they can design it, supervise its construction, and evaluate the results, but the materials themselves are the building. Effective teachers know that they play an integral role in learning, but that they do not make people learn. To echo the American bumper sticker: Learning happens.

This is the position that I take now, but let me go back with you to how this change started for me. Perhaps this story will illustrate the twistings and turnings of change in individual practice. I have been teaching for about 25 years. In the late 1970's, about five years into my career as a teacher, I found that I was getting bored. Bored with the same lessons, the same student indifference, the same classroom feeling of pushing everything up hill, of trying to put toothpaste into the tube. Things felt pretty automatic. I knew I was a good teacher, because people told me so (and that was my downfall). But I was bored. I didn't realize it and I couldn't put my finger on it because I had lots of other status-quo explanations for what was (and wasn't) happening: It was 'the kids,' it was 'the book,' it was 'the department', and so on ... But regardless of the explanation for the status-quo, I was bored.

I happened to go a seminar that spring. I wasn't looking for anything in particular, just a chance to get out and maybe pick up some new activities or ideas. The seminar would be OK, it would be different from teaching; but it wouldn't affect my basic state of mind. Or so I thought. I still remember how it started. The presenter came in, sat down, looked at each of us in the group of forty or so, and asked, "How many of you have ever thought that you might be boring?" There were some chuckles, but mostly there was a stony, embarrassed silence. The presenter then raised the stakes. Looking at a man sitting next to me, he said, "I can tell you're a boring teacher." Well, he got us going. We argued that we weren't boring and we gave reasons why. We were good teachers! If indeed some, or a very few, of our classes might be (just a little bit) boring, it certainly wasn't our faults. Things got pretty heated, and finally a woman said what I had on my mind (but was too chicken to say). She told the presenter that she "knew she wasn't boring because she was a good teacher. She knew she was a good teacher because parents, colleagues, and administrators told her so, and most of her students liked her, and many of them did well later on."

The presenter let her finish. Then he smiled and said to her, "... And that is precisely why you are a bad teacher." I won't bore you with what happened next; I can't remember actually and it really isn't the point. As things went on, a number of people got up and left; many stayed and argued with him; some were intrigued, and some of us just got more annoyed, confused, and bothered by what he was saying. What if he were right? How did I know I was any good as a teacher? I'd been going on everyone else's opinions, but where was my own evidence. How could I know for myself? What if I were a boring teacher?

Converting 'bored' to 'boring' in teaching was a turning point for me. The idea that initially had been so hard for me to take started to melt into my thinking, and it really bothered me. Over the next few years, I stumbled along as I tried to figure out if I was doing any good and how I could know. It always seemed to come back to the students, or more precisely to their learning processes, and to the blinding assumption of egotism: namely, that what I was doing as a teacher was central. I had to stop thinking so much about me and what I was doing, and look closely at my students and what they were doing. I had to re-learn to see my teaching in terms of their learning.

Once I got over the initial shock, I began to enjoy the whole thing. It was quite fascinating to always be looking at what I was doing, trying to figure out why things had happened as they had, and what I could do differently. The interesting thing was that although I thought it would be more work, in fact it wasn't. I found that I wasn't working harder, but I was working smarter. Things like the fact that we actually 'did' less material, but we did it much more thoroughly, that there were always leftovers from the previous class – a question or an issue or something to do more with – so classes flowed into one another. And when tests came, my students seemed more confident of what they knew and better able to approach and solve what they didn't.

A number of years later, I saw a colleague – a fellow teacher educator – doing a workshop in which he posed the question to participants: 'What are you doing that your students could be doing in the service of their learning?' That question struck me as the way to unpack the challenge of understanding teaching in terms of learning. First of all, the natural response is to think of things that you <u>must</u> do as teacher, otherwise the students won't learn. These are almost all habitual decisions such as modeling language in the lesson or being the one who corrects students' mistakes. If you stay with this question, you begin to see how much this assumption of egotism is in operation. You realize how much you are guided by assumptions and not by what students are actually doing or can do. How do you know you <u>have to</u> model? Have you tried another way? What happened? Or the same with correction: What exactly do you need to do for this particular student to correct the mistake he just made?

The more I probed, the more I found that much of what I took for granted was just that: things that you take for granted because they are part of the landscape of teaching, part of the socio-cultural environment. They are what teachers 'should' do and have always done: teachers always model, teachers always correct, and so on. These are the status-quo explanations of teaching from the socio-cultural environment, from the people and values that surround the classroom but they may, or may not, be borne out by what is actually going on in the classroom itself. To me, the question 'What are you doing that your students could be doing?' really exposes these status-quo explanations. It forces me to question what I do and that is what reflective teaching is, nothing more or less than constantly probing the assumptions you make about teaching and learning by testing them honestly and directly against what is happening with your students in each lesson you teach.

To do so, you need to do a couple of things. You need to be clear about what you assume about teaching. This usually involves talking to other people and explaining yourself so you can hear yourself put what you take for granted into words. You need to be watchful, and not to be blinded by your expectations. If you start a lesson by thinking it will be difficult for this class for instance, you won't be able to see how it actually goes. You need to reassess everything on a regular basis, to rethink each lesson after it is over. And finally, you need to re-explain what happened to yourself and to others. Putting new words on old events forces clarification. So, these four things make up the process of reflective teaching: Be clear about what you assume; be watchful about what is actually happening; reassess what you assume in light of what happened; and re-explain it by putting words on what you have seen and experienced.

Closing: Returning to the punch line

In my experience, reflective teaching is not a Leggo-type of change. It doesn't start with doing things differently. Nor is it a splash of water in the glass – some new ideas that bounce in and out of your status-quo explanations for what you do. In my experience, reflective teaching is an ice cube. It is an idea that takes hold and melts, infusing your thinking about your work and thus transforming it. This brings us back to where we started, to the socio-cultural environment and the fact that 'What you do is shaped by where you do it.'

To make an ice-cube type change – transforming the way something is done – changes not only the person doing the action but also the environment – the way in which people work together and the things that they value. It changes not only the teacher and her teaching but also, eventually the institution itself. Change as substitution – the Leggo approach – can leave the outer frame of the institution untouched. One way of doing things is simply substituted for another but the whole is not redefined. Change as integration – the water in the glass approach – does not affect the whole either. New ideas are added to the old, replacing some and maintaining others but the whole of the system remains intact, as it was.

Change as transformation is different. The new melts into the old, transforming it as it goes. For this reason it takes time, and there is no fixed outcome or endpoint. But when it is successful, the whole system is different as a result. Learning a new language can be a transformative change. When you become fluent and comfortable in the new language you are different, although you can't point to how or when exactly it happened. The same is true for teaching. When you get really engaged in the question of learning – how it works (and doesn't work) and what you can (and can't do) in the process – it makes you different as a teacher and as a person.

Several years ago, I completed a longitudinal research study in which we looked at how and why teachers changed their thinking and actions in teaching.[10] Jerry was a teacher in the research cohort group; he taught junior high school French in a rural town. Jerry made a comment that ended up becoming the title of the study. As I was interviewing him in the last year of the study, I asked him how his teaching had changed. 'It hasn't changed.' he told me. I gulped, inwardly at least, and I asked him to go on. 'Well, I'm not doing much differently in my teaching ... except that I am.' Having watched Jerry teach over the past three years, I could confirm that he had indeed become more effective in reaching students and getting them to learn French. 'I guess,' he concluded, 'that I do the same things but I do them differently.'

Jerry's phrase, 'the same things done differently,' responds to the conundrum that I outlined at the beginning of this paper. To understand individual development within the context of schools, we must capture this notion of transformative change in teaching. We have to better grasp how and why the ice cube melts. I began this paper with a riddle about the socio-cultural context, namely if 'what you do is shaped by where you do it,' then how can you do something in a different way while you are in the same place? This riddle is the ice cube of the seeming contradiction of transformative change in education: How can you do the same things, but do them differently? May this ice cube melt for you for a long time to come.

References

Banathy, B. H. 1992. *A systems view of education*. New Jersey: Educational Technology Publications.

Clark, E. 1998. The design solution: Systems thinking. *Encounter*. 11(1). 64.

Dewey, John. 1938. *Experience and education*. New York: Collier Macmillan.

---

[10] See Freeman (1991)

Freeman, Donald. 1991. 'To make the tacit explicit:' Teacher education, emerging discourse, and conceptions of teaching. *Teaching and Teacher Education.* 7(5/6). 439-454.

Freeman, Donald. 1992. Language teacher education, emerging discourse, and change in classroom practice. *Perspectives on Second Language Teacher Education.* ed. by J. Flowerdew, T. Brock, & S. Hsia, 1-21. City Polytechnic of Hong Kong: Hong Kong.

Freeman, Donald. 1996. Renaming experience/reconstructing practice: Developing new understandings of teaching. *Teacher learning in language teaching.* ed. by D. Freeman & Jack C. Richards, 221-241. New York: Cambridge University Press.

Freeman, Donald. 1998. *Doing teacher-research: From inquiry to understanding.* Boston MA: Heinle and Heinle Publishers.

Fullan, M. 1993. *Change forces: Probing the depths of educational reform.* London: Falmer Press.

Kelly, P. 1980. From innovation to adaptability: The changing perspective of curriculum development. *Curriculum change: The lessons of a decade.* ed. by Galton, 65-80. Leicester, U.K.: Leicester University Press.

Kotter, J. 1996. *Leading change.* Cambridge MA: Harvard Business Schools Press.

Markee, N. 1997. *Managing curricular innovation.* New York: Cambridge University Press.

Section II: Language Teaching and Learning

Teaching is at Most Hoping for the Best
N.S. Prabhu

**Perspectives on EAP Oral Communication Instruction:
Beliefs, Principles and Instructional Models**
Joan Morley

Grammar as a Metasemiotic Tool in Child Literacy Development
Geoff Williams

**Integrating Language and Content Teaching
through Collaborative Tasks**
Merrill Swain

Pragmatics and English Language Teaching
Jenny Thomas

**Pragmatics and Language Teaching Revisited:
Some Implications for the Teacher**
Asim Gunarwan

Teaching English as an International Language in Japan
Nobuyuki Honna

Language Learning Strategies: A Malaysian Perspective
Florence G. Kayad

Learner Autonomy and the Language Teacher
David Crabbe

Text and Task: Authenticity in Language Learning
Andrea H. Peñaflorida

**Educational Innovations in the Thai National English Textbooks
for Primary Schools: "On the Springboard"**
Chaleosri Pibulchol

TEACHING IS AT MOST HOPING FOR THE BEST

N. S. Prabhu

There is an ambiguity in the way we use the term 'teaching'. We sometimes talk of teaching as if it meant the causing or bringing about of learning in the learner, so that the performance of teaching necessarily implies the occurrence of learning. Teaching in this sense is the obverse of learning: something can be said to have been taught only if it has been learnt; any failure in learning necessarily indicates a corresponding failure in teaching. The terms 'teach' and 'learn' thus refer to two sides of the same event, in the way the terms 'buy' and 'sell' (for instance) do. If something has been sold, it has necessarily been bought, and it is a contradiction to say something like "John sold the house to Peter but Peter didn't buy it". If teaching means the causing of learning, it is similarly contradictory to say that the teacher taught something but the learner did not learn it.

More often, however, we use the term 'teaching' to refer to the activities and procedures carried out by the teacher, independently of how successful they are in their aim of bringing about learning. Used in this sense, teaching is a separate event from learning, not another side of the same event. It is entirely sensible to say that the teacher has taught something but the learner has not learnt it, just as it is sensible to say something like "John sent a message to Peter but Peter didn't receive it". Teaching and learning, that is to say, are not the obverse of each other; they are like sending and receiving, rather than like selling and buying.

Which of the two senses of 'teaching' is preferable or desirable in the discussion of language pedagogy? It is tempting to say that 'teaching' should mean the causation of learning because the causation of learning is, after all, the only real purpose of all teaching. It seems clear that teaching which is divorced from learning is of little educational value, being at best a form of routine or ritual, and it therefore seems necessary to resist any discussion of teaching as a separate event from learning. Indeed this line of thought often leads to (or gets reinforced by) an idealistic stance, from which it becomes unenlightened to talk of teaching as distinct from learning.

But in reality we do talk of teaching most of the time as an activity distinct from learning. We discuss teaching objectives, teaching content, teaching materials, teaching procedures, etc, which are all matters different from the occurrence of learning, though meant to be conducive to it. We do of course discuss learners' needs, learners' backgrounds, learners' role in classroom activities, etc, but these too are matters of teaching, rather than of learning, since they are all inputs to decisions about what should be done in a given classroom, how, when, etc, that is to say, decisions to be made in teaching.

The point I am making is not that we always discuss teaching and seldom learning, or even that we discuss teaching more often than learning. We do discuss various concepts and theories of what the process of learning might be like – concepts such as memorization and retrieval, habit-formation, intake and internal representation, sequence of acquisition, etc. But we regard this as a discussion of learning, as distinct from that of teaching. Even when we consider what forms of teaching might be supportive of a certain process of learning, we see ourselves as inter-relating two distinct matters, namely, the activity of teaching and the phenomenon of learning. Teaching is thus seen to be a separate matter from learning, not just the other side of it. Teaching is what the teacher does; learning is what happens to the learner.

The question I want to ask here is: why is this so? Why do we treat, or need to treat, teaching and learning as separate, though related, events, like sending something and receiving it, rather than as two sides of a single event, like selling something and buying it? Why do we not (or can we not) treat teaching as strictly the causation of learning, so that there is only one event involved, seen as teaching from one point of view and as learning from another? I want to discuss three possible answers to this question.

The first and most obvious answer is that we are unable to consider learning to the same extent as teaching. There is a large disparity in our knowledge of the two. As Brumfit pointed out forcefully some fifteen years ago (1984, 59), teaching is an intentional activity which can be planned, carried out with deliberate effort, controlled or regulated, and observed as it happens. One can decide to do it or not to do it, to do it one way or in another, to speed it up or slow it down, to stop or continue it, etc, and what is done can be observed, recorded, reviewed or studied. In contrast, learning can happen with or without the learner's intention, or even willingness, and cannot be started or stopped, speeded up or slowed down, either by the teacher or by the learner. It is something that cannot be planned, deliberately put into operation, controlled, observed or recorded. Learning, that is to say, is unpredictable and intangible, unlike teaching which is much more tangible and fully predictable. This means that we cannot talk about learning with anything like the certainty and specificity available for our discussion of teaching; and, further, we cannot claim, or assume, that what we know and say about teaching is relevant, to any extent, to learning. We cannot, that is to say, treat learning as the obverse of teaching because we have too little knowledge or control of learning, and also because our differential knowledge of teaching and learning is indicative of a major difference between the nature of teaching and that of learning, quite unlike the case with two sides of a coin.

A second possible answer to the question of why teaching and learning cannot be treated as the obverse of each other is that there is a large mismatch between the workings and outcomes of the two. Not only does teaching not always result in the relevant learning but also the learning that does result is often unrelated to what the teaching has aimed at. Allwright highlighted this fact, several years ago, when he asked, "Why don't learners learn what teachers teach?" (1984). He was concerned not with the problem of learners' failure to learn but rather with the puzzling fact that what learners do learn is frequently quite different from what teachers try to teach. As an explanation of this puzzle, Allwright suggests that learners have their own intentions, preoccupations and priorities in the classroom, which are not based on the teacher's intentions, aims and expectations. Learners, that is to say, have their agendas for learning, based on what they consider important, what they find interesting, what they experience as a problem or hurdle on the way, etc, as well as on what they see of fellow-learners' agendas, efforts, successes and failures. Seen in this light, what happens in the classroom is that teachers pursue their teaching agendas while learners pursue their (varied, individual) learning agendas, and the different agendas work at cross purposes much of the time. Far from being two related events, teaching and learning appear as independent, unrelated events, often in conflict with each other. Learners' agendas are no doubt less explicit, less stable and less perceptible than teachers' agendas but one can see enough evidence of their existence, says Allwright, if one sheds a preoccupation with the teaching agenda.

Perhaps we should pause here to ask what 'learning' means in this discussion. The term 'learning' can refer to two distinct things: one, the thing that happens in the learner's mind when something gets newly internalized, assimilated or organized; and two, the thing that a learner does with the aim of internalizing something new. The former is a piece of development; the latter a piece of action. When Brumfit says that learning, unlike teaching, is imperceptible, unpredictable and unavailable for advance planning, he is thinking of learning as a mental event, a form of internal development. When, on the other hand, Allwright talks about learners' agendas, perceptions and efforts to learn, he is thinking of learning as physical or verbal procedure, a form of activity. 'Learning' in this sense of physical activity is quite close to the sense of teaching: learners doing such work as asking questions, referring to books, participating in group work or conferring with one another about what should be done, would all be learning, i.e. effort by learners to learn, for Allwright. It can equally well be called self-teaching, i.e. effort by learners to teach themselves. Allwright's argument would then be that teachers' agendas for teaching differ from learners' self-teaching agendas, and that 'learning' (in the sense of a mental event) is relatable to learners' self-teaching rather than to teachers' teaching.

Let me now go on to a third possible reason why learning cannot be the obverse of teaching. This takes its cue from Brumfit's point about learning being internal to the learner's mind, and considers the possible nature of that mental phenomenon. Learning, as we have noted, can happen with or without the teacher's teaching. It can also happen with or without the learner's intention or conscious effort, or even willingness. Neither the teacher nor the learner can tell whether it will happen or not, or even know whether it is happening or not at a given point of time. It is something that happens, not something that is done. We can only recognize it after it has happened, from the resultant ability or behaviour of the learner; and, based on our experience of recognizing similar happenings in different learners, we can sometimes say what sort of learning is likely to happen if and when it happens. What makes it happen is completely internal to the learner's mind, therefore completely inaccessible to us. Further, it may well be the case that nothing is certain to make it happen even within the learner's mind: the happening (which we can conceive of variously as a connection being made, a pattern being formed, a reorganization taking place, etc) may be a matter of probability or chance. Learning, that is to say, is essentially an accident. It is an accident as far as our knowledge as teachers or self-teachers goes; it may also be an accident more inherently – a truly chance phenomenon in the mind, subject at most to a degree of probability. Seen this way, learning is similar to a thought, idea or image arising in our minds. We cannot make an idea arise, or tell when or whether it will arise; we can only recognize it after it arises. The arising of an idea is an accident, as far as we can tell and perhaps also by the very nature of that phenomenon. I am suggesting that learning as a mental event is similar to the occurrence of ideas, images and thoughts – beyond our conscious control and probably a matter of chance by its very nature.

Learning is also an individual phenomenon, varying from one learner to another in terms of the time at which it happens, the pace at which it progresses and the stage which it reaches either over a given period or ultimately. This is in a sense obvious, in that we know from experience that no instance of teaching leads to the same learning, or non-learning, in all the learners. Learning happens in some learners at some points of time, and does not in others. It happens more often in one learner and less in another, or more often over one stretch of time than over another. No group of learners ends up with the same amount of learning, even though the teaching has been the same. It is common to attribute this variation to such things as the learners' varied backgrounds, varied levels of motivation, varied learning styles, etc, but the point we have just made about the accidental nature of learning provides a different – I think more natural – explanation of it. If learning is inherently a chance phenomenon in the•mind, it follows that its occurrence will vary from one mind to another, from one time to another, etc, in a way that is unpredictable and unexplainable in terms of other factors. Differential learning need not be the result of differences between individuals; it can simply be due to the fact that there can be no consistency where accident and chance are involved.

Learning is not just an individual event; it is a personal – in some sense 'private' – event. I have already likened the occurrence of learning to the occurrence of an idea in the mind. When one is looking for an idea, one is in a state of uncertainty about whether or not the search will be successful; the more intently one is looking, the more acute is the uncertainty, amounting to a state of vulnerability. Something like this is true of the occurrence of learning: there is always an accompanying uncertainty or sense of risk, especially when there is an effort being made to learn, and a corresponding expectation or hope that learning will occur. Also, when a piece of learning or an idea does arise – or, rather, when there is a recognition of its having occurred – there is a moment of intense intellectual pleasure or satisfaction, which is entirely personal and private in that it is independent of any recognition or reward from outside. It is facts such as these – that there is a state of insecurity and vulnerability when a piece of learning is being looked for or hoped for, and there is a feeling of intellectual fulfilment when a piece of learning is seen to have occurred – that make us regard learning as a personal and private event. Neither the sense of vulnerability nor the feeling of fulfilment is open to a sharing with others; indeed, they are states of mind which react negatively to intrusion from others, thus making the occurrence of learning less likely to occur.

Learning, then, is accidental, individual and private – the opposite of teaching which is deliberate, public and most often directed to groups. Not only are teaching and learning separate, but they have characteristics which firmly rule out their being two sides of the same event.

And yet, learning does occur when teaching is done, or occurs much more than if no teaching is done. No one would doubt that, other things being roughly equal, a group of learners who are taught a language will learn some of that language while another group which receives no teaching will learn none. The conclusion to be drawn from our discussion of the 'difference between teaching and learning' is not that teaching does not help learning. The conclusion is only that specific pieces of teaching cannot be expected to bring about corresponding pieces of learning, and that teaching in general can only help to promote learning overall – perhaps by creating some conditions which increase the probability of the occurrence of learning.

This has implications for the way we discuss teaching and the direction of our effort to develop better teaching. It is in general futile to try to match teaching to learning more and more precisely, or to prefer one form of teaching over another on the grounds that it provides a more direct (or more perceptible) route to learning. Teaching can only help learning indirectly and as a general, overall support. We need to accept that we can have no direct access to or influence on learning whatever form of teaching we may do, and then ask if there are certain things which are nevertheless more of a support to learning than others and, equally, if there are things which are likely to be unhelpful. I will draw attention to one or two such things in the rest of this paper.

Let us consider syllabuses. A language teaching syllabus is thought to be a specification of what is to be taught and learnt, that is to say, what learning is to be caused by the teaching. It is not to be a specification of what the teacher is to do, indicating the teaching activities or procedures to be employed; it is expected to be a statement of what the learner is to learn, that is to say, what is to happen to the learner. What the teacher is to do is thought to be a matter of methodology, quite distinct from a syllabus. A syllabus, it is argued, has to indicate what the learning outcome or 'content' is to be, both overall and in relation to each part or unit of teaching. But such a 'content syllabus' (as it is often called) assumes implicitly that learning outcomes can be specified in advance of teaching, and that specific pieces of learning can be brought about by specific units of teaching. This assumption is so prevalent and so firmly set in the profession that any proposal for a procedural syllabus, specifying teaching activities instead of learning outcomes, is resisted or rejected, sometimes painstakingly (e.g. Widdowson 1990, 144 -150). A procedural syllabus is, however, much more in line with the observations we have made about the nature of learning and the possible relationship between learning and teaching. A content syllabus is at best a form of pedagogic delusion.

There is also a form of pedagogic idealism which claims to increase the efficiency and accountability of teaching by targeting it more and more precisely, and minutely, to expected learning. It advocates specific objectives for all teaching – the more specific, and clearly specified, the better. Each little piece of teaching should be carried out with a corresponding piece of learning clearly in mind, and evidence on the achievement of the piece of learning is to be sought as soon after the teaching as possible. This can be an effective way of promoting the teaching enterprise either in the eyes of the public or with people like sponsors and clients, but it is so unrealistic that the only way of sustaining it is by reducing learning to some form of intentional activity (e.g., memorization or recall of facts or statements; repetition of a rehearsed piece of behaviour) or by telling the learners themselves what they are going to learn, what they are learning or what they have just learnt, at every stage – that is to say, by making the learners partners in the pedagogic delusion.

One effect of a preoccupation with expected learning outcomes is that it prevents one from recognizing unexpected ones when they occur. I have argued that teaching is in no position to predict specific learning, but that does not mean that learning does not occur, unpredictably, when teaching is done. A great deal of learning does in fact happen in this way – so much so that I think the bulk of what gets learnt, and perhaps the most important elements of it, constitute such incidental, untargeted learning, triggered by the general condition of teaching rather than aimed at specifically by it. As Newmark (1966) put it some thirty years ago, "if each phonological and syntactic rule, each complex of lexical features, each semantic value and stylistic nuance had to be acquired one at a time –..., the child learner would be old before he could say a single appropriate thing, and the adult learner would be dead". Learning is so normal and natural to human beings (in particular, language learning) that it happens all the time. If it cannot be directly caused, it cannot be stopped either. We tend not to see it as teachers only because we tend to be over-focused on the pieces of learning we aim to bring about. If we reduced the focus on such expected learning, we will perhaps begin to see more of the unexpected, incidental learning that occurs.

Not only does teaching help to bring about learning, in some general and indirect way, but also it is very likely that one form of teaching helps more than another. We are familiar with the sad story of method-comparison research in the past, which based itself on what learning was specifically aimed at by each form of teaching. It was assumed, in fact, that the more specifically teaching was related to learning, the more dependable or revealing the comparison would be. But there is a different way of approaching the matter. If learning is normal and natural, given some general condition, one can ask what the norms of the phenomenon are.

How much learning can be expected, for example, from certain (sizeable) quantities of exposure to, or contact with, the language? A careful pursuit of this question can hopefully lead to a broad specification of the level of learning (more likely, levels over a certain range) that can be regarded as the norm – in a way comparable to the norms of IQ in relation to a young person's age. The availability of such norms would make it possible to judge particular forms of teaching over fairly large stretches of time. It would also, from another point of view, stop us from setting educational goals too ambitiously. There is at present no usable basis for indicating possible attainment levels for language teaching programmes: attainment levels are set wishfully, rather than knowledgeably, sometimes to please the powers-that-be or under pressure from them. Such unrealistic targets can have the same kind of effect as over-specific objectives, namely, a substitution of the appearance of learning for actual learning.

Developmental norms for language learning can help us make what may be called macro-judgements about forms of teaching. But the daily act of teaching calls for a variety of micro-judgements about one or another aspect of the ongoing teaching activity. These judgements cannot be based on whether or not particular teaching activities result in particular learning outcomes, as teaching cannot be related to learning in that way. The micro-judgements need to be guided, instead, by what may be called the teacher's cumulative experience and, arising from it, an evolving feel for the occurrence of learning. Perhaps when teaching is free of the blinkering effects of a content syllabus and the negative effects of over-specific objectives, teachers in the classroom will be able to recognize, in an intuitive way, more and more of the learning that takes place in learners as a general effect of the teaching being done. Perhaps, too, these small-scale intuitive judgements at the classroom level and the larger-scale judgements to be made in relation to developmental norms will together (and in interaction with each other) give us the best basis we can have for preferring one form of teaching to another.

Let me conclude with a brief, point-form summary of my argument:

1. Teaching and learning cannot be related to each other directly or specifically, as they are very different kinds of event.

2. But teaching does help to bring about learning in a general way, and it is likely that one form of teaching does this more than another.
3. We therefore need to explore ways of organizing teaching without making assumptions of a specific relationship between teaching and learning, and also ways of making judgements about different forms of teaching.
4. Such exploration leads us to propose that teaching needs to use a procedural rather than a content syllabus, and needs to avoid specific objectives. It also needs to have some developmental norms to relate itself to, and a larger scope for the teacher to exercise intuitive judgements.

Proposals such as these do not aim to make learning more directly relatable to teaching; they try, instead, to be consistent with the fact that the two are not directly relatable. Given the wide difference between the nature of teaching and that of learning, teaching will always be a matter of hoping for learning to occur, rather than of making it occur.

References

Allwright, R. L. 1984. Why Don't Learners Learn What Teachers Teach? *Language Learning in Formal and Informal Context.* ed. by Singleton, D. M. & Little, D. G. Dublin: IRAAL.

Brumfit, Christopher. 1984. *Communicative Methodology in Language Teaching.* Cambridge: Cambridge University Press.

Newmark, Leonard. 1966. How Not to Interfere with Language Learning. *International Journal of American Linguistics.* 32(I, II).

Widdowson, H. G. 1990. *Aspects of Language Teaching.* Oxford University Press.

PERSPECTIVES ON EAP ORAL COMMUNICATION INSTRUCTION: BELIEFS, PRINCIPLES AND INSTRUCTIONAL MODELS

Joan Morley

Slowly but surely over the last decade one emerging development in the field of English Language Teaching (ELT) has been a new level of serious instructional attention to oral communication skills, including attention to aspects of speech and pronunciation. Whereas traditional language education, particularly for adults, has valued literacy skills far more highly than oral skills, often affording the latter limited time and less than well-informed instruction, recently in some quarters this has begun to change. It is encouraging to observe that a number of programs in a variety of ELT settings in different parts of the world are moving to revise curricula so that speech in general, and pronunciation in particular, are being brought into the mainstream of instruction with a learner goal of oral communicative competence. Overall, the basic premise underlying these changes is the undeniable fact that intelligible pronunciation is an essential component of communicative competence.

This paper focuses on English for Academic Purposes (EAP) programming where gradually a new look in oral communication course work is emerging as it has become clear that written communication is not the only language skill needed if one is to succeed, not just survive, as a fully participating member of an English-speaking educational or professional community. Part of the apprenticeship for membership in such communities entails learning not only the written genre, but also the spoken genre of its transactional and interactional communication (Brown and Yule, 1983) including the oral discourse that marks someone as an in-member of that group (Swales, 1991).

Descriptive details of English for Academic Purposes (EAP) programming in this paper are referenced to the program at the University of Michigan English Language Institute (ELI). The Michigan ELI, over the last twelve years, has developed a comprehensive EAP program with a curriculum of over thirty credit courses a year for University of Michigan international students. Of the thirty courses, ten focus on various facets of oral communication, thirteen feature different kinds of written communication, and six provide special kinds of instruction for international teaching assistants. In addition, there are three advanced ESP intensive summer programs, one in Legal Studies, one in Business Studies, and one in general EAP. Most of the ELI courses are targeted to meet the needs of advanced graduate students who are pursuing doctoral studies in a range of colleges and departments across the university. A Speaking Clinic and a Writing Laboratory provide individual services, year round.

This paper will present five perspectives on recent developments in oral communication instruction, in general, and speech/pronunciation, in particular. The first section reviews two agents of change, catalysts for the current developments in speech/pronunciation instruction. Part 2 discusses some pre-planning guidelines for program development. The next part examines beliefs and principles. Part 4 outlines the Michigan approach paradigm for communicative speech/pronunciation teaching. Part 5 closes the presentation with some thoughts on program responsibilities and learner outcomes, cross-dialectal adaptation, and training English teachers for the next millennium.

Agents of Change

Two factors have figured prominently as catalysts in bringing about changes both in attitudes toward speech/pronunciation instruction in ELT, and in instructional theory and pedagogy. The first is a reality factor: *extensive numbers of learners in need*. It cannot be stressed enough, that there is a steadily increasing pressure on the field from a virtual population explosion of adult and teen learners whose urgent needs for intelligible, functional oral communication skills are not being met in traditional programs.

The second factor is the emergence of some innovative developments in speech/pronunciation instruction. Chief among these are substantive changes in teaching principles and practices toward a model which is based on a communicative-cognitive approach to speech/pronunciation instruction (Morley, 1991; Anderson-Hsieh, 1989).

Learner Problems and Unmet Learner Needs

Clearly, many different groups of adult and teen second language speakers have poor to unintelligible speech patterns, which may place them at a serious disadvantage. As has been observed elsewhere (Morley, 1991, 1987; Wong, 1985) there are today increasing numbers of such potentially at-risk speakers of English in a variety of settings virtually everywhere. They lack intelligible speech patterns for academic purposes and, more importantly, for successful language performance in a whole range of professional and vocational career contexts. Their communication breakdowns occur, in the words of Bolinger (1986, p. 2), when their speech patterns "...do not communicate *what* the speaker wants, *when* the speaker wants?" Second language speakers may experience one or more of the following problems.

Complete breakdown in communication

Speech is incomprehensible resulting in a complete breakdown in communication. In short, the speaker's 'accent' (that is, features of poor intelligibility and/or communicability) is such that it precludes functional oral communication. (See Figure 1, *Speech Intelligibility/Communicability Index*.)

Ineffectual speech performance

Speech patterns result in basically ineffectual communication in educational, occupational, social, and/or personal business transactions. Speakers are judged to lack credibility and are perceived not to inspire confidence in their knowledge of 'content' or their ability to make intelligent decisions. Many problems of this nature are reported in the workplace and among international graduate student instructors in university settings.

Negative judgments about personal qualities

Speech patterns trigger 'foreignerism' stereotyping and listeners make negative judgments about personality traits. Beebe's research (1978, p. 3) reported that native speakers described pronunciation errors as sounding "...'comical', 'cute', 'incompetent', 'not serious', 'effeminate', or 'childish'..."

Anxious apprehensive listener reactions

In a conversation with a non-native speaker who has poor intelligibility, many native speakers report that they experience very uncomfortable apprehensive feelings as the interaction proceeds. Even though they *seem* to understand what the second language speaker is saying *at the moment,* they feel a continuous undercurrent of anxiety, afraid that communication will break down as the interaction moves along. They report that they keep to superficial 'social' topics, shift topics frequently, speak more loudly and more slowly, and often terminate the interaction as soon as possible. This serves to rob the non-native speaker not only of natural language practice encounters, but of opportunities to develop congenial social relationships, as well.

Pejorative stereotyping

Based on speech patterns alone, listeners have been found to make serious negative judgments about non-native speakers, assigning them to a variety of undesirable categories. As demonstrated in the research of both Lambert (1967) and Labov (1972), listeners judged speakers they had never seen nor met before as to their personality, intelligence, ethnic group, race, social status – even their height – simply from listening to the way they pronounced a few words.

Accent discrimination

Language discrimination is a fact of life. As an example of accent discrimination in today's world, legal recourse (or lack there of) in the United States serves as a confounding example.

In the United States the 1964 Civil Rights Act, among other areas of potential discrimination, clearly forbids an employer to discriminate against a job applicant on the basis of linguistic traits linked to national origin. However, employers have considerable latitude in matters of language, and employer violations are widespread in the United States, perhaps at a level as high as 10% of businesses, although only a very small percentage of these infringements of civil rights result in litigation. Cases are often settled out of court and plaintiffs generally have very little success in winning their cases (Lippi-Greene, 1997, 1993; Morley, 1996; Matsuda, 1991).

Innovative Developments in Speech/Pronunciation Instruction

The second agent of change has been the growing influence of a small groundswell of innovative developments in speech/pronunciation education. Not since the 1940's, 50's, and 60's, (which witnessed the rise and decline of dialog memorization and audio-lingual pronunciation practices) followed by the pronunciation-barren 1970's and 80's (when more and more programs gave less and less time to speech/pronunciation, and many programs dropped it entirely) has there been such a theoretically and pedagogically sound reformulation of the speech/pronunciation component of ELT instruction, as that which is emerging today.

While it is true that changes in the oral communication speech/pronunciation facet of ELT have lagged far behind developments elsewhere in the field, there now seems to be a serious movement toward re-examining and reformulating principles and practices. When the restless winds of change began to blow across the field in the 1960's and 70's and when the enormous developments riding on those winds took place, there seemed to be no theoretical or pedagogical 'slot' for speech/pronunciation.

In ELT pedagogy, as new sights were set to concentrate on language functions, task-based methodologies, communicative competencies, learner strategies, and realism and authenticity in learning activities and materials, the familiar ways and means of teaching pronunciation certainly did not seem to fit. In truth there was not a clear model beyond 'articulatory phonetics' where both the process (viewed as non-communicative drill-and-exercise gambits) and the product (viewed as having a minimal success ratio for the time and energy expended) were found wanting.

But major changes have been taking place rapidly in recent years in a number of different kinds of programs in disparate parts of the world. In March 1998, at the academic session of the newly constituted TESOL Interest Section of Speech/Pronunciation, there was a three-hour panel discussion on *International Perspectives on Teaching Pronunciation* with eight people coming from Australia, Austria, Canada, the UK and the US, each presenting information on current work in their region. And in a seven-hour pre-convention institute participants came together from six countries to share their expertise: Austria, Brazil, Mexico, the UK, the US and Venezuela.

The cornerstone for change in new programs is a revised conceptualization of speech/pronunciation instruction in which, by and large, the notion of an articulatory phonetics approach as the conceptual basis for teaching has been abandoned. In its place, attention to the sound system is subsumed under an expanded and comprehensive communicative-cognitive framework, one that encompasses, among other things, the pragmatics of functional language use, the contexts of communicative interactions, a learner-centered view that takes into account the learners' cognitive involvement and self-monitoring, and attention to the affective dimension of language learning. In sections two, three, and four of this paper, particulars of these changes will be discussed and exemplified.

Pre-Planning Guidelines for Program Development

In this section, following from the above discussions of learner problems and some of the current directions, two pre-planning guidelines for program design will be presented. The first guideline involves three basic steps in program pre-planning and the second discusses goal setting.

Steps in Pre-Planning

In looking at current developments, a first question that must be asked is, 'How do today's new programs approach the task of re-designing instruction?' and the answer is found in the specification of three fundamental steps in program preplanning.

Step One: Needs and uses analysis for long-range goals

Establish long-range oral communication goals based on a projection of the language functions learners will need in their English-speaking interactions (that is, the WHY of communication). This step entails analyzing both the nature of the spoken *discourse patterns* learners are predicted to need in order to execute those functions, and *the language situations, contexts and specific settings* involved (that is, the WHY and the WHERE of communication). (See Morley and Brown, forthcoming.)

Step Two: Speech/pronunciation assessment

Evaluate the nature of each individual learner's overall speech patterns, especially in terms of intelligibility and its impact on speech

Goal One: Functional intelligibility

The intent of this premier goal is to help the learner develop clear spoken English which is (at least) reasonably easy to understand and not distracting to listeners.

Goal Two: Functional communicability

The intent of this goal is to help the learner develop spoken English that serves his or her individual communicative needs effectively toward a satisfactory sense of communicative competence. (See Canale and Swain, 1980, on communicative competencies: linguistic, discourse, sociolinguistic and strategic.)

Goal Three: Increased self-confidence

The intent of this goal is to help the learner become more comfortable and confident in using spoken English, to overcome feelings of embarrassment and shame, to develop a positive self-image, and to experience the self-realization of growing empowerment in oral communication.

Goal Four: Speech-monitoring abilities and speech modification strategies for use beyond the classroom

The intent of this goal is to guide learners toward developing speech awareness, personal self-monitoring skills, and speech modification strategies and techniques which will enable them to continue to develop the three above goals (intelligibility, communicability, and confidence), both during the class term and beyond. (Note: See Wenden, 1991, and Oxford, 1990, for strategies information.)

Beliefs and Principles

Above all else, the defining concept driving the current trends in speech/pronunciation teaching is one of communication – with the belief that the proper place of this component of the ELT curriculum is in its role as "...an integral part of oral communication – a part of the entire speech communication act – not something set aside from the mainstream in a drill-bound laboratory..." (Morley, 1994, p. 66.)

The tenets of the emerging belief system outlined below, have guided the formulation of the pre-planning steps and the setting of learner goals, and the construction of the approach paradigm which will be discussed in part four. They have been developed and used over the past several years in designing course offerings in the oral communication curriculum of the Michigan EAP program. They represent a significant shift and a broadened scope from traditional practices which usually focus on a much narrower view of 'pronunciation'. In fact, they are the harbingers of a whole 'new look' as deftly captured in the following comment by Anderson-Hsieh, "...while the pendulum has begun to swing back in the direction of more emphasis on pronunciation, it is swinging back in a different arc, and we are now at a very much different place..." (Anderson-Hsieh, 1989, p. 73).

Taken all together, the following 'beliefs' form a philosophical base upon which informed pedagogical decision-making can be carried out. They can be used as a guide for a teacher setting out to develop a course to fit the specific needs of a given clientele – as informed by information gathered in the pre-planning stage. It is important to make two additional comments here:

- Customized course work is important; it is no longer a case of 'one size fits all' lesson planning.
- Selectivity is important; it is no longer a case of teaching everything in the book.

1. A communicative-cognitive-affective approach to speech/ pronunciation instruction

The basic component of this belief system is that instructional planning and implementation must be learner-centered and it must be designed to guide learners in the achievement of three long-range goals:

- sufficient *intelligibility* to support functional communication
- learners' *cognitive involvement* in developing speech awareness, learning strategies, and personal self-monitoring and speech modification skills
- learners' *affective involvement* in developing self-confidence and a positive self image

communicability. (See Figure 1, *Speech Intelligibility/Communicability Index.*) Prepare a detailed inventory of speech/pronunciation strengths and weaknesses for each learner. With reference to the impact on intelligibility, prioritize the 'problem areas', and place them along an interference-distraction continuum. (See evaluation instruments in Morley's annotated bibliography, forthcoming.)

Step Three: Course design

Design a speech/pronunciation course syllabus which integrates two types of instruction. Determine the major speaking activities and their communicative tasks – as a 'first layer' focus. Add a complement of pronunciation activities – as the 'second layer' focus. Specify learner-centered self-involvement goals so that, early on, students can learn to self-monitor. (Consult a reputable annotated bibliography of recommended student texts and teacher reference books (Murphy, 1997, and Web Site <http://www.gsu.edu/~esljmm/furtherreading.htm>). See also Grant, 1995, for suggestions on writing your own materials.)

Setting Learner Goals

The second essential part of program pre-planning is setting learner goals, both class goals and individual goals. The former, based on the speech profiles of all class members, needs to be a limited set which combines macro-level global features of speech and micro-level discrete-point features of pronunciation. (See Figure 2, *Dual Focus: Speech Production and Speech Performance*, Morley 1994.) The latter needs to be a personal short-list of priority goals for each individual learner. It is important for teacher and student to work together assessing speech patterns and formulating a set of personal priorities for modifications of speech/pronunciation during the course.

The following four basic goals are ones which form a backdrop against which learners can focus on self-monitoring and self-modification of specific macro and micro features of speech/pronunciation. Note that neither 'perfect pronunciation', nor 'near-native pronunciation', nor 'mastery of pronunciation' – traditional goals that have proved patently unattainable, now or in earlier times – are recommended here as viable goals.

2. A reformulation of the domain of speech/pronunciation

This expanded view of what constitutes the domain of speech/pronunciation is a feature central to this belief system, and may seem like heresy to some traditionalists. It encompasses a multi-dimensional concept which integrates attention to four elements.

- suprasegmentals
- segmentals and phonotactics
- voice quality features, articulatory settings, and other paralinguistic features used in oral communication
- elements of body language and other extralinguistic features used in oral communication

(Morley, 1991; Murphy, 1991; Pennington and Richards, 1986)

3. A central focus on suprasegmentals

A basic belief of this system is one that calls for a redirection of priorities within the sound system to a focus on the critical importance of a wide range of suprasegmental features of spoken English. In the case of intonation, for example,· **it not only complements meaning, it creates meaning**. Candlin, in his preface to the Brazil, Coulthard, and Johns', book on *Discourse Intonation and Language Teaching* (1980), commented that, "In essence the argument (for a discourse approach) hinges on the inseparability of the meaning of intonation from discoursal context." (Candlin, 1980, p. xi.) And, in tandem with intonation, a variety of other prosodic features are critical to one's transmission of meaning.

This does not mean that attention to vowel and consonant sounds, their combinations, and their reduced, elided, and assimilated forms in context are excluded; of course, they continue to be an important focus of instruction.

4. A two-layer speech/pronunciation course syllabus developed to fit the needs of the specific clientele

A 'layered' framework provides an important design concept which integrates two types of instruction. Planning the first layer involves choosing a sequence of major (and minor) speaking activities and their communicative tasks, referenced to the needs-and-uses assessment. Planning the second layer involves periodically adding a complement of speech/pronunciation elements and practice activities, fitted in as appropriate, and referenced to the learners' needs. Once again, a one-size-fits all curriculum is no longer viable.

5. *Changing perspectives on the roles of learner and teacher*

This part of the belief system focuses on revised expectations, roles and goals, for both learner involvement and teacher involvement. A key part of the learner's role is the development of speech awareness, self-awareness and self-monitoring under the guidance of a speech/pronunciation teacher-facilitator. A key part of the teacher's role is not unlike that of a 'coach': a voice 'coach', a speech 'coach', or even a sports 'coach'. In this real-life drama, the student is the 'performer' of a complex communicative-cognitive-motor skill and the teacher-coach is the 'director'. (See Figure 3, *Learner Awarenesses and Attitudes*, and Figure 4, *Teacher as 'Coach' Responsibilities.*)

6. *Individualization and the uniqueness of each learner*

Individualization in the speech/pronunciation class values the uniqueness of each ESL learner. Each learner has created his or her own distinctive pattern of spoken English. Personalizing this, each of us, whether an L2 speaker or an L1 speaker of a given dialect, speaks with our own ideolectic 'accent'. It is unlike that of anyone else, the product of a variety of influences. Instruction must take this into account and guide each learner in developing a satisfactory personal pattern of spoken English, one which supports effective comfortable oral communication.

7. *Increased attention to the reciprocal link between listening and speaking*

This focus is essential to the system in its reaffirmation of the importance of instruction that features a strong link between auditory skills and speech/pronunciation skills – reception and production.

8. *Explicit attention to sound-spelling relationships*

While this is another belief which may sound like heresy to some, it is clear that information on a range of important sound-spelling relationships and specific guidance on using English orthography can be useful tools in helping students learn to predict and produce certain pronunciation patterns.

The Michigan 'Approach' Paradigm for Communicative Speech/ Pronunciation Teaching

The quest for the ultimate method has been, in H. H. Stern's words, our "...century-old obsession..." and our "...prolonged preoccupation..." as we have searched in vain for the magic method that would serve as the final answer (Stern, 1985, p. 251). On the same topic Nunan neatly summarized his view in the following way: "It has been realised that there never was and probably never will be a method for all, and the focus in recent years has been on the development of classroom tasks and activities that are consonant with what we know about second language acquisition, and that are also in keeping with the dynamics of the classroom itself." (Nunan, 1991, p. 228) Prabhu noted that discussions of 'best method' often focus on 'it depends', and comments, "That there is no best method therefore means that no single method is best for everyone, as there are important variations in the teaching context that influence what is best." (Prabhu, 1990)

H. D. Brown bids us abandon the search for the perfect method and to turn instead to a concept of 'strategic approach'. In a recent paper, *After Method: Toward a Principled Strategic Approach to Language Teaching* (1993), Brown defines *approach* in the traditional way (following Anthony, 1963) as "...a theory of language and language learning..." and notes that, "One's approach to language teaching is the theoretical rationale that underlies everything that teachers do in the classroom."

Brown's thesis is that the field's search for the 'ultimate method' has outlived its time, that we should, instead, "...get on with the business of unifying our *approach* to language teaching and of *designing effective tasks and techniques* that are informed by that approach".

In the spirit of this perspective, the following paradigm for a speech/pronunciation instructional program is offered. It is a three-part approach framework, and not unexpectedly its component parts – *language, language learning*, and *language teaching* – draw upon the source disciplines of linguistics, psychology, and education which the field of ELT has long found instructive. Each of the three parts of the approach is outlined briefly below.

Language and Linguistic Matters

The defining mark of this approach is that spoken language instruction and assessment are based upon a language model which encompasses a micro-level linguistic focus and a macro-level linguistic focus. (See Figure 2.)

The **micro level** focuses on speech production and outlines seven areas of discrete pronunciation points.

- precision and accuracy in articulation of vowel and consonant sounds; articulatory clarity in multi-syllabic words and phrasal units
- neutral vowel use; reductions; contractions; lengthening /shortening patterns of vowel use
- consonant combinations, both within and across word boundaries; elisions; assimilations
- syllable structure and precise syllabic boundaries; linking and blending words across word boundaries; phrasing and pause points
- control of pitch change points and intonation patterning
- control of speed, timing, and rate variations; rhythm and variations of vowel length related to stress; taking time to articulate clearly
- control of volume; sustaining energy level across the entire length of an utterance

(See Morley 1988, 1991, and 1994, for a detailed discussion.)

At this point, it is important to stress that the communicative speech activities drive the instructional sessions, into which pronunciation instruction, per se, is programmed as an adjunct, not by chance, but by design.

Thus the communicative speech activity of the lesson provides the practice ground where students can stabilize their abilities to manipulate prosodic and vocal features at will with emerging ease and accuracy and to adjust vowel and consonant pronunciation, in order to express intended meaning and increase intelligibility in context. Within this framework, then, teachers can insert instruction on appropriate pronunciation aspects of speech production and provide whatever discrete-point attention a given student or a whole class needs.

At the **macro level**, or global level, instruction focuses on the synthesis of many components of communicative oral discourse including the following features.

- an appropriate level of speech intelligibility and communicability in extended oral discourse (See Intelligibility/Communicability Index.)
- enhanced vocal effectiveness in oral discourse; communicative use of vocal quality features
- overall fluency and smoothness in on-going planning and structuring of speech as it proceeds
- overall accuracy, precision, and clarity in contextualized speech, both sounds and prosodic features
- expansion, refinement, and communicative command of grammatical structures in context
- expansion and communicative command of field-specific, general-academic, and general-purpose vocabulary words and phrase units; increasingly rapid retrieval time
- effective use of appropriate and expressive non-verbal features of oral communication

To support students' development of macro-level spoken discourse competence, a series of intellectually interesting and challenging speech activities needs to be designed. A format can be constructed in which assignments ask each student to prepare and present a short information-and-opinion talk on an important (to the students) issue-oriented topic, and to lead a follow-up discussion, in which they get practice in responding to interactive comments and questions from their classmates. This format also gives them an opportunity to practice spontaneous, off-the-top-of-the-head speaking, during which they can continue to try to exercise a modicum of self-monitoring and self-correction.

This format provides the practice opportunity a learner needs in order to perform the simultaneous acts of:

- propositional spontaneous speaking

while at the same time

- monitoring speech production and speech performance toward increasingly intelligible and effective patterns of oral discourse.

More importantly, this tasking gives learners the demanding kind of practice which forces them, within a guided framework, and for natural communicative purposes, to access-and-retrieve, over and over and over again, from their developing repertoire of English

The importance of this act of 'access-and-retrieval' cannot be underestimated. Ultimately this is the only way students can build the automaticity and the sufficiently rapid retrieval time which will enable them to participate successfully in the rapid real-time/real-life 'fast speech' speed of communicative interactions.

Language Learning and Psycholinguistic Matters

Within a communicative approach to speech/pronunciation instruction, it is essential to focus on the three critical dimensions of learning that involve the learner as a whole person. These three components of human learning are: the cognitive-intellectual, the psychological-affective, and the physical-performative.

1. Cognitive/intellectual component of learning
- **Language information** (and *cognitive* learning strategies)
  a. speech awareness and long-range goals
  b. study awareness and short-range goals
- **Procedural information** (and *metacognitive* learning strategies)

(Note: See Wenden, 1991, and Oxford, 1990, for strategies information.)

Attention to intellectual frameworks seems to help adult and near-adult learners enormously. The following learning objectives are intended to help learners develop speech awareness and study awareness in order to engage their intellectual involvement in the learning process.

2. Psychological/affective component of learning and affective objectives

- **Learner self-involvement** (and *cognitive, metacognitive* and *affective* strategies)
  a. recognition of self-responsibility;
  b. development of self-monitoring skills
  c. development of speech modification skills
  d. recognition of self accomplishment
- **Comfortable, supportive classroom atmosphere** (and *affective* and *social* strategies)
  a. fosters supportive teacher-student interactions
  b. fosters supportive student-student interactions

Affective objectives serve the powerful psychological component of learning. The first critical part of the affective component, *learner self-involvement*, is essential as speech/pronunciation study is most profitable when students are actively involved in their own learning, not passively detached repeaters of drills. Research shows that self-involvement is the primary characteristic of good language learners. And the greatest aspect of this is self-monitoring, a skill which will empower learners to continue to manage their own learning, whether in or out of class

3. Physical/performative component of learning and practice objectives

- **Speech/pronunciation practice** with a focus on integration of these three components
  a. linguistic components (phonetic/phonological patterning)
  b. paralinguistic components (vocal communication strategies)
  c. extralinguistic components (body and gestural communication)
- **Pronunciation-oriented listening practice** (and *meta-cognitive* strategies)
- **Spelling-oriented pronunciation practice** (and *cognitive* strategies)

Practice objectives serve the physical component of learning.

Language Teaching and Educational Matters

Overall, in this paradigm teachers must plan lessons that provide for a range of integrated practice modes designed to carry out both 'production' and 'performance' dimensions of speech/pronunciation, with a two-layered focus that integrates communicative tasks and pronunciation activities. Plans must include attention to speech/pronunciation practice, pronunciation-oriented listening practice, and pronunciation sound-spelling practice.

1. **Speech/pronunciation practice** for maximum benefit must go far beyond imitation and provide three different practice modes which can be included from the very beginning. (See Morley, 1994.)
   a. **Imitative practice** (dependent practice) needs to be used sparingly and only to establish controlled production. Once learners are able to produce the item, they need to move on quickly to rehearsed practice.
   b. **Rehearsed communicative practice** (guided self-practice and independent self-practice) needs to be used to stabilize a modified or new speech/pronunciation feature as soon as students can produce it at will.
   c. **Extemporaneous communicative practice** (independent practice) must be used to habituate and integrate modified speech patterns into naturally occurring creative speech.
2. **Pronunciation-oriented listening practice** facilitates the development of auditory perception and discriminative listening skills for all dimensions of speech/pronunciation. (See Gilbert, 1987.)
3. **Pronunciation sound-spelling practice** helps learners relate spoken English and written English quickly and accurately so they can become truly literate in English. An awareness of spelling patterns as cues to stress and rhythm

patterns can be very useful to learners. (See Dickerson, 1994.)

Some Final Thoughts on Program Responsibilities and Learner Outcomes, Cross-Dialectal Adaptation, Research, and Training English Teachers for the Next Millennium

Program Responsibilities and Learner Outcomes

To prepare learners for English-language communication in today's world, a responsible speech/pronunciation program will stress three essential learner outcomes.

Learner process

In the outcome relating to learner process, the program must guide students in learning how to become positive self-involved learners, how to become active forceful partners in their own learning, and how to develop personal skills and strategies for monitoring and altering their own speech patterns.

Learner product

In the matter of learner product, the program is responsible for helping students work toward developing a satisfactory level of intelligibility and eliminating distracting patterns of speech performance, and encouraging them to strive for increasingly effective levels of communicability. It is essential that teachers help learners develop a stock of speech-monitoring abilities and speech modification strategies that they can use both during and after the instructional period.

Adaptation attitude

Finally, there is a third matter which has begun to find its way into educational considerations. And that is the role of the program in guiding learners in developing an attitude of speech/pronunciation adaptation. Adaptation is complex; it requires one part linguistic competence, one part discourse competence, one part sociolinguistic competence, and one part strategic competence, in Canale and Swain terms (1980). But it must also have a large amount of *goodwill* and an open philosophy toward adapting one's own English dialect when in contact with dialect speakers from the many world Englishes around the globe.

Variation and Adaptation: Some Thoughts on Cross-dialect Communication and Speaking English Internationally

As noted above, it is important to consider the topic of variation and adaptation, in terms of cross-dialect communication and speaking English internationally. For both *second language* speakers of English, and *first language* speakers of the myriad Englishes around the world – personalizing this, for any one of us who intends to use English internationally – it is essential to broaden the base of our philosophy toward speech-monitoring and speech modification. As cross-dialect communicators, we need to consider seriously the importance of developing these skills. This will enable us to adapt aspects of our mode of speaking English in the two-way reciprocal communicative context where our interlocutors can be expected to use different dialects of speech/pronunciation. It is essential to help students develop an attitude of openness and adaptation, in both linguistic and non-linguistic patterns of behavior. It will help prepare them to be more comfortable as cross-dialect and cross-cultural speakers. As noted by Baxter (1980, p. 53), "Adaptation is not an easy process, requiring in the speaker a variety of communicative skills and an awareness of what is entailed in cross-cultural communication. It also requires a willingness to modify, temporarily or even permanently, one's cultural identity."

A not-unusual situation is one of transplanted native speakers of a world English dialect which differs from that of the speech community in which they find themselves living. One example is professionals in a variety of fields who take up residence in places where an English dialect different from their own is spoken, perhaps as an L1, perhaps as an L2. Their adjustment might be more comfortable if they received specific training in three 'A' areas: LANGUAGE ADAPTATION, CULTURAL ADAPTATION, and ATTITUDE ADJUSTMENT. Another example is international graduate student teaching assistants in North American universities who may need guidance from a speech/pronunciation teacher in addressing the need to adjust their attitude, as well as to apply their speech/pronunciation monitoring and modifications skills.

Finally, it is important to say again that these three areas LANGUAGE ADAPTATION, CULTURAL ADAPTATION, and ATTITUDE ADJUSTMENT are important considerations not only for non-native speakers, but in fact for any native speaker of any given dialect of world English. In a lifetime which may include travel or work in countries where English is used as a lingua-franca, all of us may find ourselves in the position of needing to adapt and accommodate in order to have successful communication. No one of us is exempt from considering seriously the role we play in the two-way street of international cross-linguistic/cross-cultural communication. And how we play that role, both linguistically and culturally, will effect the outcome of our communicative encounters and our comfort level – as citizens of the world.

Teacher Training and Research for the Next Millennium

In her plenary address at TESOL in March 1998, Anne Pakir spoke on *Connecting with English in the Context of Internationalization.* Among many provocative thoughts she laid out for our consideration, were the following: "There are about six billion mouths to feed in the world, of which a billion and a half utilize English to a greater or lesser extent, to buy their daily bread, whether in a metaphorical or literal sense. These global numbers prompt the questions: 'Who will be using English in the next millennium? What are the implications for teachers of ESL? Should they change their ways of teaching in preparation for the next millennium?'"

Teacher Training

Personalizing this, my response to Pakir's last question was a resounding "Yes!" If, as a field, we are to provide more effective speech/pronunciation instruction, then there must be significant changes in many teacher preparation programs. The ELT teacher who is equipped to meet the challenges of the multi-faceted role discussed here needs background knowledge in linguistics, psycholinguistics, sociolinguistics, and educational theory and practice, among many other things.

Note that linguistics was first in the above list of knowledge needed, and while some colleagues today suggest minimizing the role of linguistics in teacher training, in my view this is a serious mistake, particularly for speech/pronunciation instructors. Tyler and Lardiere presented a provocative paper on this linguistics issue at the last Georgetown

University Roundtable in 1996. They note that "...the relationship between linguistic study and language pedagogy is alive and well and...linguistic study continues to be of central importance to language teachers." In support of their position they note that now more than ever linguists have a solid contribution to make to pedagogy by providing information and insights on pragmatics, semantics, discourse analysis, and sociolinguistic issues, as well as the core areas of phonetics, phonology, syntax, and morphology.

In another venue, at the 1998 TESOL panel on *International Perspectives on Teaching Pronunciation*, weakness in linguistic background was cited by a number of panelists as a serious weakness in teacher training. Mendelsohn (1998) pointed out, as a basic flaw, that teacher trainees are not getting adequate training in theoretical background in the teaching of phonetics and phonology, and that lacking this, "...they are extremely nervous to tackle the teaching of pronunciation." Murphy (1997) in reporting on his recent survey of phonology courses in training programs in the U.S., comments that "...courses focused on topics in phonology represent important opportunities for preparing language teachers to meet the speech intelligibility needs of L2 learners." He adds, however, that his findings also suggest that trainees "...would benefit from considerably increased faculty assistance in applying conceptual understandings to the teaching of pronunciation." (Murphy, 1997, pp. 741 and 755)

The following list of minimum requirements (Morley, 1994) also places phonetics and phonology as the first and most fundamental requirement in teacher training for speech/pronunciation. This knowledge base established, attention can then be broadened to the other requisite areas. Morley's recommendations include four primary areas as basic to preparation for teaching speech/pronunciation.

- Phonetics and phonology, and (particularly) applied phonetics
- The structure of oral discourse and discourse phonology
- Theory and practice in current directions in second language teacher-education in general, and in speech/pronunciation teaching in particular.
- Englishes and cultures around the world

Research.

Finally, but in point of fact a priority concern for the field, there is a serious paucity of both theoretical and pedagogical research in oral communication/speech/pronunciation. There are so many areas that should be investigated that it boggles the mind, so many that it is not reasonable to attempt to detail them here. However, one of the services the new TESOL Speech/Pronunciation Interest Section can perform (following the lead of the BALEAP organisation) is setting up a research-oriented clearinghouse which will provide on-line annotated summaries of research completed and abstracts of research in progress, so that people around the world have a way to access information.

Coda

One of the intents of this paper was to underscore the fact that the 'treatment of accent', as it is sometimes flippantly misnamed, can no longer be trivialized nor relegated to a peripheral corner of the second language field. Speech/pronunciation must be a fundamental component of a communicative task-based approach to second language learning and teaching, and instruction is a complex enterprise – one of the most challenging in foreign and second language teaching today.

References

Anderson-Hsieh, Janet. 1989. Approaches toward teaching pronunciation: A brief history. *Cross Currents: The Journal of the Japanese Association of Language Teachers.* 16(2), 73-78.

Anthony, Edward. 1963. Approach, method, technique. *English Language Teaching.* 17(1), 63-67.

Baxter, James. 1980. How should I speak English? American-ly, Japanese-ly or internationally? *Teaching English pronunciation.* ed. by Adam Brown. London: Routledge. 53-71.

Beebe, Leslie. 1978. Teaching pronunciation (why we should be). *IDIOM.* 9(1), 2-3.

Bolinger, Dwight. 1986. *Intonation and its parts.* Palo Alto, CA: Stanford University Press.

Brown, H. Douglas. 1993. After method: Toward a principled strategic approach to language teaching. *Georgetown University round table on languages and linguistics, 1993.* ed. by James E. Alatis, Carolyn A. Straehle, Brent Gallenberger, and Maggie Ronkin. Washington DC: Georgetown University Press. 509-520.

Brown, Gillian and Yule, George. 1983. *Discourse analysis.* New York, NY: Cambridge University Press.

Canale, Michael & Swain, Merrill. 1980. Theoretical bases of communicative approaches to second language teaching and testing. *Applied Linguistics.* 1(1), 1-47.

Candlin, Christopher. 1980. Preface. *Discourse, intonation and language teaching.* David Brazil, Malcolm Coulthard, and Catherine Johns. London: Longman. xi.

Celce-Murcia, Marianne, Brinton, Donna and Goodwin, Janet. 1996. *Teaching pronunciation: A reference for teachers of English as a second language.* New York, NY: Cambridge University Press.

Dickerson, Wayne B. 1994. Empowering students with predictive skills. *Pronunciation theory and pedagogy: New views, new directions.* ed. by Joan Morley. Alexandria, VA: TESOL Publications. 17-35.

Gilbert, Judy. 1987. Pronunciation and listening comprehension. *Current perspectives on pronunciation.* ed. by Joan Morley. Washington, DC: TESOL Publications. 29-40.

Grant, Linda. 1995. Creating pronunciation-based ESL materials for publication. *Material writers' guide.* ed. by Patricia Byrd. Boston, MA: Heinle and Heinle. 107-123.

Labov, William. 1972. *Sociolinguistic patterns.* Philadelphia, PA: University of Pennsylvania Press.

Lambert, William. 1967. A social psychology of bilingualism. *Journal of Social Issues.* 23(1), 90-109.

Lippi-Green, Rosina. 1994. Accent, standard language ideology, and discriminatory pretext in the courts. *Language in Society.* 23(1) 163-198.

Lippi-Green, Rosina. 1997. *English with an accent: Language, ideology, and discrimination in the United States.* London and New York: Routledge.

Matsuda, Mari J. 1991. Voices of America: Accent, anti-discrimination law, and a jurisprudence for the last reconstruction. *The Yale Law Journal.* 100(1), 1329-1407.

Mendelsohn, David. 1998. Teacher training in speech/pronunciation. *International perspectives on teaching pronunciation.* Audio recording of TESOL 1998 Speech/Pronunciation panel. Alexandria, VA. TESOL Publications.

Morley, Joan. 1987. Preface. *Current perspectives on pronunciation.* Washington, DC: TESOL Publications. i-iii.

Morley, Joan. 1988. How many languages do you speak? Perspectives on pronunciation-speech-communication in EFL/ESL. *Nagoya Gakuin University Roundtable on Linguistics and Literature Journal.* Nagoya, Japan: Nagoya Gakuin University Press. 19(1), 1-35.

Morley, Joan. 1991. The pronunciation component in teaching English to speakers of other languages. *TESOL Quarterly.* 25(3), 481-520.

Morley, Joan. 1992. *Extempore speaking practice.* Ann Arbor, MI: The University of Michigan Press.

Morley, Joan. 1994. A multidimensional curriculum design for speech/pronunciation instruction, *Pronunciation theory and pedagogy: New views, new directions.* ed. by Joan Morley. Alexandria, VA: TESOL Publications. 64-91.

Morley, Joan. 1996. Second language speech/pronunciation: Acquisition, instruction, standards, variation, and accent. *Georgetown university round table on languages and linguistics, 1996.* ed. by James E. Alatis, Carolyn A. Straehle, Brent Gallenberger and Maggie Ronkin. Washington DC: Georgetown University Press. 140-160.

Murphy, John. 1991. Oral communication in TESOL: Integrating speaking, listening, and pronunciation. *TESOL Quarterly.* 25(1), 51-75.

Murphy, John. 1997. Phonology courses offered by MATESOL programs. *TESOL Quarterly.* 31(4), 741-764.

Nunan, David. 1991. *Language teaching methodology: A textbook for teachers.* New York: Prentice Hall.

Oxford, Rebecca. 1990. *Language learning strategies: What every teacher should know.* New York: Newbury House.

Pennington, Martha C. 1996. *Phonology in English language teaching: An international approach.* New York, NY: Addison Wesley Longman.

Pennington, Martha C. & Richards, Jack. 1986. Pronunciation revisited. *TESOL Quarterly.* 20(2), 207-225.

Prahbu, N. S. 1990. There is no best method – why? *TESOL Quarterly.* 24(2), 161-176.

Stern, H. H. 1985. Methods that work: A smorgasbord of ideas for language teachers. Review of Oller and Richard-Amato (1983). *Studies in Second Language Acquisition.* 7, 249-251.

Swales, John M. 1991. *Genre analysis.* Cambridge: Cambridge University Press.

Tyler, Andrea and Lardiere, Donna. 1996. Beyond consciousness raising: Re-examining the role of linguistics in language teacher training. *Georgetown University round table on languages and linguistics, 1996.* ed. by James E. Alatis, Carolyn A. Straehle, Brent Gallenberger, and Maggie Ronkin. Washington DC: Georgetown University Press. 270-287.

Wenden, Anita. 1991. *Learner strategies for learner autonomy.* London: Prentice-Hall International.

Wong, Rita. 1985. Does pronunciation teaching have a place in the communicative classroom? *Georgetown University round table on languages and linguistics, 1985.* ed. by Deborah Tannen and James E. Alatis. Washington DC: Georgetown University Press. 17-28.

LEVEL	DESCRIPTION	IMPACT ON COMMUNICATION
1	speech is basically unintelligible; only an occasional word/phrase can be recognized.	accent precludes functional oral communication.
2	speech is largely unintelligible; great listener effort is required; constant repetitions and verifications are required.	accent causes severe interference with oral communication.

COMMUNICATIVE THRESHOLD A

3	speech is reasonably intelligible, but significant listener effort is required due to speaker's pronunciation/ grammatical errors which impede communication and cause listener distraction; on-going need for repetitions and verifications.	accent causes frequent interference with communication through the combined effect of the individual features of mispronunciation and the global impact of the variant speech pattern.
4	speech is largely intelligible; while sound and prosodic variances from NS norm are obvious, listeners can understand if they concentrate on the message.	accent causes interference primarily at the distraction level; listener's attention is often diverted away from the content to focus instead on the novelty of the speech pattern.

COMMUNICATIVE THRESHOLD B

5	speech is fully intelligible; occasional sound and prosodic variances from NS norm are present but not seriously distracting to listener.	accent causes little interference; speech is fully functional for effective communication.
6	speech is 'near-native'; only minimal features of divergence from NS can be detected; near-native sound and prosodic patterning.	accent is virtually non-existent.

Figure 1: Speech Intelligibility/Communicability Index, (Describing Speech and Evaluating Impact on Communication)

NOTES ON SPEECH EVALUATION:

1. Elicit a speech sample of several minutes. The sample should be sustained impromptu speech, not just answers to simple questions or 'rehearsed' biographical comments. The sample should be spontaneous speech, perhaps on a topic such as:

   (a)   what the student wants to be doing in 5 years

    (b)   what makes the student's life interesting

    (c)   what makes a happy family

2. Try to listen to the speech sample as if you were an untrained language listener. Err on the conservative side with consideration of the 'lay' listeners whom the student will meet.

3. In a few descriptor phrases summarize the student's strengths and weaknesses in three areas: (a) use of vowel and consonant sound segments, including combinations, reductions, contractions, elisions, assimilations, etc.; (b) use of features of stress, rhythm, and intonation, and vocal quality features, rate, volume, etc.; (c) features of general 'communicability'. (Use the Dual Chart as a reference.) Comment on how each of these factors impacts communicative intelligibility, and assign a level number as Speech Intelligibility/Communicability Level (SI-CL), using [+] and [-] notations as necessary. Monitor student progress through periodic SI-CL re-evaluations. Give students practice in speech analysis of intelligibility/communicability so that they are equipped to carry out both self-assessment and peer critiquing.

SPOKEN ENGLISH	
MICRO LEVEL	**MACRO LEVEL**
SPEECH PRODUCTION: **DISCRETE PRONUNCIATION POINTS**	**SPEECH PERFORMANCE:** **GLOBAL SPEECH PATTERNS**
A focus on specific elements of pronunciation *	A focus on general features of speech/ communication **
• precision and accuracy in articulation of vowel and consonant sounds; articulatory clarity in multi-syllabic words and phrasal units	• an appropriate level of speech intelligibility and communicability in extended oral discourse (See Intelligibility/Communicability Index.)
• neutral vowel use; reductions; contractions	• enhanced vocal effectiveness in oral discourse; communicative use of vocal quality features
• consonant combinations, both within and across word boundaries; elisions; assimilations	• overall fluency and smoothness in on-going planning and structuring of speech as it proceeds
• syllable structure and precise syllabic boundaries; linking and blending words across word boundaries; phrasing and pause points	• overall accuracy, precision, and clarity in contextualized speech, both sounds and prosodic features
• control of pitch change points and intonation patterning	• expansion, refinement, and communicative command of grammatical structures in context
• control of speed, timing, and rate variations; rhythm, and variations of vowel length related to stress; taking time to articulate clearly	• expansion and communicative command of field-specific, general-academic, and general-purpose vocabulary words and phrase units; increasingly rapid retrieval time.
• control of volume; sustaining energy level across the entire length of an utterance	• effective use of appropriate and expressive non-verbal features of oral communication

Figure 2: Dual Focus: Speech Production and Speech Performance

*A focus on *discrete point pronunciation features*: vowels, consonants, and baseline features of stress, rhythm, and intonation.
** A focus on *general elements/global patterns* of 'communicability' in spoken. English.

- **Learner Role, one of 'Speech Performer'**

- **Learner Awarenesses and Attitudes**

    1. **Speech awareness.**
    2. **Self-awareness of features** of speech production and speech performance.
    3. **Self-observation skills** and a positive attitude toward self-monitoring processes.
    4. **Speech-modification skills.**
    5. **Awareness of the learner role as one of a 'speech performer'** modifying, adjusting or altering a feature of speech/pronunciation, and the teacher role as one of assisting students as a 'speech coach'.
    6. **A sense of personal responsibility** for one's own learning, not only for immediate educational and personal needs, but for future career needs.
    7. **A feeling of pride** in one's own accomplishments.
    8. **Building a personal repertoire of speech monitoring and modification skills** in order to continue to improve speaking effectiveness in English when the formal instructional program is completed

Figure 3: Learner Awareness and Attitudes

- **Teacher Role, one of 'Speech Coach'**

- **Teacher Responsibilities**

  1. **Conducting speech/pronunciation diagnostic analyses**, and choosing and prioritizing those features that will make the most noticeable impact on modifying the speech of each learner.
  2. **Helping students set both long-range and short-term goals**.
  3. **Designing group program scope and sequence; designing personalized programming** for each individual learner in the group.
  4. **Developing a variety of instructional formats, modes, and activities** (e.g., whole class instruction; small-group work; individual one-to-one tutorial sessions; pre-recorded audio and video self-study materials, computer-assisted programs etc. Overall, providing genuine speech task activities for practice situated in real contexts or carefully chosen simulated contexts).
  5. **Structuring in-class speaking (and listening) activities** with invited NS and NNS guests participating.
  6. **Planning field trip assignments** in pairs/small groups for real-world speaking practice.
  7. **Monitoring learners'** speech production and speech performance at all times, and assessing pattern changes, as an on-going part of the program.
  8. **Encouraging student speech awareness and realistic self-monitoring**.
  9. **Always supporting each learner in his/her efforts**, be they wildly successful…or not so successful.

Figure 4: Teacher as 'Coach' Responsibilities

GRAMMAR AS A METASEMIOTIC TOOL IN CHILD LITERACY DEVELOPMENT

Geoff Williams

Introduction

Over the last decade, young learner's knowledge of grammar has become one of the most actively discussed questions in language and literacy pedagogy. It is also an issue of intense community interest, evident in media discussions internationally and fuelled, of course, by concern about literacy standards. Sometimes it has been the intensity of community interest rather than the development of educational and linguistic theory which has encouraged policy makers to re-inscribe grammar to school curricula, with very problematic results.

Though some educators continue to maintain that learning grammar is ineffectual, requoting research evidence which informed the Bullock Report during the mid-1970's (1975), many more actively seek useful, sophisticated resources to describe language for and with learners, and effective pedagogies through which to work with grammatical descriptions in classrooms. As Carter pointed out during the height of the British controversies over the LINC materials:

> It is not tenable to claim that there is no connection between explicit grammar study and enhanced language performance in spite of research evidence (largely pre-1970's) disavowing such a connection, not least because such research... investigated grammar teaching based on 'old-style' descriptive frameworks and methodologies. A new approach to grammar brings with it further questions for classroom practice and classroom-based research, about which it is essential for us to retain an open mind (Carter, 1990:118).

Indeed, there have been further questions about pedagogy in the decade following Carter's comments, though evidence of actual use of a 'new approach to grammar' in curricula of the 1990's is harder to find. It is the possibility of such a new approach to grammar of the kind Carter suggests, and a qualitatively different pedagogy in young learner's education, which forms the background for this paper.

I would like to begin with a rather straightforward assertion and a reservation about the range of the assertion. The assertion is that children, through their play, demonstrate a great deal of curiosity about language itself as they learn to use language in the early years of life and that such play is very significant for their development. The reservation is that very little of our understanding of language play has influenced current approaches to grammar learning and teaching.

There is a large body of evidence, much of it informal and anecdotal but no less important for that, to support a claim for the developmental significance of language play. Some of the most interesting evidence was described in the 1930's, in Chukovsky's accounts of children's play with nonsense verse. He demonstrated, for example, how children delighted in making up impossible sentences, experimenting boldly with the boundaries of commonsense ideas and language. Such play, he argued, does not just accompany language learning but is an integral part of that learning because it is a mode of enquiry into language itself, and of relations between language and experience (Chukovsky, 1968). Many other scholars have followed Chukovsky's lead in taking language play seriously, including quite notably Catherine Garvey, who comments:

> almost all the levels of organisation of language (phonology, grammar, meaning) and most phenomena of speech and talking ... are potential sources of play (Garvey, 1977: 61)

My reservation about the absence of theorized accounts of play in grammar learning obviously requires some expansion. I do not mean, of course, that there is an absence of playful materials to make learning parts of speech more enjoyable for learners. There is no shortage of books with a title such as "Fun with grammar". Indeed, even in the nineteenth century the outstanding illustrator of children's books, Walter Crane, produced a beautiful text of this kind to make the burden of learning traditional school grammar a little easier. Crane was the predecessor to our contemporaries who design interactive digital packages to make grammar more palatable, though he was much more aesthetically interesting than some of them.

However, it is not play with grammar in the sense of making it more picturesque or palatable that I wish to foreground here. Rather it is play in the sense that Gregory Bateson discussed in one of his metalogues, 'About games and being serious' (Bateson, 1972). He writes of serious play, deeply engaged play with ideas – the sort of play toddlers engage in with blocks when they so intensely explore relations between structure, potential and outcomes. Bateson considers serious play as an exploration, often collaborative in form, in which there is an intent to develop new understanding. In particular, he values playful conversational muddles, suggesting these as a highly desirable alternative to interaction in which people are constrained to speak in clichés.

> ... the whole point of the [GW conversational] game is that we do get into muddles, and do come out of the other side, and if there were no muddles our "game" would be like canasta or chess ...

> (Bateson, 1972: 19)

It does seem that a lot of current grammar teaching and learning is like playing chess in this sense: clear-cut, well-bounded and highly rule-governed, without the possibility for new, fragmentary, insight. It is not at all like the playful, serious, muddling exploration Bateson argues to be so important in the development of thought.

Exploratory play of this kind is, of course, rather dangerous. If things are allowed to get into a muddle, how can we be reasonably confident that they won't stay that way? We are, after all in an era of intense scrutiny of learning outcomes when it is definitely unfashionable and perhaps even perverse to think of muddling play with grammar as being either possible or desirable.

The danger of such play is a question which Bateson himself recognised. In the same metalogue, he makes the following comment:

> And then you asked "What sort of order should we cling to so that when we get into a muddle we do not go mad?" It seems to me that the "rules" of the game is only another name for that sort of order (ibid.)

He is not then talking about play in the sense of an absence of order, but rather play under a different order. In the language of the late twentieth century, it might be represented as play in a different discourse.

In research, which two colleagues and I have been conducting in Sydney, we have attempted to explore what such a different order might be. Two features of order have been at the centre of our research questions: the kind of grammatical resource which might usefully be introduced to children at the beginning of their systematic explorations of relations between structure and meaning – different rules of the game about language; and the kind of learning theory which might enable us to plan for, interpret and evaluate children's work – different rules of the game about pedagogy.

In this paper, I will introduce some of the findings we have so far. The specific focus is the *evolution* of children's understanding of grammatical concepts, and their ability to use these concepts in literacy work. I will describe some features of the very first phase of the children's work, then take samples from facets of their discussions and their writing to consider evidence about learning. The two grammatical concepts central to the paper are Theme and Process, which I will define shortly. The paper is structured in two strands, each of which sample the children's work over several months, first through Theme and subsequently Process.

The orientation of this work has been to grammar as a 'tool' for understanding language use: a tool that is simultaneously both accessible to children and powerful enough to enable learners to see new possibilities for what they might accomplish with the tools. The metaphor derives from two sources, a theory of language and a theory of learning.

The theory of language and of grammar is systemic functional grammar' (Halliday, 1994; Martin, 1992; Matthiessen, 1996), which we selected for several reasons. First, it is explicitly designed to assist language teachers and learners to understand language in use. Consequently, it provides important hypotheses about relations between context of use and patterns of language features implicated in registers appropriate to those contexts. Second, because it is grammatical description pushed well towards meaning it invites questions about the facility with which learners might be able to use meaning as a way of attending to features of structure. Third, the key unit of analysis in the theory is text, a semantic unit which the analysis of grammatical structure is designed to describe. A pedagogical approach which begins from a unit of meaning is likely to produce quite different learning outcomes from one which begins with a primary interest in sentences.

However, a key and rather obvious question is: can young learners actually use descriptive concepts derived from such a theory? Is such a grammar accessible to, and productive for, learners? More specifically, can young children even begin to engage in deep exploratory play with texts, with such a grammar as the ordering frame for their explorations?

The concept of grammar as a 'tool' also derives from Vygotsky's theory of learning, and in particular his discussion of learning through semiotic mediation. The features of his theory particularly relevant to this discussion are the functions of sign mediation in the development of higher mental functions, the significance of interaction in the development of thought, and the evolution of scientific concepts.

Interestingly, Vygotsky was himself an advocate of the important role of grammar in children's intellectual development. In *Thought and language* he commented specifically on the utility of learning grammar for assisting children to become more self-aware about language use (Vygotsky, 1986:184), though his thinking on this issue is not often brought into major texts about early literacy pedagogy.

Vygotsky drew a systematic distinction between two forms of learning: on the one hand 'natural' learning, given more or less directly by biological development, and on the other hand, 'sociocultural' learning in which 'higher mental functions' evolve. The development of higher mental functions necessarily requires the use of sign mediation, and signs are typically social constructs. Therefore, higher mental functioning is necessarily the result of social interaction in and through signs. It is in this sense that signs are a form of semiotic 'tool' through which the range and abstraction of thought are qualitatively altered in human ontogenesis.

Even such comparatively simple operations as tying a knot or marking a stick as a reminder change the psychological structure of the memory process. They extend the operation of the memory beyond the biological dimensions of the human nervous system and permit it to incorporate artificial, or self-generated stimuli, which we call *signs*. This merger, unique to human beings, signifies an entirely new form of behaviour. The essential difference between it and the elementary functions is to be found in the stimulus-response relations of each. The central characteristic of elementary functions is that they are totally and directly determined by stimulation from the environment. For higher functions, the central feature is self-governed stimulation, that is, the creation and use of artificial stimuli which become the immediate causes of behaviour.

(Vygotsky, 1978:39)

In Vygotsky's view, signs are intellectual tools which can make possible qualitatively different levels of thinking. For our work, the entailed question is: what kind of metalinguistic signs enable what kinds of thinking about language?

Since signs-as-tools are accessed through social interaction, it was the *use* of signs in discourse which was of most interest to Vygotsky. His most famous formulation of his general position on learning through interaction was:

Any function in the child's cultural development appears twice, or on two planes. First it appears on the social plane, and then on the psychological plane. First it appears between two people as an interpsychological category, and then within the child as an intrapsychological category.

(Vygotsky, 1981: 63)

Since this statement has been used so extensively in the language education field, it is important to underscore some features particularly relevant to the research. Vygotsky does not argue here merely that social interaction is important for development. Rather, his position is that there is an *inherent* link between forms of social interaction and forms of higher mental functioning. The link between social interaction and higher psychological functioning is inherent because of the specific mediational role of language. The term 'interaction' sometimes is used as a general gloss in language education, disassociated from the materiality of sign use and without explanatory power. For Vygotsky, the reason for the key theoretical status of interaction is that it makes intellectual resources available to the child through semiosis in interaction. The details of material practices in sign usage are therefore of critical importance to learning outcomes.

The third feature of his theory which we have found helpful is his thoroughly evolutionary understanding of concept development. From the familiar point that there are basic, qualitative differences between the early conceptual development of children and the full conceptual development of adults, Vygotsky argued against the commonsense view that children's intellectual development proceeds additively through incremental gains and, alternatively, asserted that:

> from the very beginning, the child's scientific and his spontaneous concepts ... *develop in reverse directions*: Starting from far apart they move to meet each other.

(Vygotsky, 1986: 192, original emphasis)

and, in a closely related comment:

> ... *the development of the child's spontaneous concepts proceeds upwards, and the development of his scientific concepts downward*, to a more elementary and concrete level.

(Vygotsky, 1981: 193, original emphasis)

That is, the instructional discourses in which children participate may chart a new path for abstract thinking, and full understanding of abstract ideas will evolve as learners are able to construct relations between commonsense understandings and new, more abstract and more technical ideas. For evaluation practices an obvious implication is that learners' partial understanding may – and it is a very complex modal – indicate development rather than merely an unproductive muddle. That concepts evolve through interaction, gradually becoming 'decontextualized' from sites of initial acquisition to new sites of application and therefore capable of being understood at a more abstract level, has been a key insight for our work.

It was, then, with these theoretical resources that we began the study of grammar with a group of eleven-year-olds, and I turn now to a discussion of this work, beginning with a description of the very first practical work involving the grammatical concepts Theme and Process.

First Moves: Beginning To Make Language An Object Of Systematic Study

The children who participated in the study were in their final year of primary schooling in an inner-suburban school in Sydney. They came from a large range of family backgrounds, in terms of both first languages and social positioning. First languages ranged from English through Tagalog, Mandarin, German, Portuguese, Italian and Spanish. In most families, parents worked in manual occupations, though there were families which ran small suburban businesses, and some parents worked in professions such as education and medicine. It is a typical profile for an inner-urban school in the inner-western suburbs of Sydney during the 1990's. The focal class was one of three in the year group: these had been arranged in parallel distributions of literacy and mathematical achievement by the school administration prior to the commencement of the work I will go on to describe.

The research was conducted collaboratively by the class teacher, Ruth French, a research associate, Joan Rothery, and me. It is important to emphasise that the teacher participated equally with the university based researchers in all phases of the project – in the design of the pedagogical approaches, certainly, but also equally in the design of the data gathering techniques and data interpretation. Similarly, Rothery and I participated in preparing teaching materials as well as in specific research activities. The close collaboration has been very useful for a first study of these phenomena, enabling us to plan responsively for the children's work and, perhaps most importantly, to ground our interpretations of outcomes in detailed observations from multiple perspectives.

Sources of data, as might be expected in an initial enquiry into this complex field, were wide-ranging. They included close classroom observation by French, Rothery and me; audio and video recordings of the children's discussions; transcripts of key discussions; interviews with individual children; French's teaching journal notes; the children's reflections in their learning journals; the children's drawings about the grammatical patterns and relations they observed; comparisons between writing by children in the focal class and one of the parallel classes, written tests of grammatical knowledge, and substantial interviews with children about changes to draft writing in the focal class and one of the parallel classes.

Our approach was to try to make this initial phase seriously playful in Bateson's sense. We first introduced a dysfunctional text to the children and invited them to critique it. The text was a recipe which it would be impossible to use for any practical purpose. (We selected this text type because French's initial analyses of the children's writing development indicated, inter alia, that this was a form of writing with which the children experienced difficulty but which they were expected to control by this stage of the NSW primary school syllabus.) The recipe was for cheese sauce.

Mr Confused's Recipe For How To Make Cheese Sauce

1. You might like to add some salt and pepper.
2. Add the milk slowly.
3. You have to gently heat the butter.
4. The flour is then added.
5. Heat the saucepan first.
6. You can pour the cheese sauce over vegetables or macaroni.
7. The grated cheese should be added slowly.
8. Stir until the butter and flour are bubbling gently.

Ingredients:
11/2 tablespoons plain flour
11/2 tablespoons of butter, margarine or oil
2 tablespoons of grated cheese
1 cup milk

It took only a very short time for the children to realize just how dysfunctional the text was. They delighted in constructing mini-dramatizations of the consequences of following the recipe for both the cook and his dinner guests. Importantly, they were critical of the sequence of the activities and the placement of the ingredients at the end of the recipe. This provided a good basis on which we were able to talk with them about the ordering of information, not only in a whole text but also within a clause, and thus introduce the concept of Theme.

In Halliday's description of English grammar, the element Theme is the clausal resource through which the reader/listener is oriented to a speaker/writer's point of departure. It is indicated in English by position rather than by, for example, a bound morpheme, which is a resource used to mark Theme in some other languages (Halliday, 1994: 37). For example, in the clause 'Mix the ingredients thoroughly' the Theme is 'mix', while in the clause 'In Singapore, there is an impressive range of cuisine', the Theme is 'In Singapore'. For thinking later in the paper about the children's use of Theme descriptions it is useful to note that a Theme may include resources for linking a clause to other clauses: for example through structural elements within a clause complex, or conjunctively across stretches of text. To illustrate, in the following clauses the Theme selection includes both 'textual' and 'topical' elements:

||| (1) Additionally, you should ensure || (2) that your personal items are fully covered.|||

Analysis of Clause 1

Additionally,	you	should ensure
textual	topical	
Theme		Rheme

Analysis of Clause 2

that	your personal items	are fully covered.
textual	topical	
Theme		Rheme

The patterning of Theme appears to be quite sensitive to register variation (Matthiessen, 1996; Hasan and Fries, 1996), and relates closely to the social purpose of a text. Further, though there is no single correct pattern which is obligatory for all writers, variation is not random so when departure from anticipated norms occurs a reader/listener will typically try to attribute some meaning to it.

Turning now to Process, in systemic functional descriptions of English grammar, processes are encoded through verbal groups, but the concept is not co-extensive with that of verb for several important theoretical reasons. For our purposes a key issue is Halliday's proposal that sub-types of process are identifiable on both semantic and structural grounds, and that the process type is the key determinant of the structural possibilities of the clause in English. To illustrate briefly, sub-types of process may be described through the following system network, drawn at a primary level of delicacy.

Reading from left to right, this network indicates that for each clause the selection of a process requires a choice from the possibilities: either Material, Mental or Verbal ... and so on.

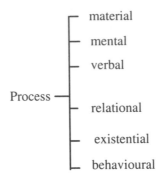

Figure 1: Types of Process Described in Systemic Functional Grammar: primary level of delicacy

Patterning of process type is also sensitive to register, though the principles which might account for variation within any one register are indeed very complex (Matthiessen, 1993). In procedural texts, there is a relatively simple pattern because the social purpose of the text is usually straightforward. In this type, Material Processes are selected, since procedural texts are organised to instruct readers in processes of doing – what action is appropriate with what clausal 'ingredients', or more formally with what grammatical Participants.

Theme	Rheme
Heat	the saucepan first.
Mix	the butter and the sugar.
Fold	the milk into the flour
Blend	all of the ingredients
Place	in the oven.

Figure 2: Typical Thematic Patterning in a Procedural Text

I now move to take up the two strands of the children's work foreshadowed at the beginning of the paper, discussing first the evolution of understandings of thematic patterning and uses of descriptions of Theme in writing, and second the development of thinking about Processes.

Using Knowledge of Theme in Classroom Literacy Work

Following the discussions of thematic patterning in a procedural text the children examined a contrastive pattern in another text type, which they were also expected to write well by this stage of their schooling. The second type was a 'recount' of some personal experience, a type of writing in which a reader is informed about the author's experience of a series of events without an expectation that there will be a dramatic complication of some kind.

The sample text through which the children were introduced to the general type, and through which they examined the thematic patterning, was an account of a holiday on the New South Wales North Coast by an eight-year-old child.

My Holiday in Coffs Harbour

On the first day we drove to Coffs. We got to Coffs at 3.30 12 seconds. That afternoon we swam at the beach. My brother was shocked when I walked deep and was only up to my ankles in water. The next day we went for a swim in the water. In the afternoon we went to the Big Banana and I got a boomerang and an ice cream. Then we went on a bushwalk in a rainforest. The next day we went on another long bushwalk but then we went for a walk behind this water-fall. The next day we went on a barbecue with some friends. And I found a natural swing. On Thursday we went to the beach in the morning and flew kites in the afternoon. On Friday we went to the Mutton Bird Hill Nature Reserve and there were lots of nests in the ground. Then we bought some prawns. And then my Dad bought me a double passionfruit twist ice cream. Then the next day we went home.

In brief, the children used the text, without prior marking-up by the research team, first to describe Processes, then the clauses which developed through these Processes, and finally the Theme selections within each clause. They were then able to compare the patterning of Theme selections in this text type with the procedural text. Here, the elements typically in Theme position were, on the one hand, the human participants in the activities – James, his brother, other members of his family – and, additionally, elements which signalled stages of time in the holiday – 'on the first day', 'the next day', 'On Thursday' and so on.

With this new knowledge, the children then engaged in writing a complex text collaboratively with the teacher, reviewed the selection of Theme, then edited their work in the light of the descriptions they were now able to make jointly with the teacher. The text was a recount of a visit to a local high school to which many of the children were to go in the following year. Since this work was conducted over several weeks, I can only mention it briefly here, drawing attention to three important aspects.

First, the writing task was in an important sense real use of language rather than an artificial classroom exercise, in that the children did produce a complex text which they 'published' attractively and which they knew would be read avidly by many people outside the class, including, of course, Rothery and me. But the issue of 'reality' is rather more subtle than the preceding formulation suggests. This task was also a kind of metaphorical space in which the children knew that they were playing with ideas about language in a serious way in order to learn more about how to use the ideas in new, non-playful contexts. It is a complexly negotiated space in which both the short-term goal orientation of producing a successful text and the long-term goal orientation of learning how to use the newly introduced and complex metalinguistic tools are simultaneously important, and known to be so by the teacher and the children[1].

Second, there was extensive collaboration between the children and French in both writing and editing the text. The theoretical basis for the approach is Vygotsky's concept of the zone of proximal development. Though the children had been introduced to the description of Theme and were newly aware of variation in thematic patterns in text types, and while they could not yet be expected to use the concepts independently, they were

---

[1] See Hasan (1995) for a discussion of short- and long-term goal orientations as features of context of situation, and Williams (1995a) for an example of the use of the concepts in an exploration of semantic variation.

in a position to engage in editing a text in a qualitatively different way from anything they had experienced previously. It is the intricate relationship between the semantically oriented grammatical description, the actual use of the description in recognisably practical activities, and reflection on the semantic effects of the grammatical patterns which appears to be crucial to the abstract learning I will describe shortly.

Finally, there was an important commitment of extensive time to this task. The children wrote the first draft of the text intermittently over three days, and then edited it through discussions over about one and a half hours of classroom discussion, a total period of time which was distributed across several days, given the age of the children. This aspect of what Bernstein has called the 'framing' of pedagogic discourse was, we suspect, crucial to the children's learning.

Soon after they completed their jointly written recount, the children went with their year peers, three classes in all, on an excursion to some cultural institutions in the city. When they returned they were asked to write an account of the excursion by each of the teachers, as is common practice in Australian primary schools. The two parallel classes had received extensive instruction in the generic structure of recounts but not, of course, any instruction in thematic patterning. It was therefore possible to compare a selection of texts written by children in the focal class and those written by children in one of the parallel classes.[2] It was also possible to compare what the children in the focal and comparison classes said about editing their first drafts, and it is these data on which I will now draw.

Meta-awareness 1: Exploratory comparisons of children's approaches to editing draft text

Six children in the focal and comparison classes were interviewed about the changes they had made to first drafts after they had completed the final version, in order to explore what use they made of their new grammatical knowledge. The interview focus was on the changes made to

---

[2] The co-researchers are very grateful to the teacher of this class for collaboration with the project, and for a readiness to assist with these comparisons. A report of some comparisons of the writing, based on clausal analysis, is available in Williams (1995b).

the texts and, even more importantly, the reasons the children gave for making the changes.

The children were interviewed individually by the Research Associate, Rothery, who was by this stage a familiar figure to them. Each child brought to the interview a copy of his or her draft text and the final version. Rothery talked with them about the specific changes, attempting to give each child broad opportunities to discuss their work, however informally. We were particularly interested to ascertain whether or not the parallel class children might informally edit their texts in similar ways to the focal group, without the benefit of the metalinguistic tools.

To illustrate the general findings I will introduce three excerpts from the transcripts: one from the focal class and two from the parallel class. They are typical of the views within each data set with respect to the children's approach to editing.

The first excerpt is from the focal class. This child, whom I shall call Kate, has Italian as her first language. We will see that she was concerned about her writing ability, and apparently looking for ways in which to improve it.

Example 1: A Student from the Focal Class and Rothery Discussing the Student's Editing of a Draft Text

CD: Well, um, I've been looking at … in this one, when I've been editing it, I have been looking at it to see to make sure that the beginning of each sentence was like, trying to get them to be new words so it is better.

JR: So you wanted variety, did you?

CD: Yes, and in the first paragraph I underlined all the Themes and I saw there was a pattern in the Themes.

JR: Oh, you did that on your own, did you?

CD: Yes.

JR: And did you find there was a pattern?

CD: I was using lots of 'we's'. 'We', 'we', 'we'.

JR: Were you? What's 'we' in the grammar?

CD: In grammar 'we's' are um ... Participants.

JR: So you had Participants as Theme did you?

CD: Yes. And so...

JR: I'm sure you had other things as well.

CD: Yes.

JR: What other things did you have as Themes?

CD: Um, I had things like ... er 'after', 'when'.

JR: 'When'. What do we call 'when'? What is that?

CD: Circumstance.

JR: Well, it's like a Circumstance because it tells us about time. But that's not the actual name we give to the grammar. What's 'and', 'so', 'but'?

CD: Conjunction.

JR: Conjunction. But it tells us about time, doesn't it? That's for sure. But a very general sense of time. So how did you ... tell me some of the things that you've ch ... oh yes, I can see how you've underlined them. You've used red, have you?

CD: Yes.

JR: What have you used red for?

CD: I've used red to underline all the Themes and then I showed Miss French and Miss French underlined all the ones I missed out on.

JR: (LAUGHS) – Did you miss out on many?

CD: Yes, I missed out on … I didn't miss out on the actual Theme but I either went too far or not far enough.

JR: Not far enough. Like in this one here you underlined the conjunction but what did you miss out?

CD: Participant.

JR: Yes, because when there's a conjunction as Theme then we also include the Participant that follows. In other words we've got, if we have a conjunction then we know there's going to be another Theme as well, usually, there's going to be another Theme, don't we?

CD: Yes.

JR: Well that's interesting. So can you tell me then about some of the changes that you've made?

CD: Um, well some of the changes I tried instead of having 'we' first I did 'first we'.

JR: So why did you change that?

CD: Because I started to use 'we' lots of times as I said before and I wanted to get a variety.

JR: And what does 'first' tell us about?

CD: It tells us about what we did before we did any of the other things, like … the first thing that we actually did.

JR: It orders, doesn't it?

(A discussion of Catherine's parents' views about her learning of grammar follows for several minutes)

JR: Well, I suppose we should get back to the recount. We wandered away from that didn't we? So you've really made a lot use of your understanding, haven't you? Do you think it's been useful?

CD: Very (STRONG EMPHASIS) useful. It's made my recounts better than what they would have been if I hadn't learnt about grammar because of, like, different clauses and conjunctions. It's also given me a variety of vocabulary and it's helped me with ... like ... I'm not very good at English. I'm better at maths and so it's sort of helps me, you know, get like even with both subjects.

JR: Oh, so you really think it's bringing you up as far as your English is concerned. That's good, isn't it? It's good that you went through and underlined the Themes. That's an interesting thing to do. I mean how did you know to do that? What was the activity you did with Miss French that um...?

CD: Um, well when we were doing our Concord recount. We sort of did that a little bit and I think it was on sections and so that when we saw we were repeating things we changed it. I thought that, because I often repeat myself a lot when I'm writing like recounts and so on I thought that maybe that would help me and to see what I have to fix up on. And once I did the first paragraph, without underlining the rest of it, I just went through it and I saw whether there were things I should work on.

Kate is quite obviously able to engage in a meaningful discussion of the writing using the concept of Theme, and she does think that her knowledge does make a practical difference to her writing. She may still have been evolving an understanding of the structural potential of Theme but she is evidently able to engage in a conversation about her use of language because she has a metalanguage with which to talk about it.

Equally striking is the fact that it is not just the description of Theme itself, but the teacher's introduction of the grammatical feature and the children's opportunity to use the description in a practical context which is the resource Kate reports she draws on in revising her work. Both the grammar and the practical use of the grammar in some context of educational activity are apparently important. We interpret this to be quite direct evidence in support of Vygotsky's claims about the significance of signs-in-use for development of abstract thought, or in this case meta-signs in use.

All of the children we interviewed in the focal class talked in similar terms about uses of the newly acquired metalanguage. Of course, not all of them attempted to describe Theme in their draft writing in quite Kate's systematic way but all of the drafts showed similar attention to editing thematic patterns.

Examples 2 and 3 are from interviews with children in the comparison class. My purpose in introducing these is *not* to examine them for evidence of an understanding of Theme – obviously, this knowledge was not available to the children and such a comparison would be invidious. However, since the children had been on the same excursion, had been asked to complete writing in the same text type and then to edit first drafts, it is possible to examine discourse about the drafts and editing comparatively.

In the interview from which the following excerpt is drawn, Rothery and the child had spoken for some minutes about spelling changes. They were near the end of the discussion when the following exchange occurred.

Example 2: An Excerpt of an Interview with a Student in the Comparison Class Who Had Written A Text in the Same Genre on the Same Topic as Children in the Focal Class

> JR: Um, I don't think there're any other big changes, are there?
>
> CD: Just spelling.

JR: Just the spelling. Do you think it's helpful to rewrite things, redraft them? Do you think it's a good idea?

CD: Yes.

JR: How does it help?

CD: It teaches you spelling (INAUDIBLE)

JR: Anything else that you change besides spelling?

CD: Um ... I don't think so.

JR: Mainly spelling is it? Uh huh.

CD: Spelling...

JR: Punctuation? Your punctuation seems pretty fine so it's mainly spelling that you change. So have you written other recounts this year?

CD: Oh ... I can't remember.

The second example is similar in the sense that the child finds it difficult to comment on specific meaning changes, but is also interesting in that as Rothery draws the child's attention to a specific grammatical feature there is evidence that the child can, even in this short time, follow the new direction of his attention and to begin to understand what Rothery describes in the language. However, before she does so there is no evidence through the entire transcript that the child has considered alternative possibilities for the *structure* of the writing during editing.

Example 3: A Second Excerpt of an Interview with a Child in another Class Who Had Written a Text in the Same Genre on the Same Topic

JR: So do you feel happier that this one is better than your other one?

CD: Yep.

JR: In what way do you think it's better?

CD: It mentions more.

JR: It makes things more clear?

CD: Yes, and more about things. I just wrote that about the computer game and in this I wrote about the games too.

JR: So more information? Is that what you're saying?

CD: Yes.

JR: More information. What about the Hyde Park Barracks? Are there drafts of that one here? That's the museum, isn't it? Where does Hyde Park Barracks start? 'They didn't have very much fear'. What have we got here? You've written a lot more here, haven't you?

CD: When I was writing, I think of more and I just write it in.

JR: Alright. That's was just sort of like ... almost like rough notes, was it?

CD: 'After lunch we went to the Hyde Park Barracks. First we went to the courtroom, then we went into the main building which the convicts built.'

JR: What are these words here like 'after lunch', 'first' and 'when'? Can you tell me what they're doing? What do they do 'after lunch', 'first', 'then'.

CD: What do you mean by (INAUDIBLE)

JR: Well, how do they help organize our text? How do they help the text? Do you understand what I mean? Um ... You don't? OK. Well, they're telling you about the sequence in time. 'After lunch' tells you about when,

110

doesn't it? 'First' tells you about 'when'. 'Then' tells you about what we did next. In recounts, you often get that. You often get a lot of focus on time (INAUDIBLE) 'After lunch', 'first', 'then' are all words that help us organize our text as far as the time is concerned. And recounts are about one thing after another, aren't they? Can you see any more words that are like that?

CD: Um ... 'when'.

JR: 'When'. That's right. That's another one that tells us about time.

All of the children responded quite readily to the discussion. There is no sense of an inability to attend to the task, nor of a lack of interest in engaging in conversation about the text. Rather, there appears to be just inexperience in thinking about any specific structural features, and a lack of access to resources with which to reflect on the text.

Reviewing the whole data set, we have formed the strong impression that the qualitative differences in talk illustrated here are systematic features of each sub-set. The concept of Theme was accessible to the children in the focal class and did seem to be used in their initial attempts at independent editing. Conversely, we could find no evidence that children in the comparison class made qualitatively similar changes through informal, non-technical means.

It is, of course, also clear that Kate and her peers had just begun to use the concept independently, and it is important to avoid any claim that they had reached a full understanding of Theme – what Vygotsky would call a full understanding of the scientific concept. Subsequently they went on to edit other text types collaboratively with the teacher, working more specifically on the relative effectiveness of different thematic patterns in information report writing. That the children's concepts were still evolving rather than fully developed by this stage of the experience is entirely consistent with what would be expected within a Vygotskyean theoretical framework.

I move now to consider the second strand of evidence, evolution of the children's understanding of Process.

Meta-awareness 2: Evolution of the children's understanding of Processes and their functions

It will be recalled that the children first considered the concept of process in their discussion of the recipe, and subsequently went on to think about processes as the central feature about which clauses develop while they were exploring thematic patterning in James's account of his holiday. These first peer discussions of processes can be compared with discussions later in the year, by which time the children had been introduced to different types of processes and some of the associated participant relations in order to assess any qualitative differences in the children's understanding of the grammatical feature.

The major argument here is that qualities of a semantically-oriented grammar enable particular effects in the description of texts to be achieved with young students, in contrast with what is enabled by a description which is oriented to initial learning about parts of speech or formal grammatical features.

Example 4 is drawn from the very first peer discussion of Processes in James' account of his holiday in Coffs Harbour.

Example 4: Students Initial Attempts To Identify Processes

CD: Annie?

CD: Mm. Huh?

CD: You're reading.

CD: 'The next day we went for a swim in the water'.

CD: 'Swim'.

CD: 'Swim'.

CD: And 'went'.

CD: Yeah, yeah 'went'.

CD: 'Swim'.

CD: I just think…

CD: No, you can 'went'. I went and you can 'swam', swim. Swim.

CD: OK … um … 'In the afternoon we went to the Big Banana and I got a boomerang and … and an ice cream'.

CD: 'Went' and 'got'.

CD: 'Went'.

CD: What a … Where is it? 'Went'.

CD: 'In the afternoon we went'. And 'got'.

CD: 'Got'. That's right.

CD: And …

CD: 'An' I got'.

CD: Are you ready?

CD: Yeah.

CD: 'Then we went on a bushwalk in the – in a rain forest'.

CD: 'Went'.

CD: Went.

CD: And 'bushwalk'.

CD: Yeah.

CD:　Not 'I bushwalk'.

CD:　Yeah, you can't do that.

CD:　I went.

CD:　Yeah. You can't do that.

CD:　'I went'.

CD:　No, you can't. OK?

Here the children rely exclusively on the sense of a process as a 'doing' word. This is not surprising, since at this stage they knew only about Material Processes, for which a useful probe is 'do'. However, the probe is vulnerable if one cannot simultaneously consider participant relations with the process, as their analyses of 'swim' and 'bushwalk' illustrate.

About five months later the children began work on a narrative text in order to consider how the grammatical patterns of some transitivity features changed at different phases of the text, and consequently achieved important meaning effects. This work was part of an exploration of the potential of systemic functional grammatical analyses to contribute to the critical analysis of text. Whereas the first phases of the project had been oriented to assisting students to better meet school expectations for their writing, this work was oriented to critical reading practices, considering how students might use linguistic analyses to become more aware of the patterning of grammatical features contributing to a construal of gender stereotyping and of a potential for change in gender relations. (For a detailed discussion of this work, see Williams, in press b.)

The text on which the discussion focussed was *Piggybook*, written and illustrated by Anthony Browne (1986). It is an ironic account of stark gender distinctions in household work, with the mother working not only in the house, doing all of the housework, but also in paid employment. In contrast, the males, a father and two sons, go off to their very important work and very important school without participating in any household jobs. Eventually the mother leaves and the males make a terrible mess of the domestic arrangements through their incompetence. They are saved from chaos only by the mother's return, on condition that they all contribute to a new distribution of work. The mother is particularly happy because one of her jobs is to mend the car.

For the phase of the work we will consider here the children had been given a worksheet with the language of *Piggybook* analysed into clauses. They could have, by this stage, completed this analysis themselves but for economy of time we gave them the text prepared for analysis of process types. In the following example, three children discuss different process types in the clauses.

Example 5: Students in the Focal Class Discussing Analyses of Types of Process during Critical Discourse Analysis

CD: Number 10.

CD: Yep, "Miss Piglet washed all the all the breakfast things".

CD: "Washed".

CD: Yep.

CD: That's a Material Process.

CD: Actually, we'll do the whole thing.

CD: OK, "made all the beds" ... I ... "made".

CD: "Made".

CD: "Made" ... Material.

CD: "Vacuumed ... vacuumed all the carpets".

CD: Yeah, "vacuumed".

CD: Your turn.

CD: OK ... "and then she went to work". Went.

CD: I'll do it. "Went" is Material.

CD: "Hurry up with the meal, Mum."

CD: "Hurry up".

CD: "Hurry up".

CD: Um ... that's a Relational Process.

CD: Oh yeh. ... But ... ok. "The boy's called every evening"

CD: Hold on, I don't think so. No, that's a Material Process. Sorry, it's Material.

CD: OK. "The boys called every evening".

CD: "called"

CD: That's a, that's ... Now that is a Verbal.

CD: Oh yeah.

CD: See cos' they talk.

    ...

CD: "When she came home from his ... when he came from his very important job" OK.

CD: "Came."

CD: There's a kind of a pattern here. Look ... hurry, called, came, hurry, called, came.

CD: Oh yeh ... hurry, called, came, hurry, called, came.

CD: Hurry, called, came.

CD: OK, that's Material. No ... yes, that's a Material.

CD: "As soon as they had eaten."

CD: Eaten.

CD: Eaten, I eaten

CD: I ate.

CD: I had, I had.

CD: Um ... had ... I had eaten.

CD: Oh, that's a tricky one. Let me think. "Had eaten." Do you think "had eaten"? Um ...

CD: We'll leave that one.

CD: Yep, because you can say "I ate", because you can change it round like I eat... I ate. I think I had. I think it's that one.

CD: OK, who cares?

CD: All right. You put I have ... and I'll put ... um, I'm not really sure. You put eaten, I eaten. OK.

CD: That's a Material too.

CD: Yep. Your turn.

CD: "Ms Piglet washed the dishes."

CD: Washed. It's a Material Process.

CD: Washed ... washed the clothes.

CD: Washed the clothes.

CD: OK. "Did the ironing."

CD: Did.

CD: Hold it. "You did." A Material or is it…?

CD: I don't know, um Relational? I think that might be a Material Process.

CD: Yes, it's a Material because um … When she vacuumed all the carpets, you know, how she did it.

CD: Yes, I hope so. "And then she cooked some more." "Cooked."

CD: Material?

CD: Yep, cos its part of the rest.

CD: OK, you can start.

CD: OK. "One evening there was no one to greet them." Um…

CD: Was.

CD: Yes, that's right. I couldn't really think.

CD: Was … the Material.

CD: Yes.

CD: Material.

CD: No, it's a … it's a Relational.

CD: Yeh, that's right. It's a Relational.

CD: Have we done that? Because I think we had another one.

CD: No, I changed it, remember, I changed it.

CD: Relational.

CD: OK. "When the boys got home from school. When the boys got home from school."

CD: Um ... got.

CD: "I got" ... Yes

CD: It's a Material? Wait.

CD: Yep ... yes ... I think it's a Material.

CD: Let's hope so.

The children's understanding of processes has obviously evolved to a much more sophisticated level by this time. Of particular interest is the confidence with which they can discriminate between process sub-types, if necessary revising an initial analysis by one of their peers to produce a more adequate one. They still do use a sense of processes as coding 'doings' of some kind, but they are not restricted to that idea and can now readily switch to other senses of processes when this is required. For example, the fact that a Participant says something becomes the basis for changing an analysis of 'called' from Material to Verbal, and the existence of something is a reason for changing from an initial description of Material to Relational.

In another group working alongside this one the children could manage an even more adroit analysis.

Example 6: An Analysis Of Existential Process By Eleven-Year-Olds

CD: OK, "hurry".

CD: Another Material Process.

CD: "Was".

CD: "Was".

CD: "Was".

CD: I'm not really sure about that, I think it might be…

CD: Yes, I think it's another Material Process.

CD: No, it's either a Relational, it could be a Relational.

CD: OK.

CD: "Inside" Hold it. "Inside the house was" means I think it is … I can't think it … Existential Process. That could be that. I'll write that down because "was" means that his wife was there, it exists.

The sophistication of this analysis is a long way from the initial sense of processes as actions. What is particularly interesting is the way these learners use meaning as a basis for their understanding of grammatical structure. As Cathy says in this transcript "'was' means that his wife was there, it exists"! It is a relatively small further pedagogical step to introduce the structural bases on which Existential Processes can be distinguished from Relationals, or Verbals from Material Processes and so on.

Having reached this level of understanding of Processes, the children were in a position to begin to examine different categories of Participants associated with each type. In the context of the discussion of *Piggybook* we introduced Actor and Goal so that the children were able to chart the frequency of these features, describe the referential domains built by the Participants and in a literal sense *see* the narrative movements. From this visual sense of the narrative movements, they were able to consider semantic effects of variation in the patterns of participant relations. Their thinking had evolved from a very simple sense of Process to an appreciation of different types of Process and then, in a major conceptual move, to a further appreciation of the potential for different roles for Participants in Material Processes.

Space precludes a more detailed description of this complex work, but to illustrate the outcome which the description of process types eventually made possible I will quote the summary statement the children produced together at the end of the unit of work.

**The Children's Summary Statement of Their Description of Relations
between Grammar and Meaning in *Piggybook***

What we learnt about the grammatical patterns in Piggybook

Beginning
All the Goals Mrs Piggott did were to do with housework
Only Mrs Piggott had Goals. This shows she is the only one doing
something TO something else.
Mr Piggott and the boys only did things for themselves; they did
not do work in the home. This shown by the fact that they didn't
have any Goals. They were the only characters that talked. They
told Mrs P to hurry up.

Resolution
At the end, everyone did an action to something – to benefit the
whole family, not just themselves. Everyone had Goals at the end.
Now the Goals for Mrs Piggott included more than housework.

The Goals had a big role in structuring the narrative. The pattern of
Actors and Goals changes at the end. This makes the Resolution.

This is a level of abstraction in thinking about text which is
uncommon in Australian primary education, indeed among some rather
more experienced students of English literature whom I currently teach, and
one which I believe to be achievable only with certain quite specific
features of semiotic mediation.

Conclusion

For the last two decades or so, the English teaching profession has
been much too constrained by reaction to limited grammatical models and
boring pedagogy. The influential research on the inefficacy of learning
traditional grammar by Harris (1965), Elley et al. (1976) and others has
been used to displace possibilities for any systematic teaching about

grammar and meaning. What has been lost or suppressed through that long reaction has been images of the new possibilities to which Carter referred in the quotation with which the paper began. I have argued that it is not productive to conceive of the 'reform' of pedagogy for grammar teaching in terms of making the presentation of traditional grammar more palatable. What will be more useful for learners is a redefinition of the discourse, a change in the linguistic and learning paradigms through which pedagogic approaches to grammar learning are articulated. A semantically oriented grammar, able to help learners reflect on the structure of language 'in' texts in context is, our data suggests, one possibility well worth pursuing in further research.

Such a redefinition cannot be undertaken by teachers working in isolation, planning individually for work with their own classes. Of course, the ingenuity and creativity of individual teachers can achieve a great deal. But a serious approach to the re-entry of grammar to language curricula for the young requires much more. Of outstanding importance are opportunities for teachers to develop their own seriously playful thinking about the structure of language. It is no coincidence that the reinscription of traditional grammar to early childhood English syllabi is accompanied by two other developments: attempts to make traditional grammar more palatable to the young and greatly reduced opportunities for further education for teachers.

References

Bateson, G. 1972. *Steps towards an ecology of mind.* New York: Ballantine Books.

Browne, A. 1986. *Piggybook.* London: Julia MacRae Books.

Bullock, A. (Chair) 1975. *A language for life.* Report of the Committee of Inquiry Appointed by the Secretary of State for Education and Science. London: HMSO.

Carter, R. 1990. The new grammar teaching. *Knowledge about language and the curriculum.* ed. by Carter, R. London: Hodder and Stoughton.

Carter, R. 1996. Politics and knowledge about language: the LINC project. *Literacy in society*. ed. by Hasan, R. & Williams, G. London: Longman

Chukovsky, K. 1968. *From two to five*. revised ed. trans. and ed. by Morton, M. Berkeley and London: University of California Press.

Elley, W.B., Barham, I.H., Lamb, H. & Wyllie, M. 1976. The role of grammar in a secondary school English curriculum. *Research in the teaching of English*. 10(1), pp 5-21.

Garvey, C. 1977. *Play*. London: Fontana Books.

Halliday, M.A.K. 1994. *An introduction to functional grammar*. 2nd.ed. London: Edward Arnold.

Harris, R. J. 1965. The only disturbing feature ... *The use of English*. 16(3), pp 197-202.

Hasan, R. 1995. The conception of context in text. *Discourse in society: Functional perspectives. Meaning and choice in language: Studies for Michael Halliday*. ed. by Fries, P. H. & Gregory, M. Norwood, NJ: Ablex.

Hasan, R. 1996. Literacy, everyday talk and society. *Literacy in society*. ed. by Hasan, R. & Williams, G. London and New York: Longman.

Hasan, R. & Fries, P. (eds.) 1995. *On Subject and Theme: A discourse functional perspective*. Amsterdam: John Benjamins Publishing Company.

Kozulin, A. 1990. *Vygotsky's psychology: A biography of ideas*. New York: Harvester Wheatsheaf.

Matthiessen, C. M. M. 1993. Register in the round: Diversity in a unified theory of register analysis. *Register analysis: Theory and practice*. ed. by Ghadessy, M. London: Pinter Publishers.

Matthiessen, C. M. M. 1996. *Lexicogrammatical cartography: English systems. Textbook Series in the Language Sciences.* Tokyo: International Language Series Publishers.

Vygotsky, L. V. 1986. *Thought and language.* ed. & trans. by Kozulin, A. Cambridge, Mass.: The MIT Press.

Williams, G. 1995. *Joint book-reading and literacy pedagogy. A socio-semantic interpretation.* Unpublished PhD dissertation. School of English, Linguistics and Media, Macquarie University.

Also reproduced as:

Williams, G. 1995. *Joint book-reading and literacy pedagogy. A socio-semantic interpretation.* Volume 1. CORE. 19 (3).

Williams, G. 1995. *Joint book-reading and literacy pedagogy. A socio-semantic interpretation.* Volume 2. CORE. 20 (1).

Williams, G. 1995b. Learning systemic functional grammar in primary schools. *Australian English in a Pluralist Australia. Proceedings of Style Council 95.* ed. by Peters, P. H. Dictionary Research Centre, Macquarie University.

Williams, G. In press a. Children entering literate worlds: Perspectives from the study of textual practices. *Literacy in schooling.* ed. by Christie, F. & Missan, R. London: Routledge.

Williams, G. In press b. Children's Literature, Children and Uses of Language Description. *Researching language in schools and communities.* ed. by Unsworth, L. London: Cassell Academic.

Vygotsky, L. S. 1981. The genesis of higher mental functions. *The concept of activity in Soviet psychology.* ed. by Wertsch, J. V. New York. M. E. Sharpe.

INTEGRATING LANGUAGE AND CONTENT TEACHING THROUGH COLLABORATIVE TASKS[1]

Merrill Swain

Introduction

Tasks have been defined in a number of ways. David Nunan (1989), in his book "Designing Tasks for the Communicative Classroom", provides several definitions of "task", showing that they all "share one thing in common: they all imply that tasks involve communicative language use in which the user's attention is focused on meaning rather than [on] linguistic structure." (p. 10)

The definition of task that Nunan adopts in his book is similar and reads as follows:

> ...the communicative task [is] **a piece of classroom work which involves learners in comprehending, manipulating, producing or interacting in the target language while their attention is principally focused on meaning rather than form**. The task should also have a sense of completeness, being able to stand alone as a communicative act in its own right. (p. 10, emphasis in original)

In this paper, I would like to expand somewhat on Nunan's definition. I would like to suggest that Nunan's definition is too limited: that a task can equally as well be **focused on form**. Consistent with Nunan's definition, though, when students focus on form, they must be

[1] Most of the research reported in this paper was supported by a grant to Merrill Swain and Sharon Lapkin from the Social Sciences and Humanities Research Council of Canada (# 410-93-0053). The current paper is an updated and re-oriented version of two other papers, one presented at the III European Conference on Immersion Programs in Barcelona, Spain in September 1996, and the other presented at the International Language in Education Conference at the University of Hong Kong, Hong Kong, December 1996.

engaged in the act of "meaning-making". In the context of this paper, the act of meaning-making should relate to the academic content under study.

Let me give one example of the sort of task I am referring to. Students, working together in pairs, are each given a different set of numbered pictures that tell a story. Together the pair of students must jointly construct the story line. After they have worked out what the story is, they write it down. In doing so, students encounter linguistic problems that they need to solve to continue with the task. These problems include how to best say what they want to say; problems of lexical choice; which morphological ending to use; the best syntactic structure to use; and problems about the language needed to sequence the story correctly. These problems arise as the students try to "make meaning", that is, as they try to construct and write out the story, as they understand it. And, as they encounter these linguistic problems, they focus on linguistic form – the form that is needed to express the meaning in the way they want to convey it.

Of course, there are many variations of such a task. Rather than a series of pictures that tell a story, there could be a series of graphs that relate to a science lesson, or pictures that relate to a math problem, or diagrams that relate to a history lesson, or tables that relate to a political science lesson, and so on. The important feature in common is that students must jointly work out the meaning of the series by talking about them, and then write out their negotiated understanding in their second language as accurately, appropriately and coherently as possible.

I will return to the story example later, after I have had an opportunity to explain why we began to experiment with such tasks in the first place.

This paper, then, has three parts. In the first part, I would like to provide you with some background for our interest in using collaborative tasks in content-based language classrooms. This will entail a brief discussion of French immersion programs in Canada, and a consideration of the roles output – that is, speaking and writing – might have in second language learning.

In the second part of this paper, I will describe a set of studies undertaken in content-based language learning contexts to suggest that certain types of collaborative tasks – those which require written output from students – are particularly useful for language learning.

Finally, in the third part of the paper, I would like to pull together the first two parts by summarizing insights about language teaching that were new for us. These insights follow from the particular theoretical perspective and line of research inquiry presented, and, I believe, have relevance for both foreign language teaching per se, as well as content-based language teaching.

So let me begin by explaining why we have begun to research the use of collaborative tasks as a means of integrating content and language teaching.

The story began quite some years ago as we researched the outcomes of French immersion programs in Canada. French immersion programs are for students who have had little or no exposure to French before starting in the program, and who attend classes taught in French. The grade seven and eight students who participated in the research discussed in this paper, like many other immersion students, were taught entirely through the medium of French until grade three. After that, they received some instruction in English, the native language of most of the students. By grades seven and eight, several academic subjects were still taught using French as the language of instruction.

Our research demonstrated quite clearly that in spite of the input-rich, communicatively-oriented classrooms the students participated in, the students did not develop native-like proficiency in French (Swain, 1985). The results from two decades of research in French immersion classes suggested that immersion students are able to understand much of what they hear and read in the target language even at early grade levels. However, although they are fairly well able to get their meaning across in French, even at intermediate and higher grade levels, they often do so with non-target-like morphology, syntax and discourse patterns. (For overviews of this research, see for example, Genesee, 1987; Swain, 1984; and Swain and Lapkin, 1986. For detailed accounts, see for example, Harley and Swain, 1984; Harley, 1986; Harley, 1992; and Vignola and Wesche, 1991.)

Early Observational Research

These findings led us back to the classroom to search for explanations of why French immersion students' French was developing in the way it was. We spent time in a number of grade three and grade six immersion classrooms, observing and recording what actually went on.

Among what we observed (see, for example, Allen, Swain, Harley and Cummins, 1990; Swain, 1996), two themes emerged which are of particular relevance here:

1. the nature of grammatical instruction; and
2. student talk, or to use the jargon, student 'output'.

First, then, what did we find out about the teaching of grammar in the French immersion classes that we observed? Our observations revealed that grammar was being taught in immersion classes. However, the main emphasis in these activities appeared to be more on manipulating and categorizing language forms than on relating forms to their meaningful use when teaching academic content. It was a relatively rare occurrence for teachers to refer to what had been learned in a grammar lesson when they were involved in content teaching, and even more rare for teachers to set up content-based tasks for the main purpose of focusing on problematic language forms. Furthermore, in general, there was considerable content teaching that occurred where little or no attention was paid to the accuracy of students' target language use.

A second theme which emerged from our observations was the quantity of student talk – both how much the students talked during class lessons, and the length of student utterances. We found that there were, on average, about two students who talked per minute in the French portion of the day, as compared to about six students per minute in the English portion of the day. Thus these immersion students, who rarely spoke French outside of the classroom context, were also speaking relatively infrequently in French in class.

Furthermore, about 50% of the time the French immersion students talked in these teacher-fronted activities, their utterances consisted of only one or two words. Utterances longer than a clause were infrequent –

consisting of about only 14%. As I will be arguing, students should get more opportunities than this for sustained oral use of the target language.

Theoretical Considerations

These observations about the nature of grammatical instruction and student output in typical French immersion classes led us to certain theoretical considerations. First, the observations about grammatical instruction led us to a recognition that, at least in an immersion setting, teaching grammar lessons out of context, as paradigms to be rehearsed and memorized, are insufficient for the achievement of grammatical accuracy. The need to integrate language teaching with content teaching was clear.

Secondly, our observations concerning the limited output of students led to a consideration of the role of output in second language learning. There has been much theoretical discussion about the role of input in second language learning. But there has been little discussion about the role of output in second language learning, except as it might enhance fluency. However, the processes involved in producing language can be quite different from those involved in comprehending language (e.g. Swain, 1995). In listening, semantic and pragmatic information assist comprehension in ways that may not apply, or may apply differently in production, in that the semantic and pragmatic information can circumvent the need to process syntax. With output, however, learners need to move from the semantic, open-ended, strategic processing prevalent in comprehension to the complete grammatical processing needed for **accurate** production. Output, then, would seem to have a potentially significant role in the development of syntax and morphology, a role that underlies the functions output may have in the learning of a second language.

Let me turn, then, to describe three functions of output that have been proposed which relate to linguistic accuracy rather than to linguistic fluency (Swain, 1995). The three hypothesized functions of output in second language learning are to promote "noticing", to formulate and test hypotheses, and to reflect on language use through metatalk.

Noticing

I have suggested that, under certain circumstances, output promotes "noticing" (Swain 1995). This is important if there is a basis to the claim that "noticing" a form in input must occur for it to be acquired (Ellis, 1994).

The important issue here is that it is **while attempting to produce** the target language (vocally or subvocally) that learners may notice that they do not know how to say (or write) precisely the meaning they wish to convey. In other words, under some circumstances, the activity of producing the target language may prompt second language learners to consciously recognize some of their linguistic problems; it may bring to their attention something they need to discover about their second language possibly directing their attention to relevant input. This may trigger cognitive processes which might generate linguistic knowledge that is new for the learner, or consolidate his or her own existing knowledge (Swain and Lapkin 1995). Example 1 is taken from a think-aloud session with a grade eight immersion student while he is writing a newspaper article about pollution.

Example 1

Student: La dé...truc...tion. Et la détruction. No, that's not a word. Démolition, démolisson; démolition, démolition, détruction, détruision, détruision, la détruision des arbres au forêt de pluie (**the destruction of trees in the rain forest**).

(Swain and Lapkin, 1995)

In Example 1, the student has just written in French "Il y a trop d'utilisation des chemicaux toxiques qui detruissent l'ozone." (**There's too much use of toxic chemicals which destroy the ozone layer.**) In his think-aloud, we hear him trying to produce a noun form of the verb he has just used. He tries out various possibilities (hypotheses), seeing how each sounds. His final solution, "la detruision" is wrong, but he has made use of his knowledge of French by using the stem of the verb he has just produced and by adding a French-sounding suffix. This example is revealing, because the incorrect solution reached by the student allows us to conclude that new knowledge has been created through a search of his own existing knowledge. His search began with his own output which he heard as incorrect. He noticed what he did not know and tried to solve it by focusing on both form and meaning in context.

Hypothesis formation and testing

A second way in which producing language may serve the language learning process is through hypothesis formation and testing. As seen in Example 1, the learner used his output as a way of trying out new language forms (hypotheses). Tarone and Liu (1995: 120 – 121) provide evidence that it is precisely in contexts "where the learner needs to produce output which the current interlanguage system cannot handle...[and so]...pushes the limits of that interlanguage system to **make** it handle that output", that acquisition is most likely to have occurred.

In Example 1, the learner was in a situation where feedback from an external source was not available and so there was nothing to test his hypotheses against except his own internalized knowledge. In more usual circumstances, however, learners are able to obtain information useful for testing their hypotheses from other sources – teachers, peers, dictionaries, grammar books, and so on. Where external feedback has been available, learners have also modified, or reprocessed (Swain 1993), their output. The fact that learners modify their speech in some, but not in all of their utterances suggests that they are only testing out some things and not others (Pica et al, 1989). It may be that the modified, or reprocessed, output that follows feedback can be considered to represent the leading edge of a learner's interlanguage.

Thus, learners may use their output as a way of trying out new language forms and structures as they stretch their new language to meet communicative needs; they may produce just to see what works and what does not. That immediate external feedback may not help or be forthcoming does not negate the value of having experimented with their language resources. However, feedback is surely important as a source of information to the learner. We will return to this point when we look at the research which examines closely what happens when students work together on a task.

Metatalk

A third function of output is its metalinguistic function. In this case, a learner uses language to indicate an awareness of something about their own, or their interlocutor's, use of language. That is, learners use language to reflect on language use, as **metatalk.** In doing so, although learners may make use of metalinguistic terminology, it is by no means essential as part of the definition of metatalk. In fact, in the case of the data we have collected from grade eight immersion students, the majority of our examples illustrate students talking about language without using any metalinguistic terminology at all. The examples demonstrate, however, how students are thinking about their target language, that is, what the hypotheses are that they hold about the target language. Example 2 is illustrative.

Example 2

Rick:	Un bras…wait…mécanique…sort?
	(An arm…wait…a mechanical [arm]…comes out?)
Kim:	Sort, yeah.
	(Comes out, yeah.)
Rick:	Se sort?
	(Comes out?) [reflexive form: se sort]
Kim:	No, sort.
	(No, comes out.) [correct form: sort]

(Swain and Lapkin, 1996)

In Example 2, Rick is wondering whether the (non-existent) reflexive form of the verb "sortir" should be used in this context. His hypotheses are apparent as he first tries out the non-reflexive form "sort", then the reflexive form "se sort". Kim is able to provide Rick with correct answers to his questions; that is, she provides useful and correct feedback to Rick's hypothesis about the appropriate form to use in this context. This metatalk[2], happening as it does here – **in the context of "making meaning"** – may well serve the function of deepening the students' awareness of forms, rules and their relationship to the meaning they are

---

[2] Metatalk is often signalled by intonation and/or stress (prosodic features).

trying to express; of understanding a relationship between meaning, form and function in a highly context-sensitive situation.

My current working assumption is that metatalk is a surfacing of language used in problem-solving, that is, it is language used for cognitive purposes. In metatalk, we are able to observe learners' working hypotheses as they struggle towards, for example, solving mathematical problems, scientific problems, or, as we are concerned with in second language learning, linguistic problems. If this is the case, then much of what is observed in metatalk when learners are faced with a challenging language production task and are encouraged to talk about the problems they encounter in doing the task should help us to understand language learning processes. It should help us to understand language learning processes because much of what is observed will be language learning **in progress**. In other words, in metatalk, noticing, hypothesis formation and testing (cognitive problem-solving), and other learning processes (e.g. comprehending) may be made available for inspection. They are available for inspection by researchers, teachers and, possibly most importantly, for students themselves as they engage in second language learning.

Thus, by encouraging metatalk amongst second and foreign language students, we may be helping students to make use of second language acquisition processes. That is, metatalk may be one pedagogical means by which we can assure that language acquisition processes operate. It is essential, however, that this metatalk – this conscious focus on language form – is encouraged in contexts where the learners are engaged in "making meaning". Otherwise, the critical links between meaning, form and function may not be formed.

Current Research

The metalinguistic function of output has been the most important for us in thinking about the type of tasks in which we could engage immersion students that might help them move beyond their current state of L2 development towards more native-like performance. In our current research, we have sought to utilize tasks that would encourage output, and so we have used collaborative tasks. We also wanted our tasks to foster the use of metatalk. Thus, we have begun to try out in the classroom different tasks that are communicatively oriented, but where communication is in part, at least, **about** language; that is, where students will talk about – consciously reflect on – their own output. One type of task that we have found effective in achieving these goals is the dictogloss task (see Kowal and Swain 1994, 1997 for details).

The dictogloss, quite different from a dictation exercise, is a procedure which encourages students to reflect on their own output (Wajnryb 1990). As Wajnryb says about the dictogloss task, "Through active learner involvement students come to confront their own strengths and weaknesses...In so doing, they find out what they need to know." (p. 10, 1990).

During a dictogloss task, a short, dense text is read to the learners at normal speed; while it is being read, students jot down familiar words and phrases; then the learners work together in small groups to reconstruct the text from their shared resources. The final versions the students have produced are then analyzed and compared in a whole class setting in order to provide students with teacher feedback on student performance. The initial text is intended to provide practice in the use of particular grammatical constructions. In second language medium teaching situations as in French immersion programs in Canada or English-medium programs in Singapore, the contents of the text can also be related to academic material the students are currently studying in class.

We have tried using dictogloss tasks in grade seven and eight immersion classes (Kowal and Swain, 1994, 1997), and have found that they have elicited the sort of student talk we hoped they would elicit: talk about the language of the text they were reconstructing, that is, metatalk. We observed students noticing things they did not know or could not say to their own satisfaction, and we observed these same students formulating hypotheses and testing them out using the tools at their disposal: themselves; each other; their dictionaries; their 'verb' book; their teacher; their L1. Additionally, students ignored some of the errors they made; they often functioned at a semantic level, wanting to use the right word as well as thinking about correct inflections and relationships between words; and they focused on many other points of grammar than the one Kowal, the teacher, had in mind in developing the particular dictogloss.

We therefore felt assured that the dictogloss had created opportunities for metatalk, which these immersion students took up. The question of interest which this raises is, of course, does this metatalk support second language learning? Or, even, is the metatalk, itself, evidence of learning occurring?

To begin to address these questions, we have conducted two additional studies. To restate, our goals for this research are both theoretical and pedagogical. Pedagogically, our research is aimed at considering teaching strategies which might focus immersion students' attention on the accuracy of their spoken and written L2, while still maintaining the "philosophy" of immersion education – that is, that second language learning be embedded in a contextually rich, content-based, curriculum. This has led us to consider tasks that would lead immersion students to focus on form while never losing sight of the meaning they are trying to convey. And theoretically, our interest is in the role that output might have in the process of second language learning.

The first study that I would like to discuss was conducted by Donna LaPierre (1994) as her MA research and involved grade eight early French immersion students. Her study served as a pilot study (see also Swain, 1998) to the research we have just completed and that I will describe shortly. In LaPierre's study it was hypothesized that when L2 learners engage in a task in which they need to talk about the language they are producing (metatalk) to complete the task, that metatalk may be a source of second language learning. The task the students engaged in, in her study, was a dictogloss.

Second language learning was tested by means of tailor-made dyad-specific post-tests. We examined what aspects of language students talked about as they reconstructed the dictogloss passage in pairs. On the basis of these episodes, test items were constructed. Thus, every pair of students had a set of test items that reflected what they specifically had considered in reconstructing the passage. These tests were administered approximately a week after the students had done the task.

Of course, as the students encountered a linguistic problem and tried to solve it, their solution could be correct or incorrect. The results show that when the students solved the linguistic problem correctly, which for these students, at least, was most of the time, approximately 80% of the relevant post-test items were correct. Furthermore, and equally as telling, when the solutions the students arrived at through their metatalk were incorrect, approximately 70% of the answers on the post-test were wrong, although they matched the solutions the pairs had arrived at. In other words, the students tended to "stick with" the knowledge they had constructed collaboratively the previous week. These results suggest rather forcefully that these language-related episodes, where students reflect consciously on the language they are producing, may be a source of, or even an occasion for, second language learning. These results also show the importance of teacher follow-up to task activity to provide feedback to students concerning their hypotheses.

The second study, which my colleague, Sharon Lapkin, and I have been working on, differed from LaPierre's in that two tasks were used: a dictogloss task and a jigsaw story construction task. The story construction task was like the one I described at the beginning of this paper. Additionally we attempted to use a pre-test/post-test design.

One goal of the study was to see if one type of task led students to focus on form with greater frequency than the other. Our original prediction was that the dictogloss task would lead students to focus on form with greater frequency than the jigsaw task. This was because our results to date using the dictogloss had clearly led students to focus on form; and our reading of the relevant literature had suggested that jigsaw tasks – one in which each participant has some, but not all, the information needed to complete the task – is the type of task where opportunities for meaning negotiation are most likely to be generated (e.g. Pica, Kanagy and Falodun, 1994). In other words, we assumed our jigsaw task represented a typical communicative task as defined by Nunan where "attention is principally focused on meaning rather than form".

Space does not allow me to consider the details of the full study (see Swain and Lapkin, 1998 for details). What is important to know at this point is that in order that the two groups be treated as similarly as possible, a pre-recorded mini-lesson on French reflexive verbs was shown on video. This was followed on the video with two students shown working collaboratively on the relevant task – dictogloss or jigsaw. This served as a model for what the students were to do immediately following the viewing of the videotape when a new jigsaw task or dictogloss was introduced for the students to do. The conversation of each pair of students in the class was tape-recorded as they did their task. About a week later, these students were tested on, among other things, aspects of language that they had talked about while they carried out the task.

What were the results?

Table 1: Language-Related Episodes (LREs)

	Class J			Class D			
	N	$\overline{X}$	SD	N	$\overline{X}$	SD	Sig.[3]
Count of total episodes	12	8.8	8.0	14	9.2	4.2	ns
Count of Lexis-based LREs	12	4.0	3.7	14	3.7	2.3	ns
Count of Form-based LREs	12	4.8	4.5	14	5.5	2.9	ns
Percent Lexis-based LREs	12	41%	21%	14	40%	19%	ns
Percent Form-based LREs	12	59%	21%	14	60%	19%	ns

First, and to our considerable surprise, the percent of form-based language-related episodes (LREs[4]) produced by the students was the same for both tasks. As shown in Table 1 above, approximately 60% of the language-related episodes generated were form-based whether the task was the dictogloss or the jigsaw. On reflection, we believe there are two reasons for this similarity.

One reason is that the mini-lesson on reflexive verbs given prior to actually doing the task served, as we had expected, to focus students' attention on language form. This is shown clearly in Example 3.

Example 3: (Class J, pair 4)

---

[3] Two-tailed t-test.

[4] A language related episode is any part of a dialogue where students talk about the language they are producing, question their language use, or other- or self-correct.

B:	Yvonne va à l'école.
	(**Yvonne goes to school.**)
A:	Se part à l'école.
	(**Yvonne leaves [uses non-existent reflexive form] for school.**)
B:	Oui. Elle…se marche
	(**She walks [uses non-existent reflexive form]**)
A:	Se part, parce que…
	(**Leaves [uses non-existent reflexive form], because**)
A:	Est-ce que c'est part ou se part?
	(**Is it leaves or leaves [in the non-existent reflexive form]?**)
B:	Part.
	(**Leaves.**)
A:	Part? Just part?
	(**Leaves? Just leaves?**)
B:	Ya
A:	Ok. Yvonne part à l'école, um…
	(**Yvonne leaves for school.**)

Here the two students talk about the correct form of the verb **partir**. They wonder if it should be a reflexive verb. In fact, the French verb **partir** does not exist in the reflexive form; but clearly these students are hesitating, most likely because of the mini-lesson they had seen on the video just preceding their doing the task. A asks B if the verb should be "part" or "se part", that is, should it be in the reflexive form or not? B supplies the correct answer, and that is the form A then uses.

The second, and perhaps more important reason, is that the tasks had in common the necessity to produce written language. It was as the students wrote that they questioned each other about how to write, focusing their joint attention on form. The activity of writing collaboratively led students to discuss their own language use as they encountered problems. They brought to conscious attention gaps in their own knowledge and worked out possible solutions through hypothesis formation and testing, relying on their joint linguistic resources.

A second major finding was that there was a wide range of student behaviour in doing the tasks. For example, although an average of 8.8 language-related episodes (LREs) were produced by student pairs in the jigsaw task, there was a rather surprisingly high range of 26 to 1 LREs produced by individual pairs. The average number of form-based LREs was 4.8 with a range of 15 to 1, and the average number of lexis-based LREs[5] was 4.0 with a range of 12 to 0.

Similarly, there was a wide range of time spent on task. Again using the jigsaw task as an example, the average time students spent on task was approximately 10 minutes out of a half-hour that they were given to do the task. However, the range of time spent on task varied from 23 minutes to a rather low 3.5 minutes.

A third major finding concerns the texts produced by the students. They were rated according to content, organization, vocabulary, morphology and syntax. The average rating of the jigsaw pairs was similar to that of the dictogloss pairs. However, the range of scores for the dictogloss pairs was much smaller than that for the jigsaw pairs, suggesting that the language model provided by the dictogloss focuses and constrains students' language production. Because the reflexive verb was the focus of the mini-lesson, we counted instances of correct and incorrect reflexive verb use in the written texts of the jigsaw and dictogloss students. Of the reflexive verbs used by the jigsaw student, approximately 60% were correct. In contrast, approximately 90% of the reflexive verbs used by the dictogloss students were correct, underlining the importance of the dictogloss in providing grammatically accurate input.

Our fourth major finding was that, like LaPierre, we found evidence of the importance of metatalk as reflected in the language-related episodes for second language learning. Example 4 is richly illustrative.

The first LRE in Example 4 relates to the use of "reveille-matin": turns 2 through 4, 9, 55-72 and 92-95 were all considered as part of this

---

[5] Lexis-based LREs involve students seeking French vocabulary and/or choosing among competing French vocabulary items. Form-based LREs involve students focusing on spelling or an aspect of French morphology, syntax or discourse.

single LRE. Turns 66 through 72, and 92 to 93 also constitute part of a second LRE focusing on the noun "le sonnement".

Example 4:

Turn 2: Kim: On peut pas déterminer qu'est-ce que c'est.
            (**One can't figure out what it is.**)
Turn 3: Rick: Réveille-matin.
            (**Alarm clock.**)
Turn 4: Kim: Et il y a un réveille-matin rouge...sur une table brune, et le réveille-matin dit six heures, et c'est tout.
            (**And there is a red alarm clock...on the brown table, and the alarm clock says six o'clock, and that's all.**)

This exchange continues for another 4 turns with Kim using "réveille-matin" three more times, and Rick once more; Rick then for some reason switches to "la/le rêve-matin" in turn 9. His hesitation in producing it suggests his uncertainty.

Turn 9: Rick: Elle est en train de dormir après que...la rêve-matin est encore sonné. Et le rê-...rêve-matin dit six heures un.
            (**She is sleeping after the alarm clock rang again. And the alarm clock says one minute after six o'clock.**)

This uncertainty continues.

Turn 55: Kim: ...il y a un réveille-matin.
             (**...there is an alarm clock.**)
Turn 56: Rick:Réveille-matin?
             (**Alarm clock?**)
Turn 57: Kim: Réveille-matin.
             (**Alarm clock.**)

Turn 66: Rick:Se réveille à cause...du son...
             (**Wakes up because...of the sound...**)
Turn 67: Kim: Réveille-matin.
             (**Alarm clock.**)
Turn 68: Rick:A cause du...
             (**Because of...**)

Turn 69: Kim: Du réveille-matin qui sonne? Does that sound OK?
(Of the alarm-clock that rings? Does that sound OK?)
Turn 70: Rick: Or what about...Jacqueline se lève a cause du...du réveille-
...yeah, qui sonne.
**(Or what about...Jacqueline [the girl in their story] gets
up because of the...of the alarm-...yeah, that rings.)**
Turn 71: Kim: OK. Or you can say, du réveille-matin, or du sonnement du
réveille-matin.
**(OK. Or you can say, of the alarm clock, or the ring of
the alarm clock.)**
Turn 72: Rick: No, réveille-matin qui sonne.
(No, alarm clock that rings.)

Turn 92: Rick: Sur la rêv-...rêve-matin.
(On the alarm clock.)
Turn 93: Kim: Sur le réveille-matin pour arrêter le sonnement.
(On the alarm clock to stop the ring.)
Turn 94: Rick: Rêve-matin?
(Alarm clock?)
Turn 95: Kim: REVEILLE-matin.
(Alarm clock.) [Stresses component meaning 'wake'.]

(Swain and Lapkin, 1998)

We do not know why Rick sometimes used "rêve-matin" after he, himself, initially suggested using "réveille-matin" to Kim (turn 3). However, it is clear from the dialogue that Rick is uncertain as to which is the correct vocabulary item. This is indicated by the pauses prior to, or even during, the use of "rêve-matin" (turns 9 and 92) and "réveille-matin" (turn 70); by his need for reassurance before writing "réveille-matin" (turn 56); and finally by overtly asking if "rêve-matin" is OK (turn 94) and getting immediate feedback from Kim that it should be "REVEILLE-matin". In writing the story, Rick correctly uses "réveille-matin" three times, though it is misspelled each time as "réveil-matin".

Key to our understanding of what might have resulted from this metatalk is a relevant multiple-choice pre- and post-test item. Students saw a picture of an alarm clock and were asked to choose the best response from: 1. Voilà mon horloge. 2. Voilà mon réveille-matin. 3. Voilà mon rêve-matin. 4. Voilà ma cloche. As a pre-test item, Kim correctly chose "réveille-matin" and Rick chose "rêve-matin". But, in the post-test, both students chose the correct response.

In this collaborative dialogue, we are able to "observe change" in Rick's use of the correct term for alarm clock. It is not a one-time shift from wrong to right, but a wavering between alternatives. The source of his learning is not only input although Kim used "réveille-matin" seventeen times during their entire conversation. Nor was the source of his learning only output, although it was probably Rick's attempt to write it (turn 56) which focused his attention on his own uncertainty about which term to use. We see here the two students engaging in talk about their own language use, stimulated by Rick's uncertainty which he realized only when he had to produce "réveille-matin" in writing. Having noticed this gap in his knowledge, he questions Kim. Here Rick's questions serve as hypotheses, and Kim's responses serve to confirm or disconfirm them.

The "sonnement" LRE (in turns 66 to 72 and continued in turns 92 and 93) is particularly interesting because "le sonnement" is not a word in French ("le son" or "la sonnerie" are the relevant words here). Although the word "sonnement" does not exist in French, Kim, in creating this word, applies a productive rule in French ("ment" is a suffix which marks many masculine nouns). Elsewhere in the transcript, Rick questions whether it is "la sonnement" or "le sonnement", and Kim immediately assures him that it is "LE sonnement". Here we see Kim and Rick applying rules to new contexts, albeit incorrectly. They solve a lexical problem in much the same way as native speakers might coin a new word, by using their existing language knowledge as a tool to create new knowledge.

Summary of Insights

Let me now turn to the third part of this paper in which I will try to summarize for you the insights about language teaching that were new for us, and that follow from our research and particular theoretical perspective.

1. In an immersion-type setting where students are to learn the academic content of school through the medium of a second language, provision of input-rich, communicatively-oriented instruction is not enough for

students to develop native speaker levels of proficiency in the second language.

2. Teaching grammar per se, disconnected from the content it conveys and the functions it serves, also is not enough to develop native speaker levels of proficiency in the second language.

3. Language instruction needs to be systematically integrated into content instruction. There are many ways to do this (see, e.g. Day and Shapson, 1991; Harley, 1989; Mohan, 1986; Snow, Met and Genesee, 1989). The use of carefully planned and structured collaborative tasks is one means.

4. Characteristics of these collaborative tasks are:
   a) students work in pairs thereby "forcing" participation.
   b) a final product of written text (or oral presentation) is required.
   c) students focus on language form as they work to express content accurately, coherently and appropriately. They are, therefore, communicative tasks. However, different from communication tasks as they are usually defined, students communicate about both language form and content.

5. Collaborative tasks provide opportunities for second language learning because:
   a) students notice gaps in their linguistic knowledge as they try to express their intended meaning leading them to search for solutions (formulate and test hypotheses).
   b) students externalize their knowledge allowing them to reflect on it, revise it, and apply it.
   c) all students participate actively and the resulting output allows them to increase their use and knowledge of the target language.

6. Collaborative tasks generate unintended consequences. Students carry out tasks according to their own needs and goals. They may not learn what the teacher intended them to learn, but nevertheless they learn what, given their state of content and language knowledge, they are able to learn.

Often together, students accomplish what they could not have accomplished alone.

7. Teachers, researchers, testers and the students, themselves, have much to learn by studying the substance of collaborative talk.

   a) Teachers can gain insights into the hypotheses students hold about language and content, helping them to orient their instruction towards erroneously held hypotheses.

   b) Researchers can gain insights into the processes of language learning as students engage in linguistic problem solving.

   c) Testers can gain insights as to what to test, and why students perform well or badly on a particular test. If the students did not consider the issues the test deals with, why should they perform well on it? Furthermore, students may have learned other things which were not tested – a credit to themselves, but not to the tester.

   d) Students can gain insights into their own linguistic shortcomings and develop strategies for solving them by working them through with a partner.

8. Collaborative tasks should not be seen as "stand-alone" activities. Teachers' availability during collaborative activities, and their attention to the accuracy of the final product subsequent to the completion of collaborative activities, are potentially critical aspects for student learning.

In conclusion, the research I have discussed is just a beginning: just a beginning in a program of research aimed at examining pedagogical strategies that will enhance the second language learning of, in our case, French immersion students. We have begun to accumulate evidence to suggest the usefulness of collaborative tasks that lead learners to reflect on their own language production as they attempt to create meaning. Such tasks not only stimulate output that can serve to focus attention and to formulate and test hypotheses, but they also provide opportunities for output to function as a metalinguistic tool. On the basis of our results to date, we see the desirability of incorporating collaborative, form-focused tasks – of the sort used in this study – in second language curricula as part of a language class, or in second language medium contexts to support academic-specific language development.

References

Allen, P., Swain, M., Harley, B. & Cummins, J. 1990. Aspects of classroom treatment: Towards a more comprehensive view of second language education. *The Development of Second Language Proficiency*. ed. by Harley, B., Allen, P., Cummins, J. & Swain, M. (pp. 57-81). Cambridge: Cambridge University Press.

Day, E. & Shapson, S. 1991. Integrating formal and functional approaches to language teaching in French immersion: An experimental study. *Language Learning*. 47, 25-58.

Ellis, R. 1994. *The Study of Second Language Acquisition*. Oxford: Oxford University Press.

Harley, B. 1986. *Age in Second Language Acquisition*. Clevedon, Avon: Multilingual Matters.

Harley, B. 1989. Functional grammar in French immersion: A classroom experiment. *Applied Linguistics*. 10, 331-359.

Harley, B. 1992. Patterns of second language development in French immersion. *Journal of French Language Studies*. 2, 159-183.

Harley, B. & Swain, M. 1984. The interlanguage of immersion students and its implications for second language teaching. *Interlanguage*. ed. by Davies, A., Criper, C. & Howatt, A. (pp 291-311). Edinburgh: Edinburgh University Press.

Kowal, M. & Swain, M. 1994. Using collaborative language production tasks to promote students; language awareness. *Language Awareness*. 3, 73-93.

Kowal, M. & Swain, M. 1997. From semantic to syntactic processing: How can we promote metalinguistic awareness in the French immersion classroom? *Immersion Education: International Perspectives.* ed. by Johnson, R. K. & Swain, M. (pp 284-309). Cambridge: Cambridge University Press.

LaPierre, D. 1994. *Language output in a cooperative learning setting: Determining its effects on second language learning.* MA thesis, OISE (University of Toronto).

Mohan, B. 1986. *Language and Content.* Reading, MA: Addison-Wesley.

Nunan, D. 1989. *Designing Tasks for the Communicative Classroom.* Cambridge: Cambridge University Press.

Pica, T., Kanagy, R. & Falodun, J. 1994. Choosing and using communication tasks for second language instruction. *Tasks and language learning: Integrating theory & practice.* ed. by Crookes, G. & Gass, S. (pp 9-34). Clevedon, Avon: Multilingual Matters.

Pica, T., Holliday, L., Lewis, N. & Morgenthaler, L. 1989. Comprehensible output as an outcome of linguistic demands on the learner. *Studies in Second Language Acquisition.* 11, 63-90.

Snow, M. A., Met, M. & Genesee, F. 1989. A conceptual framework for the integration of language and content in second/foreign language instruction. *TESOL Quarterly.* 23, 201-217.

Swain, M. 1984. A review of immersion education in Canada: Research and evaluation studies. *Studies on Immersion Education: A Collection for U.S. Educators.* Sacramento: California State Department of Education, 87-112.

Swain, M. 1985. Communicative competence: Some roles of comprehensible input and comprehensible output in its development. *Input in Second Language Acquisition.* ed. by Gass, S. and Madden, C. (pp 235-253). Rowley, Mass.: Newbury House.

Swain, M. 1993. The output hypothesis: Just speaking and writing aren't enough. *The Canadian Modern Language Review.* 50, 158-164.

Swain, M. 1995. Three functions of output in second language learning. *Principle and Practice in Applied Linguistics: Studies in Honour of H.G. Widdowson.* ed. by Cook, G. & Seidlhofer, B. (pp. 125-144). Oxford: Oxford University Press.

Swain, M. 1996. Discovering successful second language teaching strategies and practices: From program evaluation to classroom experimentation. *Journal of Multilingual and Multicultural Development.* 17, 89-104.

Swain, M. 1998. Focus on form through conscious reflection. *Focus on Form in Classroom Second Language Acquisition.* ed. by Doughty, C. & Williams, J. Cambridge: Cambridge University Press.

Swain, M. (in press). Collaborative dialogue: Its contribution to second language learning. *Revista Canaria de Estudios Ingleses.* 34.

Swain, M. & Lapkin, S. 1995. Problems in output and the cognitive processes they generate: A step towards second language learning. *Applied Linguistics.* 16, 371-391.

Swain, M. & Lapkin, S. 1996. Focus on form through collaborative dialogue: Exploring task effects. Paper presented at the Annual Conference of the American Association of Applied Linguistics, Chicago.

Swain, M. & Lapkin, S. 1998. Interaction and second language learning: Two adolescent French immersion students working together. *MLJ* 83 (3).

Tarone, E. & Liu, G-Q. 1995. Situational context, variation, and second language acquisition theory *Principle and Practice in Applied Linguistics: Studies in Honour of H.G. Widdowson.* ed. by Cook, G. and Seidlhofer, B. (pp 107-124). Oxford: Oxford University Press.

Vignola, M-J. & Wesche, M. 1991. Le savoir ecrire en langue maternelle et en langue seconde chez les diplomes d'immersion francaise. *Etudes de linguistique appliquee* 82, 94-115.

Wajnryb, R. 1990. *Grammar Dictation.* Oxford: Oxford University Press.

PRAGMATICS AND ENGLISH LANGUAGE TEACHING

Jenny Thomas

Introduction

In this paper, I shall discuss the applications of pragmatics to the teaching of languages. I shall begin with an overview of the different areas covered by pragmatics, at each stage trying to show its relevance for the language teacher. I shall focus particularly on two areas of cross-cultural pragmatics – pragmalinguistics and sociopragmatics. I shall conclude by addressing the question of why pragmatics should be assigned a more prominent place in language teaching syllabuses.

I would like to begin with an anecdote. When I was sixteen and just beginning A-levels, I took part in the Bristol-Bordeaux school exchange. It was a cross-cultural experience in more than one sense – not only was this my first trip abroad, I also found myself placed in a strict, upper-class, girls' boarding school in the middle of a large town, a school with a very different ethos from the easy-going, mixed, rural and largely working-class day school I attended at home. Within hours of my arrival, an incident occurred which, more than thirty years later, I still remember with hurt and embarrassment. I recount it here because it illustrates neatly many of the points I would like to make regarding the importance of introducing students to basic notions in pragmatics before they spend time in the target culture.

The first lesson I attended was on current affairs and the class was beginning a new topic – countries which had been divided for political reasons. I remember feeling rather pleased that here was a subject I could discuss on equal terms with my French classmates – I knew about Germany, Korea and Vietnam and, as might be expected, I was quite knowledgeable about Ireland. So engrossed was I in the discussion that I failed to notice that the other groups had fallen silent. The teacher said: *Mademoiselle, voulez-vous vous taire?* Not realising that she was speaking to me, I carried on talking. She repeated her request; this time I understood from the reaction of the other students that she was addressing me and that she seemed to be asking me if I wanted to do something. I did not understand what I was being 'invited' to do, so I cautiously replied '*Non, merci*'! The teacher made a tremendous and quite unnecessary fuss about my alleged rudeness, first bringing in the *censeur*[1] and then someone from the exchange programme. This apparently trivial incident affected the way I was treated throughout the whole of my time at the school and made my first experience of life in a foreign country very miserable.

So what had gone wrong? The first problem was a straightforward linguistic (grammatical) difficulty – I was familiar enough with the imperative forms *tais-toi* and *taisez-vous*, but I had never come across the infinitive *se taire*. All the other problems were pragmatic in nature, involving address forms, T- and V-forms,[2] indirectness, speech acts and different politeness norms. I will comment on these and other pragmatic issues which could usefully be brought to the attention of students of modern languages.

What areas are covered by pragmatics?

Pragmatics is generally held to deal with the following areas:

- the disambiguation of meaning in context
- the assignment of complete meaning
- distinguishing sentence meaning from speaker meaning
- the investigation of how listeners arrive at particular meanings
- the investigation of *why* people speak as they do

The first three areas are at the more 'linguistic' end of pragmatics (what I shall term 'pragmalinguistics'); the last two relate to more 'social' aspects of pragmatics (I term this 'sociopragmatics'). I will deal with each of the areas in order.

---

[1] The *censeur* is the person responsible for discipline in French secondary schools.

[2] T- and V- forms relate to the pronouns of 'power and solidarity' (Brown and Gilman 1960), such as tu/vous (French), du/Sie (German), ты/вы (Russian), etc.

The disambiguation of meaning in context

Many (in fact most) words/phrases are ambiguous when taken out of context. And, from the point of view of the hearer, many words and phrases are ambiguous even in context. Ambiguity is a semantic property, but the process of disambiguating meaning[3] in context involves pragmatic reasoning. Let us take a simple example. The word *bank* has a number of possible meanings, including *financial institution* and *embankment* (e.g. of a river). It is rather difficult to conceive of situations when the two different meanings might genuinely be confused, but the following is a case in point:

Example 1

[A boy 'joy-rider' was telling an interviewer about an occasion when he had stolen a car, had been chased by the police and had crashed, injuring himself badly][4]

'At the end of the road was a bank, a steep mud bank'

As I listened to the boy's account, I assumed (given the reference to *road*) that *bank* meant *financial institution*. However, as the account unfolded and more details were given I was obliged to revise my initial interpretation; the reference to *steep mud* made it clear that the boy was referring to *an embankment*.

Disambiguation is probabilistic

The process of disambiguation is probabilistic. In example 1, I initially misunderstood the meaning of *bank*, but revised my interpretation in the light of more evidence. However, probabilities vary between languages. For example, the word *station* in British English almost invariably means *railway station*. In American English, it could equally well refer to *bus/coach station, train station*, etc. An unfortunate example of such failure to assign the **most probable** interpretation occurred when

---

[3] And also resolving structural and referential ambiguities (see Thomas 1995: 2–16).
[4] *Barnados*, Radio 4, 18.7.95.

150

the French actor, Gérard Depardieu, was being interviewed on American television.

Example 2

Discussing an incident from his early childhood, Depardieu said:

J'ai assisté à un viol

What Depardieu meant was 'I **witnessed** a rape', but his words were translated as 'I **took part in** a rape.' The French verb *assister à* means, in order of probability, *to attend*, *to witness* and only lastly *to assist/to take part in*. It is important to note that this was a possible interpretation of Depardieu's words, but not the most likely. Not surprisingly, Depardieu came in for a great deal of unfair criticism for what he was reported to have said.

Interpretive bias

Psycholinguists (e.g. Kess and Hoppe, 1981) have shown that in interpreting grammatical ambiguity there is almost always 'bias' (by which they mean that one meaning is generally seen first by most people). The same is true in the pragmatic process of resolving ambiguity (we saw in example 1 how the word *bank* was first assigned the meaning *financial institution* by a native speaker of English and only later re-interpreted in the light of more 'evidence'). Cross-culturally, however, the bias in interpretation may be different. Consider the following examples.

Example 3

In the Hotel Mercure in Grenoble I read the following advertisement for fine wines:

Des plaisirs raffinés à des prix incroyables

The Hotel helpfully provided the following interpretation for its English-speaking guests:

Refined pleasures at an incredible price!

151

Unfortunately, the semantically equivalent *incroyable/incredible* has a different interpretive bias in the two languages. In French, the most likely interpretation is *incredibly low* prices. In English, it would be *incredibly high* prices! The same process operates in my next example. When I was a 'lectrice' at Reims University one of the chaplains was a painfully shy man, with a terrible stammer. I asked one of his colleagues why this man had been appointed, of all things, chaplain to overseas students and was told:

Example 4

Puisqu'il parle toutes les langues **indifféremment**

[Literally: because he speaks all languages indifferently/ without distinction]

At the time, I thought this reply·was tremendously witty and I laughed uproariously. It was many years before I realised that exactly the same phenomenon was in operation here as in example 3 – a **positive** interpretative bias in French ('he speaks all languages equally **well**') and a **negative** interpretative bias in English ('he speaks all languages equally **badly**'). And the same positive/negative French/English bias can be observed in example 5, said to me (in English) by a French-speaking guest in my house:

Example 5

Your cat is peculiar!

I must admit to having been momentarily offended by this unwarranted criticism of my pet, but after we had talked about it I realised that his remark was a translation of the French *Votre chat est particulier*. Again we see that the French word *particulier* means 'individual (+GOOD)' ('unique'), whereas the semantically equivalent English word *peculiar* means 'individual (+BAD)' ('odd', 'weird', 'strange').[5]

---

[5] A member of the audience at which a talk based on this paper was first given offered me an example where the interpretive bias operates in the other direction. He told me that he had once said (in English) to a French student that

What is homonymous in L1 may not be homonymous in L2

The term **homonymy** refers to words which are spelt and pronounced in the same way but have completely different meanings, such as *(vampire) bat* and *(cricket) bat*. Homonymy is one form of ambiguity (ambiguity can also be caused by problems to do with reference or grammatical structure).[6]

This is a small and rather obvious point – a word which is homonymous in one language is unlikely to be homonymous in another. In spite of the best efforts of teachers and dictionary makers, students seem to find this linguistic fact hard to grasp.[7] For example, several years ago I was teaching on a first-year course in stylistics and the students had been asked to undertake an analysis of *Spring* by Gerard Manley Hopkins. One of the students was from Iceland and she interpreted the word *thrush* as *fungal infection* instead of *songbird*! There then followed a phenomenon which I have often noticed – having come up with an improbable interpretation of an unknown word, she then 'twisted' the meanings of other words with which she **was** perfectly familiar to fit in with this implausible reading.[8]

---

the change in his written work was dramatic. The student was extremely upset, since he interpreted *dramatic* (French *dramatique*) as *dramatic change for the worse*, whereas the English speaker meant *dramatic improvement*.

[6] See Thomas (1995) pp 5–16.

[7] Of course, there are occasions when words are ambiguous in the same way, even in non-cognate languages – for example *bank/banque* is ambiguous between *financial institution* and *embankment* in both French and English. Examples such as this make the message 'beware ambiguity!' even harder to drive home to students.

[8] Shortly after this event, I found myself doing exactly the same thing. A friend had asked me to translate from Russian an article concerning mitochondria in rats. I translated it without a dictionary (biological terms tend to be very similar in the two languages), but in the very first line I came across the expression печени крысы (*from the liver of a rat*) but I misread it as печёной крысы (*from a baked rat*). (I should perhaps say in my own defence that I was working from a very smudgy mimeograph and the diacritics were illegible.) Even to a non-scientist the idea that rats might be baked in order to extract the mitochondria seemed extremely improbable, but nevertheless I found myself twisting the sense of other words which I knew perfectly well in order to fit in with the 'baked rat'. I have observed this phenomenon over and over again –

Hopkins's charming poem of hope and re-birth was transformed into a grim image of disease, decay and death.

What is polysemous in L1 may not be polysemous in L2

Homonymy relates to two (or more) different meanings of a word. Polysemy refers to situations where a word has different, but clearly related meanings. Thus, the *neck* of a bottle and the *neck* of a giraffe refer to very different entities, but nevertheless contain related concepts. A word which is polysemous in L1 may not be polysemous in the same way in L2 (indeed, it may not be polysemous at all). The ways in which **extensions** of meanings occur are predictable only to a degree. For example, the word *wing* (*aile* in French, крыло in Russian) has as its basic meaning *the wing of a bird*. In all three of these non-cognate languages (and, I dare say, in most other languages) the word can also be applied to *the wing of an aeroplane* and *the wing of a building*. As we move further away from the most basic, core meanings, the range of applicability is less predictable.

The polysemy of *wing* in English, French and Russian			
.	English	French	Russian
Wing of an aeroplane	✓	✓	✓
Wing of a building	✓	✓	✓
Wing of a stage	✓	✓	✗
Wing of a political party[9]	✓	✗	✓
Flank (of an army)	✗	✓	✓
Position in football	✓	✗	✗
Blade (of a propeller)	✗	✓	✗

when doing translations otherwise intelligent people seem willing to distort a text entirely, rather than abandon an initial hypothesis about the meaning of an unknown word, however extraordinary! I have never seen this phenomenon discussed, but I call it the 'baked rat syndrome'!

[9] And this meaning may itself be extended. On the way to a Conference at which this paper was given, I heard the following on the car radio: 'I read this in *The Daily Express*, the militant wing of *The Daily Mail!*' (BBC Radio 4, 10.4.96).

Note that Russian seems to have fewer polysemous meanings of *wing* – I have not been able to find an example which occurs in Russian but not in English and French. Some languages seem to have wholly idiosyncratic polysemous usages. For example, *Flögel* (literally *wing*) also means *grand piano* in German – presumably because the lid, when raised, looks like a wing. As far as I am aware, this particular extension of core meaning does not occur in any other language.

As I noted above, some words are polysemous in one language but not in another. An example which I discuss elsewhere (Thomas, 1995: 7) shows how the Hebrew word צילום (*tzilum*) has three (closely related) meanings: x-ray, photograph, photocopy (xerox). There is no comparable polysemous word in English.

The lessons for the language teacher are, I think, clear: students should be made aware of the phenomenon of polysemy. They need to understand the concept of *core meaning*, to make educated guesses about the range of probable extensions of meaning and to identify usages which are likely to be idiosyncratic or language-specific. In other words, they need to start to think about **cognitive** aspects of language use. The same cognitive processes are involved in the assignment of complete meaning.

Assigning complete meaning

The meaning of many (perhaps most) words is underspecified by its semantics. For example, **deictics** such as *there*, *then* are only truly meaningful in context. Pragmatic reasoning is required in order to 'fill out' the complete meaning. The same is true of grammatical words such as *and* and *for*. Consider the following examples – in each sentence, the word *for* has a slightly different meaning:

The girls were punished for playing truant
(because they...)

I gave her an omelette for her lunch
(to eat for...)

I gave her £2 for her lunch
(so that she could buy...)

She was given three years for burglary
(as a punishment for ...)

That remote control is for the video, not the television
(belongs to ...)

Sue was awarded the CBE for services to education
(in recognition of ...)

The underspecifying of meaning is particularly obvious in the case of deictics and grammatical words such as conjunctions and prepositions. But we can observe a very similar phenomenon with most words. Consider the word *university* in each of the following sentences – in each case it has a slightly different meaning:

It's difficult to park at the university
(place/buildings/geographical location)

Relations are good between the town and the university
(group of people)

The university is £3,000,000 in debt
(legal entity)

The role of the university is changing
(institution)

The university is offering premature retirement to ...
(the administration)

When I was at university
(life-stage)

We can 'fill out' the meanings in a similar, but not identical way, in other languages. In French and Russian, for example, all but the last two usages would be possible. (Both French and Russian would require you to say 'when I was a student (at university).')

Process of transfer of meaning (metonymy)

Pragmatic reasoning is necessary in order for the hearer to 'fill out' the meaning of words and also to interpret metonymy. One of the most common forms of metonymy is using one entity to refer to another as in the following standard examples:

Example 6

[One waitress to another in a snackbar]:

'The ham sandwich just left without paying'

Example 7

[Nurse to doctor]:

'The coronary infarction has just died'

My next example of this type of metonymy was actually addressed to me when I was in Canada and caused me considerable offence. I was having a meal in a restaurant with a friend, and the steaks were given different names, according to their size – the 16 oz fillet steak was a *lumberjack*, the 8 oz steak a *lady lumberjack*, etc. I was unaware of this quaintly sexist naming convention, since I had not looked at the meat menu but my (male) companion, unable to face 16 oz of meat, had ordered the 8 oz steak, in spite of its unmanly designation.

Example 8

Waitress to me:

'Are you the lady lumberjack?'

Another very common form of metonymy is 'place' for 'institution' metonymy, where 'Brussels' stands for 'the EC Commission' (example 9) and 'Fleet Street' for 'newspaper journalists' (example 10):

Example 9

Brussels has agreed to foot 70% of the cost of compensating British beef farmers

Example 10

Fleet Street has whipped up panic over 'Mad Cow Disease'

A third very common form of metonymy is 'whole' for 'part' (as in example 11, where *car* stands for *the petrol tank of the car*) or 'part' for 'whole' (as in example 12 where *eyes and ears* stands for the whole person).

Example 11

I'll fill up the car.

Example 12[10]

Member of French Resistance:	Remember, the Resistance has eyes and ears everywhere.
Gary Sparrow:	Don't you have any whole people?

Metonymy (transferring meaning) occurs in all natural languages, but it seems that not all metonymic processes occur in all languages. This is an area which is not well researched, but a recent study by Baranov and Dobrovol'skij (1996) suggests that different languages favour different forms of metonymy. It would be interesting to get students to explore the processes of metonymy which exist in their own and other languages. Example 13 illustrates 'container' → 'contents' metonymy. This form of metonymy does occur in English (e.g. the school broke up for the holidays) but is very much more common in Russian:

---

[10] This example is taken from an episode of the BBC comedy series *Goodbye Sweetheart*, broadcast in April 1998.

Example 13

[Аудитория means auditorium/lecture hall]

Аудитория смеялась – the lecture theatre laughed

Example 14 illustrates 'activity' $\rightarrow$ 'time of activity' metonymy, where an activity (lunch) also stands for the time at which that activity occurs (lunchtime). I am not aware of being able to use this type of metonymy in English or French:

Example 14

Пригласить оа обед – to invite to lunch

Прийти в обед – to come at lunch(time)

Ambiguity, meaning extension and metonymy are all semantic phenomena. Disambiguation and the resolving of issues of meaning extension and metonymy are pragmatic processes. Semantics tells us what a word/sentence *could* mean; pragmatics tells us what it *does* mean in a particular context.

Distinguishing sentence meaning from speaker meaning

There are semantic and pragmatic aspects to meaning. Semantic meaning (the meaning of a word/sentence) is a two-part relationship: **X** means **Y** (see Leech, 1983: 6). Examples 15 and 16 contain examples in which someone is asking for clarification of the meaning of an unknown word.

Example 15

[This example is taken from the 'context-governed' section of the British National Corpus.][11]

Lecturer: About fifty percent of our anthropogenic CO_2 has
been locked away in this system in the ocean and at

---

[11] For details of the British National Corpus, see Burnard, L (ed.) 1995.

the moment there is considerable er research effort being directed to try and work out just how much more carbon dioxide the ocean will continue to absorb.

Student: What does anthropogenic mean?

Lecturer: From human sources.

Example 16

[A police officer (P) was being interviewed about investigations into a bizarre series of murders of homosexuals]

P: But his cards were being kited in the West End on Monday 23 December.

Int: What does *kited* mean?

P: *Kiting* is police slang for *fraudulently using stolen credit cards*.

Pragmatic meaning is a three-part relationship: **S** means **Y** by **X**. It concerns not what the **words** mean, but what the **speaker** means by those words. Example 17 is an illustration of someone asking for clarification of **speaker meaning**. Note that the meaning of the **actual words uttered** is not a problem; the problem is that the questioner does not know **why** the chairman said what he did (was he genuinely *thanking* her for attending, *welcoming* her, *criticising* her for arriving late?).

Example 17

[A arrives at a meeting which she was supposed to attend]

Chairman: It was good of you to come.

A: What do you mean?

To summarise: semantic meaning is a two-part relationship **X** means **Y** (see Figure 1). As soon as we introduce the speaker into the equation (**S** means **Y** by **X** – see Figure 2), we are dealing with pragmatics.

X	means	Y
anthropogenic		from human resources
kiting		fraudulent use of credit cards
bank		financial institution
		embankment
assisté à		to attend
		to witness
		to assist/take part in
incroyable		Incredible
coronary infarction		heart attack
lady lumberjack		an 8 oz steak
Fleet Street		headquarters of national newspapers

Figure 1: Word/sentence meaning

Speaker	means	Y	by	X
Joyrider		embankment		bank
Depardieu		witnessed		assisté à
Hotel		incredibly low		incroyable
Speaker		when she was a student		at university
Nurse		patient with coronary infarction		coronary infarction
Waitress		person who ordered 8 oz steak		lady lumberjack
Politician		newspaper journalists		Fleet Street
Chairman		welcome		It was good of you to come

Figure 2: Speaker Meaning

In technical terms, we distinguish between **locution** – the actual words uttered and **illocution** – what the speaker means by those words (Austin 1962). For example:

LOCUTION: Is that you car?

ILLOCUTION: The speaker would like the addressee to give him/her a lift into town.

The act performed by the illocution (in the previous example a request) is known as a **speech act**. The same speech act can be performed using different words. For example, the speech act of requesting the addressee to close the door could be performed as follows (adapted from Levinson 1983: 264–5):

Shut the door!
Could you shut the door?
Did you forget the door?
Put the wood in the hole!
Were you born in a barn?
What do big boys do when they come into a room, Johnny?

Each of these six utterances *could* perform the same speech act (of requesting the addressee to close the door). However, it would be foolish to imagine that they are interchangeable. The choice of speech act strategy (e.g. direct imperative *versus* indirect hint) is determined by both linguistic (pragmalinguistic) and social (sociopragmatic) considerations.

Cross-cultural differences in choice of speech act strategy

It is observably the case that, in the same situation, different language/culture pairings will make different choices regarding the speech act strategy to be used. I was once waiting for a plane at Copenhagen Airport, when the following announcement was made – first in English and then in Russian – for passengers on an Aeroflot flight:

Example 18

Russian:

Траⱳзитⱳые пассажиры рейса xxx СУ Москва Стокхольм, ѳемедлеⱳⱳѳ пройдите ѳа сосадку ѳомер 7.
[Transit passengers on Aeroflot flight number SU xxx from Moscow to Stockholm go quickly to Gate No. 7].

English:

Transit passengers on Aeroflot flight number SU xxx from Moscow to Stockholm ~~are kindly requested to proceed immediately~~ to Gate No. 7.

The announcement in Russian involves a bald-on-record strategy (see Brown and Levinson, 1987: 94*ff*) – a direct imperative (пройдите) 'aggravated' by the adverb *immediately*. In precisely the same circumstances, English employs a negative politeness strategy (ibid. 147) – an explicitly polite performative (*request*) hedged by an adverb (*kindly*).

We can see a very similar phenomenon in example 19: Spanish employs a direct imperative where English again employs a negative politeness strategy – conventional indirectness + the politeness particle *please*.

Example 19

Spanish:

Deme un kilo de patatas y dos de peras
Give me one kilo of potatoes and two of pears

English:

Can I have ... please
or
I'd like ... please

These differences in usage are objectively observable and reveal systematic differences in usage between the languages concerned. The question is, do the differences stem from the fact that a Russian (or Spanish) bald-on-record strategy 'corresponds' in terms of politeness to a negative politeness strategy in English, or do the different choices in the two languages reflect different social perceptions? It is not possible to answer the question with certainty in relation to any one occurrence, but it is useful here to introduce the distinction between **pragmalinguistics** and **sociopragmatics** (see Thomas, 1983). Pragmalinguistics relates to the pragmatic force associated with a particular linguistic structure in a given language, whereas sociopragmatics relates to the **underlying reasons** for choosing one form over another.

Pragmalinguistics

The pragmatic force associated with a given linguistic structure in one language may be different from the force associated with the corresponding linguistic structure in another. Cross-cultural pragmalinguistic failure occurs when the pragmatic force mapped by the non-native speaker onto a given linguistic structure is systematically different from that normally assigned to it by a native speaker of the target language, or when speech act strategies are inappropriately transferred from L1 to L2. I have discussed the first aspect of pragmalinguistic failure extensively in a previous article (Thomas 1983, 101−103) and will offer just a brief summary here.

Learners often wrongly assume that a particular syntactic form will have the same pragmatic force in L1 and L2. Leech (1983: 160*ff*) notes that in English the positive interrogative form (*Have you anything to declare?*) is generally much politer than the negative interrogative form (*Haven't you anything to declare?*) and the same would be true in many other languages (e.g. French). However, in many Slavonic languages, the opposite is the case − negative interrogatives are politer. In Russian, for example, it is more polite to say *Couldn't you tell me the way to the station?* than *Could you ...?*.

We have already seen above that some words which are semantically equivalent in two languages may have a different 'interpretive bias'. Thus *prix incroyable/incredible price* could mean 'an incredibly low price' or 'an incredibly high price' in either French or English, but the former is the more likely first interpretation in French, the latter in English. There is a similar pragmalinguistic phenomenon which often causes problems for learners: words/phrases which are syntactically/semantically comparable in two languages may be pragmatically different. For example *of course/конечно* [konyeshno] are **semantically** equivalent in English and Russian. In English, however, its use often implies fault or ignorance on the part of the addressee, as in the following (invented) examples:

A: Is there a postal collection on Sunday?
B: Of course.

A: Would you like something to drink?

B: Of course.

In Russian (and in many other Slavonic languages), there is no such negative implication. *КоШечШо* would be a perfectly civil response in both these contexts – a better translation would be *sure!* or *great!* or *you bet!*

Earlier I noted that the same speech act could be performed using a range of different utterances. However, the forms are by no means interchangeable, and the form most typically used in one language may be different from the form most typically used in another. We have already seen that in French classrooms a teacher might say to a student: *Voulez-vous vous taire?* (literally: *Would you like to be quiet?*). This does not mean that the teacher is enquiring into the student's taste in classroom interaction – it is a conventionally polite request, but one which definitely expects compliance. In comparable circumstances in an English classroom the teacher would use a straightforward imperative form, with or without a politeness particle (*Be quiet!* or *Please be quiet!*). We have seen then that inappropriate choice of speech act form may be due to i) inappropriate transfer of a strategy from L1 to L2; or ii) failure to recognise the pragmatic force of a particular form in L2. A third possibility, which I have not previously discussed, is that there may be a lack of direct correspondence between speech acts in L1 and L2. In technical terms, the **components/attributes** of a speech act in language A may be different from those in language B. Coleman and Kay (1981) have shown that 'lying' typically contains the following features:

+ SAYING SOMETHING WHICH IS UNTRUE
+ KNOWING IT TO BE UNTRUE
+ WITH INTENTION TO DECEIVE

In a really 'good' example of a lie all these features would be present (e.g. you borrow your friend's dictionary without asking and then flatly deny having done so). In a less typical example of a lie only two features would be present (e.g. at the time you took the dictionary you mistakenly thought it was your own), while if only the first feature were present, most people would hesitate to classify an utterance as a lie at all (e.g. on the platform at the station someone asks you if the Birmingham train has gone yet. You say 'no', but you are mistaken). In the case of lying, it is probably the case that a similar array of features would be present in most languages/cultures, but this is not true of all speech acts. 'Apologising' is notoriously tricky between English and Japanese. In English, an apology includes the following features:

+ EXPRESSION OF REGRET BY S FOR X
+ RESPONSIBILITY OF S FOR X

In Japanese, the notion of responsibility for X is not necessarily present in an apology. On the other hand, it is sometimes claimed that Japanese apologise when it would be more appropriate to thank (e.g. if a fellow passenger offers to help you take your luggage down from the rack in a train). This misunderstanding occurs because the scope of the speech acts of apologising and thanking are different in English and Japanese – the expression スミマセン (*sumimasen*) in Japanese includes both the notion of thanking and apologising for causing inconvenience to another person.

It is often the case that speech acts cover a different range of phenomena in two different languages/cultures (for a discussion of this in relation to Polish see Bonikowska 1985). In English, for example, we have quite a wide range of verbs describing how a speaker might get a hearer to do something (*invite, ask, request, order, command*, etc). The features related to each speech act verb are slightly different (presupposing, for example, different power relations or whether or not the desired end is seen as pleasurable/beneficial to H or not), as in the diagram below:

Invite	→	Suggest	→	Request	→	Order
+GOOD FOR H		+GOOD FOR H		-GOOD FOR H		-GOOD FOR H
						+S HAS POWER OVER H

Chinese has fewer speech act verbs covering this spectrum, which can lead Chinese learners of English to *invite* someone to do something not necessarily seen as pleasurable or beneficial to H.

Again, the implications for language teaching are, I think, obvious. We need to ask:

- What forms are available in L1 and L2? (e.g. Direct imperative, modals, etc).
- Of the available forms which is the favoured form?
- What supportive moves typically accompany the speech act (e.g. grounding, mitigation/ aggravation, politeness particle, honorific, etc. See Blum-Kulka *et al* 1989)?

Sociopragmatics

Sociopragmatic failure arises from cross-culturally different assessments of social value. In all naturally occurring languages and in all societies we find **indirectness**. Broadly speaking, we can also say that in all societies the factors governing indirectness will be the same and can be summarized as follows:

- **Power relationship**

  - How much power does your addressee have over you? The greater the power differential, the greater the degree of indirectness is likely to be (you are more likely to use indirectness to your boss than to your son);

- **Social distance**

  - How well do you know the other person? (The better you know your addressee, the smaller the degree of indirectness is likely to be);
  - How close to you is the other person (e.g. is the addressee a close friend/relative)? (The closer your addressee is to you, the less indirectness is likely to be used);

- **Size of imposition**

  - Are you asking a large or small favour (e.g. are you asking to borrow a biro for a moment, or to borrow someone's car for the weekend?)? The greater the imposition, the greater the degree of indirectness is likely to be. Note that 'imposition' does not necessarily relate to material goods – it could also relate to information. In Britain you would probably ask the time very directly, but you would be more indirect about asking someone about the size of their salary;

- **Rights and obligations**

  - What are the relative rights and obligations of the speaker and addressee? If you are requesting something which you see as your right (e.g. asking the taxi driver to take you to the station) you are likely to be much more direct than if you are asking a favour (e.g. asking your next door neighbour to drive you to the station).

Negotiating pragmatic parameters

Note that each of the dimensions which I have listed is not 'given', even within a particular culture. Each of them may be negotiated in interaction, as in examples 20 (negotiation of size of imposition) and example 21 (negotiation of social distance).

Example 20

[C is just about to go off to university. She is trying to persuade her mother, P, to part with some drinking glasses. With each successive utterance, C diminishes the value and desirability of the glasses, so that by the time she actually makes the request it is very difficult for her mother to refuse]:

C: Mum. You know those browny glasses.
P: Mm.
C: The ones we got from the garage.
P: Mm.
C: Do you use them much?
P: Not really, no.
C: Can I have them then?

Example 21

[J and D are meeting for the first time. D reduces the social distance between them by rejecting *Title + surname* as an address form, and offers instead the diminutive form of his first name].

J: Dr Galašinski?
D: Darek.
J: Darek.

It is possible to increase or decrease any of the parameters which I have listed. In practice, cultures appear to vary as to which they favour. Little research has been done in this area, but informal observation suggests to me that British culture favours reducing the size of the imposition, American culture seems to favour reducing social distance. In some 'T/V-languages'[11, 13] such as French or German, there may be explicit negotiation about the use of *tu/du* or *vous/Sie* (see Béal 1988).[12] In Russian, it would be more usual simply to 'slip' from ты to вы – to ask permission would be rather crass.

Refining pragmatic parameters

Each of the five parameters I listed above are capable of further refinement and the number and nature of the sub-divisions may vary from culture to culture, and so may their relative importance. For example, Spencer-Oatey (1992) has shown how the concept of **power** can be refined – she lists six different types of power:

Reward power – the speaker has power over the hearer because S has control over positive outcomes (e.g. S can give H high marks, a positive recommendation, etc)

Coercive power – the speaker has power over the hearer because S has control over negative outcomes (e.g. S has the power to punish or damage H)

---

[12] T- and V- forms relate to the pronouns of 'power and solidarity' (Brown and Gilman 1960), such as tu/vous (French), du/Sie (German), ты/вы (Russian), etc.
There is a vast literature on address forms and on the use of T/V forms. See, for example, Braun (1988), Brown and Gilman (1960 and 1989), Delisle (1986), Kroger and Kim (1984), Wolff (1988), Wood (1991).

Expert power – the speaker has power over the hearer because S has some special knowledge or expertise which H needs.

Legitimate power – the speaker has power over the hearer because S has the right to prescribe or request certain things by virtue of role, age or status (e.g. S can require you to do certain things because S is your teacher, a police officer, etc)

Referent power – the speaker has power over the hearer because H admires and wants to be like S in some respect (e.g. because S is a sports idol, a pop star, a national hero).

The type of power to which a person aspires – and more particularly the type of power which S will make explicit – varies greatly from culture to culture. In Britain, for example, people are likely to aspire to expert power or referent power and are reluctant to make explicit their 'legitimate power'. In other cultures (Japan, for example) it is important to make very clear early in a relationship where you stand relative to one another in terms of age, status, etc.

Cross-cultural interpretations of pragmatic parameters

Earlier I listed the main **types of consideration** which influence sociopragmatic decision-making in **any** society (and, in particular, the degree of indirectness used). However, although the parameters themselves appear to be universal, the way in which they are interpreted will vary greatly from culture to culture. I have already noted that in different cultures different types of power may be invoked. It is also important to note that the 'same' relationship may be interpreted differently in different cultures. For example, some version of the parent-child relationship exists in most cultures, but in some this relationship implies a close, non-authoritarian relationship (and might be encoded using a T-form),[13] in others it is distant and authoritarian (and would probably be encoded using a V-form). In the same way, in some languages/cultures (e.g. France) university students and older school children are addressed with the V-form

---

[13] T- and V- forms relate to the pronouns of 'power and solidarity' (Brown and Gilman 1960), such as tu/vous (French), du/Sie (German), ты/вы (Russian), etc.

and possibly a title + last name (*monsieur/ mademoiselle*); in others (Russia, UK) they are generally addressed with the T-form (Russian) and their first name throughout their school and university career (this, of course, was one source of my difficulties in the incident at school in France). Different norms of address can be observed in similar workplace settings (such as universities) in different countries (see Chick, 1989; Tanaka, 1994) and in different varieties of English. A former student of mine from Hong Kong was very insulted when she was addressed as *Ms*, while her British classmates were deeply offended by *Miss/Mrs*. I myself felt very affronted at seeing myself referred to in India as *Dr Jenny Thomas (Miss)*, when my male colleagues did not receive a corresponding *(Mr)*. And, of course, to complicate matters, all these norms may change over time (see Nevalainen and Raumolin-Brunberg, 1995).

In a similar way, cultures differ greatly in their perception of the relative rights and obligations associated with particular roles, events, etc. For example, when I was a university teacher in the former Soviet Union, I was often taken aback by what seemed to me to be the undue licence which Soviet teachers assumed with regard to their students – it was not unusual for teachers to criticize their students' manner of dress, or to send them on errands to the shops, or to tell them in a peremptory manner to clean the blackboard. Such behaviour would be unthinkable in the context of a British university, but the Soviet students seemed untroubled by it, so I assume it was considered to fall within the teachers' rights and the students' obligations.

Perhaps the most striking cross-cultural differences relate to perceptions of 'size of imposition'. For example, in the former Soviet Union, cigarettes were very inexpensive and you could ask a complete stranger for one very directly. In the UK, cigarettes are very expensive, and a degree of indirectness might be needed even to obtain one from a friend. Asking to borrow someone's car in Britain is definitely a 'big deal' and the request would need to be couched in very indirect terms. In the US, it is less so and would require less indirectness. I noted in relation to example 19 that, in Spanish, one would ask for potatoes at a greengrocer's in a manner very much more direct than would normally be considered appropriate in English. Is this because asking to be served with potatoes is considered a 'greater imposition' in England than in Spain, or is it because different speech acts are favoured in the two languages? In other words, are we dealing with a pragmalinguistic or a sociopragmatic question? My guess is that it is the former, but it is never possible to resolve the issue with certainty in relation to any one example.[14]

I have already noted that 'size of imposition' does not relate to material goods alone – it can also relate to other sorts of 'goods', particularly information. I have been told that in Laos it is quite common to ask someone – particularly a foreigner – how much he or she weighs! This is clearly information which in Western countries (and outside the doctor's consulting room) could only be sought with the greatest circumlocution. To be offended by questions they consider too direct and too personal, or unwittingly to cause offence, is a common experience for people travelling in foreign lands.

Cross-cultural differences in observance of Gricean norms

The philosopher of language H P Grice set out four maxims (Quality, Quantity, Relation and Manner) which help us to interpret indirectness (for a simple overview of Grice's work, see Thomas, 1994a and 1994b or 1995 chapter 3). When a speaker **blatantly** fails to observe a maxim, an implicature is generated. Suppose, for example, that someone spills a cup of coffee over my computer keyboard and I say: 'Great. That's just what I wanted!' My comment is so blatantly untrue (it flouts the maxim of Quality), that the hearer is forced to look for another interpretation – in this case, I **mean** exactly the opposite of what my words say. Broadly speaking, we can say that the maxims operate in the same way in all languages/cultures. However, several writers (see, for example, Keenan 1976) have pointed out that in some societies speakers may not observe one or more of the maxims, and yet not generate an implicature. This can be explained by the phenomenon of **suspending** a maxim. For example, if I say 'A chimpanzee comes into a pub...' it is obvious that I am telling a joke and hearers will interpret the rest of my story accordingly; the maxim of Quality is temporarily suspended. The same would be true in other

---

[14] In fact, the distinction between pragmalinguistics and sociopragmatics is ultimately not sustainable. But, as I shall show in the final section, it is a useful concept in relation to the application of pragmatics to language teaching.

situations – we do not, for example, expect the whole, unvarnished truth in funeral orations.

Just as the maxims may be suspended/observed differently within different speech events within a single culture, so cross-culturally there are differences in the way in which the maxims are observed. Travellers have observed that in some countries (India, for instance) people asking how far it is to their destination may be given an overly optimistic answer (e.g. they may be told that it is an hour's easy walk, when in fact it is a day's walk over poor terrain!). Foreigners will accept the information at face value and may be badly misled – they may even think of the locals as liars. Within the community, however, people will know how to decode such apparently misleading information – they will know that the local resident does not want to upset them by giving them bad news – and they will adjust their interpretation accordingly. In such cases, the maxim of Quality ('say what you know to be true') is suspended.

Keenan (1976: 70) has observed that in the Malagasy Republic people frequently appear not to observe the maxim of Quantity in that they:

> ...regularly provide less information than is required by their conversational partner, even though they have access to the necessary information.

For example, a woman might refer to 'a boy', which in most societies would imply that she did not know the identity of the boy in question. In a Malagasy context, however, the woman might well be referring to her own son, but she deliberately refrains from naming him in order to avoid drawing down upon him the attention of malign spirits. Keenan suggests that this is a counter-example to Grice's theory, but it is probably better seen as another instance of 'suspending' a maxim. The non-observance is systematic and readily understood by all members of that community. Among members of the acting profession in Britain, it is common to refer to 'The Scottish Play'. An outsider might assume that they could not recall the title *Macbeth*, but this is not the case – it is because they believe that uttering the name brings bad luck. This non-observance of the maxim of Quantity is systematic and understood by all members of the acting profession.

Cross-cultural differences in observance of interpersonal maxims

Leech (1983) introduces the **Politeness Principle** which, he claims, explains 'why people are often so indirect in conveying what they mean'. Subordinate to the PP are a series of interpersonal maxims, such as the Modesty maxim, the Generosity maxim, the Agreement maxim, etc (see Leech 1983, chapter 6). Leech himself notes that there are cross-cultural differences in the way in which his interpersonal maxims are observed; he gives an example (1983: 136–8) of the greater emphasis placed upon Modesty in Japanese society. The same cross-cultural variation can be found in relation to the observance/non-observance of other maxims.

Leech's **Agreement maxim** 'Minimize disagreement between *self* and *other*; maximize agreement between *self* and *other*' (Leech 1983: 132) is a case in point. Of course, it is perfectly normal in all societies that people will disagree with one another, but cultures vary in the degree to which the **expression** of that disagreement is acceptable. An examination of any stretch of naturally occurring (informal) interaction in British English will reveal many instances of disagreements prefaced by 'Yes, but...'. The *yes* is a surface-level nod in the direction of the Agreement maxim, an interpersonal 'sweetener' warranting the subsequent disagreement. Other cultures (and other speech events in British English[15]) tolerate much more direct contradiction (see, for example, the contributions by the Indian parent in the now-famous *Cross Talk* data). In Japanese, by contrast, disagreements are often so indirect that non-Japanese do not recognise them as such. I worked with a Japanese PhD student for more than five years before I understood that when she said: '(Oh.) Do you think so?' she was actually disagreeing with me.

Maxim clashes

It is perfectly normal that 'clashes' should occur between Grice's conversational maxims and Leech's interpersonal maxims – for example, it is often difficult to be both truthful and tactful or both truthful and modest, to observe both the Quantity maxim and the generosity maxim. When such clashes occur, different cultures resolve those clashes in different ways. For example, in many Western cultures in a clash between Quality

---

[15] In academic discourse, for example, very direct (even bald-on-record) contradictions are tolerated.

('truthfulness') and politeness, Quality tends to prevail; in some Asian cultures (as I discussed in an earlier example), the opposite is the case. A clash often occurs between Quantity and Generosity: in some countries (e.g. China, Greece, Ukraine) it is customary to offer food/drink many times (the actual number of times varies) before it is accepted (in other words, Generosity prevails over Quantity); in Anglo-Saxon cultures the opposite tends to be the case.

Politeness

Politeness is a vast field within pragmatics (for a brief overview see Thomas 1995, chapter 6) and there is a huge literature on politeness in cross-cultural interaction. Politeness theory has often been inaccurately criticised as ethnocentric. Some of the criticism, however, is justified. An early paper by Lakoff (1973), for example, starts with 'Give options'. Allowing options (or, more accurately, giving the appearance of allowing options) is absolutely central to Western notions of politeness but, as Spencer-Oatey (1992: 17) notes, it has little place in the Chinese conception of politeness. Just as a polite Chinese host will choose your dishes for you in a restaurant without consulting you (and will often go so far as to place the most select morsels directly onto your plate), so the linguistic expression of optionality in, say, inviting someone to one's home, is not seen as polite. Spencer-Oatey (1992: 30–33) suggests that all the research on politeness can be summarised in terms of these three sets of dimensions: individuals will select the point on the scale according to their cultural values.

a) **Need for consideration**

autonomy   ⟵————————————⟶   imposition

b) **Need to be valued**

approbation   ⟵————————————⟶   criticism
interest/concern   ⟵————————————⟶   disinterest

c) **Need for Relational Identity**

inclusion   ⟵————————————⟶   exclusion

equality   ←——————————————————→   superordination/
subordination

The importance of pragmatics in English language teaching

I have identified ten areas of pragmatics which are relevant to the language learner and teacher. All the areas are important and demand new and different approaches to teaching, but as we move from the pragmalinguistic to the sociopragmatic end of the spectrum, greater sensitivity is required on the part of the teacher.

PRAGMALINGUISTICS

Ʌ

Disambiguation
Interpretive Bias
Polysemy
Assigning complete meaning
Metonymy
Choice of speech act form
Gricean Maxims
Interpersonal maxims
Indirectness
Politeness

ⴸ

SOCIOPRAGMATICS

Learners do not automatically acquire the pragmatic norms of the target language/culture. I used to believe (Thomas 1983) that teaching the pragmalinguistic norms of another language/culture is no more difficult than teaching, say, differences in syntax or lexis. I now think that while sensitizing learners to pragmalinguistic differences does not threaten the student's sense of individual or cultural identity, it does force the student to view the world differently and demands new (cognitive) approaches to the study of language.

Alerting learners to potential sociopragmatic differences between L1 and L2 is more important and more difficult. More important because sociopragmatic 'errors' are often not identified as such and are often attributed to, say, rudeness on the part of the non-native speaker. More difficult because learners may feel that they are being asked to adopt a different system of values, perhaps even to take on a new personality. Teaching sociopragmatics requires great sensitivity and demands new (social) approaches to the study of language. But these are worthwhile challenges for the language teacher – sensitizing learners to pragmatic issues makes them look at the world in new ways and is an important means of challenging ethnic and national stereotyping.

References

Austin, J. L. 1962. *How to do things with words*. Oxford: Oxford University Press.

Baranov, A. N. & Dobrovol'skij, D. O. 1996. Cognitive modeling of actual meaning in the field of phraseology. *Journal of Pragmatics*. 25 (3), 409–429.

Béal, Christine. 1988. On se tutoie? Second person pronominal usage and terms of address in contemporary French. *Australian Review of Applied Linguistics*. 12 (1), 61-82.

Braun, Frederike. 1988. *Terms of address: problems of patterns and usage in various languages and cultures*. Berlin: Mouton de Gruyter.

Blum-Kulka, S., House, J. & Kasper, G. (eds.) 1989. *Cross-cultural pragmatics: requests and apologies*. Norwood, New Jersey: Ablex.

Bonikowska, M. P. 1985. *The speech act of complaining*. Unpublished MA dissertation, Department of Linguistics and Modern English Language, Lancaster University.

Brown, P. & Levinson, S. C. 1987 [1978]. *Politeness. Some universals in language usage*. Cambridge: Cambridge University Press.

Brown, R. & Gilman, A. 1960. The pronouns of power and solidarity. *Style in language*. ed. by Sebeok, T. A. (pp 253–276). New York: Wiley.

Burnard, L. (ed.) 1995. *Users' reference guide to the British National Corpus*. Oxford: Oxford University Computing Services.

Chick, Keith. 1989. Intercultural miscommunication as a source of friction in the workplace and in educational settings in South Africa. *English across cultures – cultures across English*. ed. by Garcia, Ofelia & Otheguy, Ricardo (pp 140-160) Berlin: Mouton de Gruyter.

Coleman L. & Kay, P. 1981. Prototype semantics: the English word 'lie'. *Language* 57 (1), 26-44.

Delisle, Helga H. 1986. Intimacy, solidarity and distance: the pronouns of address in German. *Unterrichtspraxis.* 19 (1), 4-15.

Keenan, E. O. 1976. The universality of conversational postulates. *Language in society.* 5, 67–80.

Kess, J. F. & Hoppe, R. A. 1981. *Ambiguity in psycholinguistics.* Amsterdam: John Benjamins.

Kroger, R. O. & Kim, U. 1984. Are the rules of address universal? III: Comparison of Chinese, Greek and Korean usage. *Journal of Cross Cultural Psychology.* 15, 273-284.

Lakoff, R. 1973. *The logic of politeness; or, minding your p's and q's.* Chicago: Chicago Linguistic Society.

Leech, G. N. 1983. *Principles of pragmatics.* London: Longman.

Levinson, S. C. 1983. *Pragmatics.* Cambridge: Cambridge University Press.

Nevalainen, Terttu & Raumolin-Brunberg, Helena. 1995. Constraints on politeness: The pragmatics of address formulae in Early English correspondence. *Historical pragmatics: pragmatic developments in the history of English.* ed. by Jucker, Andreas H. (pp 541-592). Amsterdam: John Benjamins.

Spencer-Oatey, H. D. M. 1992. Cross-cultural politeness: British and Chinese conceptions of the tutor-student relationship. Unpublished Ph.D. Thesis. Lancaster University.

Tanaka, Noriko. 1994. An investigation of Japanese address terms: how to address colleagues in a teachers' room at school. *Meikai Journal* 7, 75-84.

Thomas, J. A. 1983. Cross-cultural pragmatic failure. *Applied Linguistics.* 4 (2), 91–112.

Thomas, J. A. 1994a. The conversational maxims. *The encylopedia of language and linguistics.* ed. by Asher, R. E. (pp 754-758). Oxford: Pergamon Press.

Thomas, J. A. 1994b. The cooperative principle of H P Grice. *The encylopedia of language and linguistics.* ed. by Asher, R. E. (pp 759–762) Oxford: Pergamon Press.

Thomas, J. A. 1995. *Meaning in interaction: an introduction to pragmatics.* London: Longman.

Wolff, P. 1988. New studies on the polite form of direct address, four epic poems, four forms of address and possibly four national temperaments. *Comptes rendus des séances de l'Académie des Inscriptions et Belles-Lettres.* Jan, 58-74.

Wood, L. A. & Kroger, R. O. 1991. Politeness and forms of address. *Journal of Language and Social Psychology.* 10 (3), 145-168.

PRAGMATICS AND LANGUAGE TEACHING REVISITED: SOME IMPLICATIONS FOR THE TEACHER

Asim Gunarwan

1. Introduction

The title of this paper pragmatically implies that a topic on pragmatic issues in language teaching is by no means new. Since a single utterance conveys a whole variety of assumptions, the title further implicates that this paper does not claim that it will present something new. To most practitioners of language teaching, what will be reviewed here is old hat. If there is anything new at all, it may be the terminologies or the perspectives from which the issues are discussed in relation to language teaching.

This paper would be more appropriately presented to language teachers in Indonesia, where despite over three decades of its development, pragmatics has not been widely welcome, even among linguists in general. Moreover, since the term *pragmatic* was formally used erroneously in the 1984 High School English Curriculum to refer to language skills that should be mastered by students, there has seemed to be terminological confusion about pragmatics among language teachers in Indonesia. There are different interpretations among them as to what pragmatics is really about and what it can offer practitioners of language teaching, be they teachers or materials writers.

With that background, the objective of this paper is to review what this field of inquiry is all about. The hope is that misconceptions about this new branch of linguistics can be amended, if not corrected. This paper also aims to highlight some notions in pragmatics which are relevant, and may be insightful, for practitioners of language teaching, foreign or otherwise. These are notions of speech act, implicature (along with the Gricean cooperative principle), and politeness. Findings of relevant cross-language pragmatic research studies are cited to show that pragmatic issues in language teaching are worth our attention.

2. Pragmatics: The State of the Art

The terminological confusion among language teachers in Indonesia surmised above may not have been due wholly to the lack of clear elucidation of what is meant by pragmatics in the 1984 High School English Curriculum. It might have been due to the fact that pragmatics has indeed been defined differently by different linguists. Levinson (1983) took one whole chapter (53 pages) to explain what is meant by pragmatics. Various definitions are offered, all of which can be understood to point to one thing in common: pragmatics studies language in relation to three aspects, namely meaning, context and communication.

That meaning is studied in pragmatics suggests that this new branch of linguistics can be considered an 'extension' of semantics, for a long time the traditional cauldron of meaning, lexical or sentential. What is worse, there was a time when pragmatics was seen as just a wastebasket for semantic problems: what could not be explained by using semantic rules (such as contradiction and tautology) was relegated to pragmatics. Unlike semantics, however, pragmatics deals with meaning in context, as alluded to above. Specifically, meaning in pragmatics refers to speaker or user meaning in real communication which, needless to say, has a concrete context: who speaks to whom, where, when, about what, how and why. Differently stated, meaning in pragmatics, unlike in semantics, refers to the intention of the speaker or, to borrow Austin's (1962) term, the *illocutionary force* of what the speaker says in real, natural communication. Pragmatics studies what the speaker means by saying X, whereas semantics deals with what X means (Leech, 1983).

The first mentions of the term *pragmatics* are often associated with Charles Morris, who, following Charles S. Peirce (Mey, 1993: 287), in 1938 discussed semiotics, the study of signs, which he divided into syntax, semantics and pragmatics. In the wider sense, not restricted to language, 'syntax is the study of the formal relations of signs to one another, semantics is the study of how signs are related to the objects to which they are applicable..., pragmatics is the study of the relation of signs to interpreters' (Schiffrin, 1994: 191).

While the study of the relation of signs to interpreters is already sixty years old now, its application to language can be regarded as starting

Pragmatics and Language Teaching Revisited

with the posthumous work of J.L. Austin *How to Do Things with Words* (1962), followed by the work of his student, John Searle, *Speech Acts* (1969). The works of these philosophers are now considered the prelude to the pragmatic approach in linguistics.

According to Mey (1993), however, the pragmatic approach in linguistics is not wholly attributable to the two philosophers. In the 1960's and 1970's, he says, there were two conflicts in the linguistics circle. One conflict was between linguists who took an abstract approach to the study of language on the one hand and those who took a practical approach on the other. The other conflict was between those who believed in (Chomskyan) 'syntactism' and those who believed in 'antisyntactism' led by Chomsky's students like George Lakoff and John Robert ('Haj') Ross. These rebellious students, along with the proponents of the practical approach to the study of language, pioneered a new 'brand' of linguistics which, as it turned out, expedited the birth of pragmatics, the conception of which is attributed to the two philosophers above.

Today, pragmatics has grown to be a full-fledged branch of linguistics. A course in pragmatics is now offered in many departments of linguistics in universities around the world. At least five books on pragmatics in English, not to mention scores of pragmatics articles, are now available. These are: Gerald Gazdar's *Pragmatics* (1979), Geoffrey Leech's *Principles of Pragmatics* (1983), Stephen C. Levinson's *Pragmatics* (1983), Jacob L. Mey's *Pragmatics: An Introduction* (1993), and Diane Blakemore's *Understanding Utterances: An Introduction to Pragmatics* (1992). There are journals such as *Journal of Pragmatics* and *Pragmatics*. There is now an organisation called International Pragmatics Association (IPrA), with headquarters in Antwerp, Belgium. This association convenes an international pragmatics conference every three years.

So many linguistic topics find their way into pragmatics that its boundaries have become difficult to assign. However, in the diversity of pragmatic topics two traditions can be identified, namely the Anglo-American tradition and the Continental tradition (Levinson, 1983: 5). The former is narrower in scope and more related to issues which are traditionally under the rubric of linguistics proper such as sentence structures and linguistic forms. The latter is wider in scope and includes discourse analysis, ethnography of communication, aspects of psycholinguistics and address terms (Fasold, 1990). According to Schiffrin (1994), the Continental tradition is closer to what in the United States is called sociolinguistics and discourse analysis.

Pragmatics has developed so rapidly that it is now relevant to talk about two levels of this field of study, namely micropragmatics and macropragmatics (Mey, 1993: 87-315). The former studies reference, anaphora, the speech act (its classification and (in)directness), and implicature. The latter deals with 'higher' units of language such as text and conversation and its related matters (including co-text, context, turns and turn-taking, coherence and sequencing). Within macropragmatics, Mey mentions two subfields, namely metapragmatics and societal pragmatics. Metapragmatics refers to 'the conditions under which pragmatic, i.e. users', rules are supposed to hold' (Mey, 1993: 277) and societal pragmatics is the study of language use in societal context and refers to societal factors like the institutions of the family, the school, the peer group and so on, 'which influence the development and use of language, both in the acquisition stage and in usage itself' (Mey, 1993: 287).

To sum up, pragmatics is now an independent field of study. It is on a level with, if not higher than, the other branches of linguistics. No longer is it considered the wastebasket of semantics.

3. Some Pragmatic Notions

3.1 Speech Acts

The term *speech act*, despite being specified with the word *speech*, does not refer only to the act of producing vocal symbols in communication. It also refers to the act of producing written symbols. Whether oral or written, what is important in the notion of *speech act* is that the symbols are produced in real communication, thus involving interlocutors, an interaction end, and interaction context. This is, among other things, what distinguishes a speech act or, to be exact, an utterance (i.e. the result of performing the act) from a sentence. A speech act is a unit of linguistic communication (Searle, 1969: 16), while a sentence is a unit of grammar. The former is concrete; the latter abstract. The relation between speech act and sentence is comparable to that between phone and phoneme.

A speech act has a pragmatic meaning. This refers to the illocutionary force or the intention of the speaker: for what purpose the act is performed. Differently stated, a speech act has a function or functions to perform, for example to tell our interlocutors how things are, to express to them our feelings or attitudes, to ask them to do things, etc. Hence, pragmatics belongs to the functionalist approach to the study of language, as opposed to the formalist approach, which studies language forms only.

A speech act can be direct or indirect. A direct speech act refers to an utterance in which the illocutionary force is expressed by way of a 'literal' act. Thus, to ask someone to move a table by saying 'Move this table' is to perform a direct speech act of ordering (or requesting). An indirect speech act, by contrast, refers to an utterance in which the illocutionary force or pragmatic meaning is expressed by performing another act. To ask someone to move a table by asking him about his ability 'Can you move the table?' is to perform an indirect speech act. What we see here is a case of two different sentence forms serving the same function, namely asking someone to move a table. In everyday language use there are many, not just two, sentence forms serving one function. The following, taken from Blum-Kulka and Olshtain (1985), illustrates the case in point: all nine sentence forms convey a request to someone to move his car.

1. Could you move your car?
2. Why don't you move your car?
3. Move your car.
4. I would like you to move your car.
5. You'll have to move your car.
6. I'm asking you to move your car.
7. You've blocked the driveway with your car.
8. I would like to ask you to move your car.
9. We don't want any crowding here.

As can be seen in the examples, the degrees of the directness of (the tokens of) the speech act vary. If we imagine a line (in pragmatics called illocutionary path) connecting the point of the origin of the speech act and its point of destination, the straightest line would be the one representing (3). Its illocutionary force is the most transparent. The curviest line would be the one representing (9), which conveys the least transparent force, the word *car* not being mentioned.

A question may arise at this juncture as to why for a given interaction an indirect speech act, instead of a direct one, is used by a speaker. One possible reason is that certain speech acts have the potential of threatening the face of the addressee, and therefore the speaker tries to mitigate the effect by restructuring his would-be utterances. Another possible reason is that it is embedded in the culture of the community. Among ethnic groups of Indonesia, for example, the Javanese have a penchant for being indirect, to the extent that what they say is often not transparent, especially when it comes to making dispreferred statements. In one study involving 142 Javanese respondents, Gunarwan (1996b) found that in criticizing, they overwhelmingly used indirect speech acts, and of these, the 'off-record' criticisms figured the most. In a study now almost completed, it has been found that, by comparison, the Batak of North Sumatra have the tendency to be straightforward or, at least, more direct than the Javanese. Another finding of the study now being conducted is that linguistic behaviour (at least as far as the execution of the prohibiting act is concerned) relates to ideology (worldview).

Another pertinent question at this point is whether indirectness correlates with politeness. Blum-Kulka (1987), in her study of indirectness and politeness in Hebrew and English involving Israeli and American students as subjects, found that this is not the case. One finding of a research project (Gunarwan, 1993) corroborates Blum-Kulka's finding. Among Indonesian learners of English who were the respondents of the study, most of whom were ethnic Javanese, to a certain degree, indirectness indeed connotes politeness; beyond that it imparts sarcasm.

3.2 Implicature

The philosopher Paul Grice (1975) shows that an utterance can have an implication, i.e. a proposition, which is in fact not a stated part of the utterance, nor is it a consequence that exists in the utterance. He calls the proposition or 'implied information' *implicature*. Since it is recovered from a conversation, the complete term Grice used is *conversational implicature*, as opposed to conventional implicature. It is 'something which is left implicit in actual language use' (Mey, 1993: 99). The significance of the notion of implicature is that it cannot be accounted for by using a syntactic or semantic rule (alone). Something else needs considering, and this is where the principles governing the conversation or discourse figure well.

The difference between conversational and conventional implicatures can be problematic. According to some pragmaticians, notably Levinson (1983: 127), conventional implicatures are ... non-truth-conditional inferences that are *not* derived from superordinate pragmatic principles like the maxims, but are simply attached by convention to particular lexical items. Mey does not agree to that definition. According to him (1993: 105) '[no] matter how conventional the implicatures, it is still the case that the conventions which govern their use are culture-specific, historically developed and class-related'. He exemplifies this by citing the use of *tu* ('impolite') and *vous* ('polite') in French. He found that there is no 'impolite' implicature in using *tu*, instead of *vous*, when ordering a drink in a Quebec bar, unlike the case in France. According to Mey this is because the otherwise impolite 'implicature' is 'cancelled out by the culture' (*ibid.*).

What is important to note here is that an implicature, conventional or conversational, can be culture-specific. One case in point is the use of speech levels (i.e. low, refined low, mid, high, elevated high, etc), which is Javanese culture-specific. In one given setting, elevated high Javanese can implicate different 'forces' depending on the dialect (Gunarwan, 1996a). In one scene of an east Javanese folk theatre performance, for instance, elevated high Javanese was found to implicate sarcasm, not the 'expected' implicature of deference.

Being an assumption which the hearer recovers from the proposition expressed by the utterance, implicature hinges upon the hearer's understanding of what the speaker said. Thus, the first thing that the hearer should know before recovering the assumption is the syntactic meaning and the semantic meaning of the utterance. Based on the context which, loosely speaking, is the sum total of everyday language use, the hearer then recovers the implicature.

Important in understanding implicature is the notion of the Gricean cooperative principle. According to Grice (1975) this is a principle which governs what should be done by an interlocutor in a conversation in order that his utterance contributes to the coherence of the whole conversation. A contribution is said to be coherent if it satisfies three maxims of Grice's cooperative principle, namely the maxims of quantity, quality and relevance. In addition, it should also satisfy the fourth maxim, the maxim of manner, namely that the contribution be perspicuous.

Grice's cooperative principle is not without criticisms. According to Sperber and Wilson (cited in Fasold, 1990: 143) all four maxims can be reduced to a matter of relevance. According to Horn (*ibid.*), only the maxims of quality and relevance are really needed in order for a hearer to recover an implicature. Quality leads to 'Q-implicatures' of the type 'I've said as much as I can [and] you can't infer anymore'. Relevance leads to 'R-implicatures' of the type 'I've said only as much as I must. I know you can work out the rest' (*ibid.*).

The importance of the Gricean maxims lies not in their observance by interlocutors in everyday language use. On the contrary, it lies in the fact that the maxims are, more often than not, violated and that an implicature can be recovered from the violation of the maxim(s). The adequacy of the Gricean mechanism thus lies in the fact that it can be used as a basis for inference: what inference can be drawn when an interlocutor violates a maxim or maxims. Levinson (1987) seems to agree to this interpretation of an inference being recoverable from maxim violation. Blakemore (1992) does not seem to agree. However, she believes that Gricean theory offers a point of fundamental importance, namely that 'understanding utterances is not simply a matter of knowing the meanings of the words uttered and the way in which they are combined' (1992: 57).

What can be inferred from the violation or non-violation of Gricean maxims is that there is more than one way of communicating a message. One way is by observing Gricean maxims letter-perfectly; this is what we call *explicating* a message – by means of an explicature. Another way is by violating the maxims; this is what we refer to as *implicating* a message – by means of an implicature. As can be seen in the nine examples of speech act for ordering or requesting someone to move the car, the eight implicatures range from very strong to very weak. Thus we can talk about a scale of implicatures, from strongest to weakest. The choice of using an explicature or an implicature and, if the latter, whether it is the stronger or weaker depends on various factors. Gunarwan (1998) found that the factors include power, solidarity (intimacy) and setting (i.e. whether or not the interaction is public or *tête-à-tête*). These are interactional factors. Cultural and societal factors can also constrain the choice. The Javanese, as alluded to earlier, have by and large a penchant for preferring weaker implicatures (to the extent that a bald-on-record 'no' would be considered un-Javanese, implying uncouthness). Still within Javanese society, the lower class prefers, so it seems, stronger implicatures.

3.3 Politeness

Language scholars who have brought forth theories of language politeness are Robin Lakoff (1972), Fraser (1978), Brown and Levinson (1987) and Leech (1983). These theories can be said to have one thing in common, namely that in real communication the speaker does not always obey the Gricean cooperative principle. The main difference in the politeness theories put up by those scholars lies in what they see as triggering the need to perform a 'polite' speech act. Lakoff and Leech see the trigger as being comprised of social rules; Fraser and Brown and Levinson see it as being the result of choosing a strategy.

In a nutshell, Lakoff believes that there are three social rules to obey if we want to be heard as being polite. The three rules relate to three aspects (Fasold, 1990: 159), namely *formality* ('don't impose or remain aloof'), *hesitancy* ('give the addressee his options') and *equality* or *camaraderie* ('act as though you and the addressee were equal – make him feel good'). Thus, in Lakoff's view, an utterance sounds polite if the speaker is not aloof, if he gives the hearer the right of choosing, and/or if he makes the hearer feel that he has rapport with him.

Unlike Lakoff, Fraser discusses language politeness not on the basis of social rules, as alluded to above, but on strategy. He does not elaborate on the notion of strategy like Brown and Levinson do. Fraser only mentions that there are eighteen types of speech act for performing a directive ('request') without showing their scalar implicatures (i.e. which implicature is more polite than another). Still, what is worth noting in his concept of politeness is that Fraser distinguishes between *politeness* and *deference*. Quoting Goffman (1967), Fraser (1978: 11) defines the former as '... the component of activity which functions as a symbolic means by which appreciation is regularly conveyed'. Thus, in the Javanese community, for example, when a speaker uses the *krama inggil* (high elevated) speech level to another (whose social status entitles him to being addressed in it), the speaker is showing his deference to the addressee: he is symbolically showing his appreciation towards the addressee. However, being deferent is not necessarily being polite in Fraser's notion of politeness. For him, politeness is a 'property associated with an utterance in which, in the hearer's opinion, the speaker has neither exceeded any right nor failed to fulfill any obligation' (1978: 10).

To explain his definition of politeness, Fraser likens an interaction to the execution of a contract, i.e. a 'conversational contract', in which politeness is related to the rights and obligations of each of the parties involved. According to this scholar, whether or not an utterance sounds polite depends on (1) whether the speaker has not exceeded his rights pursuant to the conversational contract and (2) whether he has fulfilled his obligations pursuant to the same contract. Otherwise the speaker's utterance will be heard as being impolite by the addressee.

Like a business contract, a conversational contract is preceded by 'negotiations' between the parties involved concerning the rights and obligations of each, without closing the possibility of renegotiating new terms of contract after the old ones have been implemented for some time – for example because of a change in the roles of each or either party. The rights of a speaker include the right to ask a question and the obligations of the hearer include the obligation to answer when asked. As a rule, there is a limit to what one may ask. Asking a too personal question can be considered impolite. Likewise, if the hearer intentionally does not answer, he may be considered not performing polite behaviour.

That these conversational rights and obligation differ from culture to culture is a truism. In one culture it may be polite to ask a person – as a form of greeting – where he is going. In another it may not be the case. To sum up, Fraser talks about linguistic or, to be exact, pragmalinguistic politeness besides talking about sociopragmatic politeness. The former refers to the linguistic form of the utterance; the latter to the 'content' encapsulated in the form. The former is a question of how; the latter of what.

Briefly, Brown and Levinson's theory of politeness centres on the notion of face, which is seen as being comprised of two 'sides', namely the positive and the negative face. The positive face refers to the self-image of a (rational) person who has the want that whatever is associated with him is affirmed. It refers to a 'person's status as an autonomous, independent, free agent' (Mey, 1993: 72). The negative face refers to the self-image of a (rational) person who has the want that he is free from obstruction from other persons. In this aspect of face, the person's 'immunity from outside interference and undue external pressure is stressed' (*ibid.*).

According to Brown and Levinson, certain speech acts have the potential of threatening the face. Such a speech act is called a face-threatening act (FTA), and in order to mitigate its force, rational speakers violate Gricean maxims, avoiding explicatures. This is politeness according to the two scholars, and since there are two aspects of face, politeness consists of two kinds: positive politeness (in the literature sometimes called affirmative politeness) and negative politeness (or deferential politeness). The former is used to protect the positive face and the latter to protect the negative face.

The basic thesis proposed by Brown and Levinson is that a speaker computes the degree of his would-be speech act or utterance by considering, in a normal situation, factors such as (1) the social distance between the speaker and the hearer; (2) the difference in terms of power or dominance between them; and (3) the relative status of the speech act within the given culture. It is on the basis of these considerations that a competent speaker decides on his strategy. Depending on the degree of the threat to the face, a competent speaker can opt for one of the five strategies proposed by Brown and Levinson (1987). These are: (1) bald on record; (2) on record with positive politeness; (3) on record with negative politeness; (4) off record; and (5) not performing the speech act. Positive politeness can be realized in fifteen ways and negative politeness in ten ways (1987: 102 and 131).

Unlike Brown and Levinson, who base their view of politeness on the notion of face, Leech (1983) bases his view of politeness on four notions: (1) cost and benefit; (2) agreement; (3) approbation and (4) sympathy/antipathy. On the basis of these notions he proposes a politeness principle which, analogous to Grice's cooperative principle, involves a set of maxims. Among Leech's maxims are tact maxim ('Minimize cost to other; maximize benefit to other'); generosity maxim ('Minimize benefit to self; maximize cost to self); approbation maxim ('Minimize dispraise of *other*; maximize praise of *other*); modesty maxim ('Minimize praise of self; maximize dispraise of self').

According to Leech, there are three scales which we should take into account in 'measuring' the degree of the politeness of a speech act. The three scales, which together form a pragmatic scale, are the cost-benefit scale, the optionality scale, and the (in)directness scale. The relative heights of the position of a speech act on the three scales will determine the degree of its politeness.

4. Implications

To my knowledge, no pragmatician has to date claimed that his or her pragmatic theory is applicable to the practice of language teaching. Fraser (1978: 19) only touched a bit on the relation of pragmatics to language teaching when he talked about whether or not the learner should be taught knowledge for conveying intention in the language being learned. Thus, in the absence of in-depth literature on this, the following should be regarded as a preliminary attempt on my part to relate pragmatics to language teaching.

One seemingly relevant implication of the theory of speech act for language teaching is that one pragmatic function can be served by more than one form, as evident from the nine sentence forms cited in Blumka and Olshtain's experiment mentioned above. Conversely, we can assume that one sentence form can implicate more than one function, as can be inferred from the fact that an utterance like 'I will come back' can be a promise, a notification, or a warning, depending on the context. Similarly, an utterance such as 'Look at the floor' can function as a description (meaning 'there is something on the floor'), a warning or a threat ('or else I'll shoot you'), a reprimand ('You have made the floor dirty') or a straightforward order (meaning 'don't look up') said to a girl learning a classical Javanese dance, for instance. What these examples further imply is that there is no one-to-one correspondence between form and function. Seen from the pragmatic perspective, thus, the old grammar "rule" that an imperative is used to give an order or a command no longer applies.

The notion of an indirect speech act (as opposed to a direct speech act) suggests that there are more than one way of communicating a message. This is a truism. But pragmatics figures well here in that it offers an explanation based on theories with sufficiently high explanatory adequacy, as exemplified by the ones proposed by Brown and Levinson or by Leech, for example. Knowledge about pragmatics would therefore be useful for the language teacher. It is not that she must know pragmatics in order to teach well. It is that pragmatics enables her to be better able to explain why in a given cultural setting and in a certain interactional event, for instance, a direct or indirect speech act is more appropriate.

That brings us to the notion of the *appropriateness* of an utterance, a term which was first introduced by Hymes in relation to the term *communicative competence* as a critique against Chomskyan linguistic or grammatical competence. Now rightfully a term in pragmatics, appropriateness becomes a requirement for a good utterance. For an utterance to be grammatical is not enough. It should also be appropriate in view of the setting in which the utterance is produced. Thus, in order to be able to communicate effectively, advanced students of a second or foreign language should be taught the notion *appropriateness*, both pragmalinguistic appropriateness (referring to form) and sociopragmatic appropriateness (referring to content). They should be taught the knowledge of when to use a direct speech act and when to use an indirect one in the language.

It is about time we commented on Fraser's 'statement' above, namely that much of the knowledge for conveying a language learner's intention need not be taught (the reason being that there was a survey finding which showed that strategies for performing speech acts were the same across the languages surveyed). In all fairness, Fraser was very cautious in saying that. He did not say it in a bald-on-record fashion, admitting that he based his observation on an unsubstantiated claim. However, even if this observation of his is true, there are two reasons that learners, advanced learners especially, need to be taught knowledge for expressing intentions the pragmatic way.

First, how a speech act is performed bears upon politeness. Even if the strategies for expressing politeness in both the learner's mother tongue and the second or foreign language are the same, the nuances of the politeness conveyed may be different across both languages. Gunarwan (1993) found that there was a significant difference in the rank orders of the politeness of directive types between Indonesian learners of English (N=173) and native speakers of the language (N=57), implying that the perception of politeness differs across cultures.

Second, even if the strategies are the same across languages, there is the question of the frequency of occurrences of each strategy in each language. One speech community might use one strategy more often than another. Even between two 'related' communities the frequencies of occurrence can be different. In a research study, Herbert (1989) compared the realisation of expressing compliments and compliment responses between South African university students on the one hand and their American counterparts on the other. Despite the fact that all subjects were English-speaking (and white) there was a significant difference between the two communities.

Without the learner's knowing the social rules governing the choice of speech act strategies in the other language, interference is likely to happen. When it does, a pragmatic error or pragmatic failure is made. Since pragmatics can be divided into pragmalinguistics (related to grammar) and sociopragmatics (related to sociology) (Leech, 1983), pragmatic errors can be in the forms of pragmalinguistic errors and sociopragmatic errors. The former results from a failure in expressing meaning correctly; the latter from a failure in identifying the situation correctly (Riley, 1989: 235).

A question might arise at this juncture whether it would not be a tall order for the language learner to be expected to know so many pragmatic principles underpinning the social rules of the second or foreign language use. It would. But for the language teacher it would not be a tall order. Knowing the pragmatics of the language she teaches or, moreover, the contrastive pragmatics of her learners' language and the target language would certainly be a boon. She would be in a better position to equip her students with cross-cultural competence.

5. Concluding Remarks

The following points are digested from the cursory review above. Since they are based on a review, no claim is made that these are original. Somewhere, some time, they must have been mentioned by someone else.

1. There is more than one way of expressing a meaning or an intention, and an appropriate one should be chosen for a given interaction.
2. A rational speaker would determine his choice for a strategy for performing an act on the basis of interactional and, probably, cultural factors.
3. A strategy for performing a speech act can be seen as an effort to save face (the speaker's or the hearer's).
4. There are indications that indirectness does not always correlate with politeness.
5. Politeness lies in the ear of the hearer and varies across languages.
6. Politeness refers to the form as well as to the message of a speech act.

The points here are meant for language teachers to consider in order for them to decide whether they are worth their attention. If indeed they are, then these points should be regarded as insights that they can incorporate into their teaching.

References

Austin, John L. 1962. *How to Do Things with Words.* Oxford: Oxford University Press

Blakemore, Diane. 1992. *Understanding Utterances: An Introduction to Pragmatics.* Cambridge: Blackwell

Blum-Kulka, Shoshana. 1987. Indirectness and politeness in requests: Same or different? *Journal of Pragmatics.* 11: 131-146

Blum-Kulka, Shoshana & Olshtain, E. 1985. Requests and apologies: A cross-cultural study of speech act realization patterns. *Applied Linguistics 5*: 198-212

Brown, Penelope & Levinson, Stephen C. 1987. *Politeness: Some Universals in Language.* Cambridge: Cambridge University Press

Fasold, Ralph. 1990. *The Sociolinguistics of Language.* Oxford: Blackwell

Fraser, Bruce. 1978. Acquiring social competence in a second language. *RELC Journal.* 9(2): 1-21

Gazdar, 1979. *Pragmatics: Implicature, Presupposition and Logical Form.* New York: Academic Press

Grice, H. Paul. 1975. Logic and conversation. *Syntax and Semantics*, Vol. 9: *Pragmatics.* ed. by Peter Cole and Jerry Morgan New York: Academic Press. 41-58

Gunarwan, Asim. 1993. The politeness rating of English and Indonesian directive types among Indonesian learners of English: Towards contrastive pragmatics. Paper presented to the Fourth International Pragmatics Conference. Kobe, 25-30 July

Gunarwan, Asim. 1996a. Language and language variety as metaphors: Evidence from the East Javanese folk theater. Paper presented to the Fifth International Pragmatics Conference. Mexico City, 4-9 July

Gunarwan, Asim. 1996b. The speech act of criticizing among speakers of Javanese. Paper presented to the Sixth Meeting of the Southeast Asian Linguistics Society. Eugene, Oregon, 9-12 May

Herbert, Robert K. 1989. The ethnography of English compliments and compliment responses: A contrastive sketch. *Contrastive Pragmatics.* ed. by Wieslaw Oleksy. Amsterdam: John Benjamins. 3-36

Lakoff, Robin. 1972. Language in context. *Language.* 18(4): 907-927

Levinson, Stephen C. 1983. *Pragmatics.* Cambridge: Cambridge University Press

Mey, Jacob L. 1993. *Pragmatics: An Introduction.* Cambridge, Massachusetts: Blackwell

Riley, Philip. 1989. Well don't blame me! On the interpretation of pragmatic errors. *Contrastive Pragmatics.* ed. by Wieslaw Oleksy. Amsterdam: John Benjamins. 231-249

Searle, John R. 1969. *Speech Acts.* Cambridge: Cambridge University Press

Schiffrin, Deborah. 1994. *Approaches to Discourse.* Oxford: Blackwell

TEACHING ENGLISH AS AN INTERNATIONAL LANGUAGE IN JAPAN: WITH A REPORT FROM AWARENESS TRAINING SESSIONS

Nobuyuki Honna

Introduction

Japan's Anglophile English teaching program has strongly indoctrinated Japanese teachers and students with the concept of English as an American language. Japanese teachers and students underestimate Japanese English, a product of their strenuous learning efforts, simply because it is different from native speakers' varieties, most probably from American English.

As they have little experience in using this language in practical situations, they are not really aware of its international spread and diversification. Actually they have no clear vision of the significant roles English can play as a language for multinational and multicultural communication.

However, once Japanese teachers and students of English discover what possibilities this international language can give them, they gradually come to understand the concept of English as an international language and develop confidence in Japanese English. They also display increasingly positive attitudes toward other non-native varieties of English.

This paper, first, explores some of the theoretical issues involved in recognizing English as a language for international communication in Japan. It, then, reports on the results of a series of lectures and workshops designed to prepare teachers and students for the awareness of English as such and Japanese English as a legitimate variety.

The English Language Teaching Situation

In Japan's school education, foreign language, although categorized as an elective subject, has always been an important component at its secondary and tertiary stages. At public junior and senior high schools, English virtually constitutes the first foreign language taught as a subject, though some schools, mostly private, offer French, German, Spanish, Russian, Chinese, or Korean in addition to English.

Most students in Japan begin studying English in junior high school at the age of twelve, and continue for six years until they graduate from senior high school at the age of eighteen. If they choose to go to college as 38% of the nation's 18-year-olds do, they will most normally study English for another two years at least. (See Figure 1 and Table 1 in the Appendix)

In a move to further intensify English teaching in Japan, the Ministry of Education issued new guidelines for the English program at the high school level in 1989 and 1990. The guidelines describe the overall objectives for the courses of study for junior and senior high schools as follows.

- For Junior High Schools: To develop a basic ability to understand and express oneself in a foreign language (read as English) and a willingness to communicate in it; to instil an interest in language and culture, thus laying the foundation for international understanding.
- For Senior High Schools: To develop an ability to understand and express oneself in a foreign language (read as English here too) and a willingness to communicate in it; to heighten an interest in language and culture, thus increasing international understanding.

In spite of the repeated reference to communication and international understanding, however, the guidelines do not recognize English as an international language. Actually, with all the spread of English as a language for wider communication, many Japanese still believe that English is the property of the U.S.A. and Britain.

As such, although team-teaching is encouraged to activate oral communication, a Japanese teacher of English is expected to cooperate only with a native English speaker in instructing a class. The case in question is the Japan Exchange and Teaching (JET) program. Sponsored by the three Ministries of Education, Home Affairs, and Foreign Affairs in a joint effort to "strengthen foreign language teaching and promote international exchange" at the local municipal level, the program started in 1987 with

813 Assistant Language Teachers (ALT's) all coming from English-speaking countries (570 from the U.S.A., 149 from Britain, 72 from Australia, and 22 from New Zealand).

The program kept expanding and, in 1995, there were 4,243 ALT's, with 2,248 from the U.S.A., 790 from the U.K., 692 from Canada, 243 from Australia, 194 from New Zealand, and 63 from Ireland teaching English, and 9 from France teaching French, and 4 from Germany teaching German. At present, they are all over the country, with every public high school receiving at least one ALT constantly.

The fallacy is obvious here. Since English is not dealt with as a global language, the three-circle distribution of English speakers in the world is not reflected. Teachers from India or Singapore who mastered English as a second or foreign language are rarely seen transmitting their learning experience to Japanese students. The result is the increased popularity of English as an Anglo/American language.

Japan's Proclivity for Native Speaker English

Actually, the conventional objective of Japan's English teaching program is unrealistic. It calls for students to acquire native-like proficiency in English regardless of the extremely limited roles allocated to the language in Japanese society. Behavioral acculturation is also presupposed as a must.

This "nativist" goal should be held largely accountable for the present low achievement. It also causes Japanese students' passive attitudes in using this language as a means of international and intercultural communication. They are ashamed if they do not speak English the way native speakers do.

Given an Anglophile goal as their guiding light, Japanese students of English cannot accept their limited proficiency as natural and inevitable. They also look down on non-native varieties of English used by other Asian and African speakers.

In a novel by a popular author, a Japanese Government official assigned to the Republic of the Philippines laments: "Three years here means ten years at my age. I went to Canada to brush up my English. Now it's almost useless. Here I have to hear their strong accented English and I'm afraid I'm bound to pick up that trill soon."

Japan's present, unrealistic English teaching model is illustrated as follows:

<u>Input</u>　　　<u>Program</u>　　　<u>Output Expectation</u>
Students ➔　American English ➔ American English Speakers

By virtue of this utter perfectionism, Japanese students tend to hesitate to interact with English speakers "until," as they often are heard to say, "they develop complete proficiency in the language." Fears of making mistakes often prevent them even from using the phrases and expressions they are learning at school.

Many students profess that their ultimate purpose in learning English is to acquire proficiency for intercultural communication. But it often looks as if their purpose in fact is to enjoy the process of the acquisition of the proficiency, but not to use the acquired proficiency, however useful it might be.

As Honna and Takeshita (1998) report, Japanese students' images of English are strongly flavored with the United States. In other words, they are obsessed with the idea that English is a language for communication between native speakers (probably Americans) and themselves, and therefore, they are extremely sensitive to native speaker varieties and tend to overlook other possibilities.

Although quite a few are inclined to see English in the light of "international communication", they do not seem to have a correct understanding of how international and how common the language actually is among people of the world. In their mind, the native speakers are a big group, while the others do not cut a clear figure. English as a language for international communication in Asia would seem to be quite an obscure idea to Japanese students.

As a result, a great majority of the students interpret Japanese varieties of English quite negatively. Comments such as "grammar-bound" and "formal" are hardly meant to be positive. They reflect the Japanese evaluation of their English as not as natural as American English. Japanese English is cynically criticized as so "full of words coined in a Japanese way" or "expressed from Japanese points of view" that it is "not communicative" or "understood only by Japanese". Not being able to produce English like Americans leads the students to a feeling of failure, inferiority, and even guilt and shame.

An ethnography of Japanese students of English will show a lot of episodes of their adamant faith in native-speaker English. Here is an example of a middle-aged government officer.

> I was studying English at Columbia University in New York. I wanted to master American English in the United States. When I was there, I met with a Japanese businessman who spoke beautiful American English. I admired him and wanted to be like him. I was glad to be assured that if you worked very hard, you could be able to speak English like a native American. One day, however, a shocking incident befell me. While he was talking about the Japanese economic situation at a party, I heard him say "Let's discuss about it from this point of view." Hey, "discuss about it" is not correct English, I told myself. Native speakers would discuss it, never discuss about it. This is a simple, plain fact, isn't it? This guy is not like a native speaker, I thought. At this disappointing moment, my respect for him, my admiration of him disappeared. Since then, I keep saying to myself, if you want to master authentic American English, you have to work really hard. I am still at it.

Japanese use of "discuss about" as well as "mention about" as an index of underdeveloped proficiency is well known among intermediate or advanced level students. But the more worrisome thing is that Japanese speakers of English are invariably reminded that they are being watched, actually heard, by their peers and colleagues.

They are extremely worried not to make mistakes in front of their compatriots. A famous American studies professor who conducted his classes in English was once heard to say "more big" in his talk.

Immediately, he was secretly known as an "English-bragging professor who says more big" among his faculty.

Examination English

Even more seriously, the nation's inclination to native-speaker English is making teachers victims of frustration and self-defeatism. Thus, out of a feeling of insecurity, many teachers become more interested in theoretical linguistics than in practical communication. In the English class, they put greater emphasis on grammatical studies than on practical lessons. This general trend is reflected in Examination English.

This term refers to the kind of English that high school students are led to learn because that is the way students' knowledge of English is evaluated at an entrance examination for higher education. Particularly, English tests given high-school students by colleges and universities contain a lot of awkward questions made to examine applicants' theoretical linguistic knowledge rather than practical communicative competence. Let me quote a couple of examples from Matsuoka (1998).

Question x: Choose one sentence from among those below whose usage is most approximate to the underlined word in the following sentence:

Taking <u>buying</u> a car, for example.

1. He denied knowing anything about the case.
2. He sat reading while I taught my little ones.
3. The boy came running out of the house.
4. There is nothing like doing a thing at once.

To answer the question correctly, the students should be informed of the linguistic idea that the gerundive use of "buying"(a car) here functions as the object of "taking" and that the parallel use might be found in answer (1).

Question y: Choose one sentence from among those below whose usage is most approximate to the underlined word in the following sentence:

<u>Working</u> means we receive a salary which enables us to buy things we need and want.

1. Do you mind my opening the window?
2. He always says, "Keeping promises makes a man trusted."
3. I remember seeing her somewhere before.
4. On leaving school, he went into business.

Similarly, to find the correct answer (2) here, the students are expected to reveal that "working" functions as the subject of "means".

Although the number of these structural questions is decreasing in college entrance examinations, the fact remains that high school teachers are highly grammar-oriented. In the same vein, some teachers contrast syntactic and semantic differences between English and Japanese. Many teachers resort to these approaches in the belief that under the circumstances analytical approaches are more useful and productive than communicative approaches.

English at the Primary School Level

In a recent development, the Central Council for Education, an influential advisory organ to the Minister of Education, published an extremely important recommendation report in 1996. In a report titled "Japan's Education in the Perspective of the 21st Century," one of the most controversial recommendations was about foreign language (actually English) instruction at the elementary school level.

The Education Council identified foreign language instruction at the elementary level not as an autonomous subject, but as part of international understanding education to be taught in a "general studies hour" or a "special activity hour". It is important, the Council report said, that children should have an opportunity to familiarize themselves with conversation in a foreign language, especially English, and thereby with various different ways of life and culture overseas.

In support of the recommendations, the Curriculum Council, another advisory body to the Minister of Education, came forth with a set of plans in 1997 to implement foreign language teaching (actually English) in public primary schools throughout the nation. While making plans to introduce foreign language studies into the primary school curriculum in 2003, the Ministry of Education had already started experimental programs in 1992 at several schools selected for curriculum research and development. Indeed, as of 1994, 87.7% of the private schools and 22.1% of the public schools were offering English in various ways in Japan.

The two authoritative advisory councils stress foreign language training as part of a program to nurture children's willingness and competence to understand foreign culture and interact naturally and live harmoniously with people from different cultural backgrounds. Yet, an analysis of those experimental programs indicates that they are extremely Anglo/American oriented.

Children are taught a lot about Halloween (trick or treat), Thanksgiving Day, or Christmas. Similarly, they are expected to talk about Japanese customs such as New Year's Day and Beginning of Spring Day. Thus, international or intercultural understanding is defined, though implicitly, as understanding Anglo-American culture, and English as a language to be used between Japanese and Anglo-Americans.

As such, the roles to be played by ALT's are increasingly emphasized. A Ministry of Education-related guideline has this to say about Assistant Language Teachers who are native speakers of English: "Children are greatly impressed by the experience of learning from a familiar foreign teacher. The pleasure of understanding ALT's native English, the pleasure of making themselves understood in English by ALT's, and the pleasure of being praised by ALT's motivate pupils greatly to learn English."

The guideline further specifies the ALT roles in teaching English at the primary school level in the following way:

1. To familiarize children with "Living English" by giving them explanations and instructions in English about learning activities, talking to them and reading picture books to them in natural rhythmical English;
2. To teach pronunciation and situationally correct usage;

3. To inform children of conventions and customs of English-speaking people;
4. To teach gestures and other non-verbal signals of English-speaking people;
5. To work together with Japanese teachers of English to facilitate the children's learning at the planning, implementation, and evaluation stages, and;
6. To work together with Japanese teachers of English to prepare teaching material.

In the projected primary school instruction of English, ALT's are envisioned as an indispensable component. They are expected to help teach children not only linguistic and communicative skills but also cultural and behavioral values. Under these circumstances, since most ALT's are from America and Britain, children are apt to be taught English as an Anglo/American language.

Actually, independent observers have noticed that children tend to admire ALT's pronunciation and downgrade other varieties. Reportedly, they often tease Japanese teachers when they do not pronounce the way ALT's do. "Teacher, your pronunciation is funny," a child derides a slightly Japanese-accented instructor. "I agree. Your pronunciation cannot be communicative," adds another, even when there is no communication problem between two instructors.

Young ALT's can be linguistically and culturally perfectionist. They sometimes insist on children imitating their pronunciation in its entirety. American ALT's are often seen demanding that children point a forefinger to the chest, not the nose when they say "I" or "me." Some observers express concern about ALT's overeagerness to see their behavioral patterns prevail in the classroom.

On the other hand, Japanese teachers' self-imposed faith in native speakers can prove counterproductive. While they fail to approximate native speaker English, they lose confidence in their own non-native speaker varieties. Out of a feeling of helplessness, they often show passive communicative attitudes toward ALT's. When there is a pedagogical problem to solve, some teachers yield to what ALT's have to say.

Of course, the purpose of the discussion here is not to denigrate ALT's. Their present and future contributions to Japan's English teaching practice should not be underestimated. The crux of the matter is Japan's propensity for native-speaker English. And underlying this is the failure to understand the exact nature of the contemporary evolution and diversification of English as an international and intercultural language.

In 2003, Japan is introducing English-language instruction as part of international understanding education to 24,000 public elementary schools all over the country. It seems that now is the time to establish English as a language for wider communication and international understanding, for multinational and multicultural understanding.

Proposed Initiatives for Improvement and Reorientation

In view of the situation, if there is to be innovation, there has to be enlightenment. Indeed, English now is a multinational and multicultural language. This is the fact that Japanese students should be prepared to take into consideration if they are to learn English as a language for international and intercultural communication.

Actually, as the spread of English progresses, non-native speakers surpass native speakers in number. For example, many Japanese business people report that they have more opportunities to use English with Asians than with Americans or British in their business interaction. Indeed, English is here to stay as an important Asian language.

At the same time, English has become a "variegated" language. Everyone who speaks it speaks it with an accent. As Americans have American English accents and the British British English accents, so do Indians Indian English traits and Filipinos Philippine English characteristics. The concomitant result is that English is increasingly de-Anglo-Americanized, and diversified in many parts of the world.

Thus, many people in the world are learning English not to assimilate themselves to the Anglo-American norms of behavior, but to acquire a working command of the language of wider communication and to express their national identity and personal opinions. In other words, no one is forced to abandon his or her native culture and behave Anglo-American in order to acquire proficiency in English.

When the Japanese speak English with Singaporeans, there is no room for American or British culture. It would be clumsy if the Japanese had to represent American ways of behavior and the Singaporeans the British version while speaking English to each other.

Consequently, it is necessary to assess Japan's English teaching model given earlier in terms of the present role English plays as a world language. It is NOT FEASIBLE and NOT DESIRABLE to expect to produce American English speakers in the Japanese public education system. The traditional model has to be modified to comply with this reality, as is shown below.

<u>Input</u>   <u>Program</u>   <u>Output Expectation</u>
Students ➔   American English ➔ Japanese English Speakers

The definition of Japanese English is difficult to describe here. Suffice it to say that it is the kind of English patterns that many students of average and above-average grades can produce after six-plus years of training in school. They should be advised that what they have learned can be a useful means for multinational and multicultural communication.

The collective energy and time spent by more than sixty million Japanese who compulsorily studied English for some six years is truly enormous, and should not be wasted. Japanese students should be encouraged to take advantage of the outcome of their educational experience. One way to achieve this is to recognize that the Japanese are ordinarily expected to speak Japanese English, not American English.

As a matter of fact, Japanese English can be an important utilitarian language. It is part of various non-native speaker Englishes used in many functions in many parts of Asia and the rest of the world. More often than not, these varieties constitute the most useful language of initial contact among many international travelers and business persons.

Standards of acceptability and correctness are not absolute but negotiable. The bottom line is mutual intelligibility. Comparative studies indicate that there are more common features than differences among these varieties. This flexibility reflects the strength of the English language and should further be promoted.

Reports from Awareness Training Sessions

Specialists in language policy studies often express an optimistic view of the future. Once Japanese teachers and students of English discover what possibilities this international language can give them, they gradually come to understand the concept of English as a multinational and multicultural language and develop confidence in Japanese varieties of English. This is witnessed in the results of a series of workshops conducted for teachers and students of English.

In these workshops, English teachers learn what it is like now that English is a multinational and multicultural language. The sociolinguisitc assumption here is that if English is perceived as an Anglo/American language, EFL students are led to use it as a means of binational communication in Anglo/American sociocultural contexts. But if English is understood as an international language, they are expected to use it as a means of global communication in multinational and multicultural contexts. (See Figure 2 in the Appendix.)

In this connection, it is important to take note of the fact that non-native speakers have more opportunities to use English with other non-native speakers than with native speakers. The audience is amazed to learn that it is the likelihood of using English with Japanese, Chinese and other Asians that motivates Thai students to learn the language. (See Figure 3 in the Appendix.)

Participants also study the thought-provoking opinions advanced by Larry Smith, Braj Kachru, and other eminent scholars involved in promoting the concepts of World Englishes. They are first astonished to read the lines from Larry Smith (1983) such as:

1. No one needs to become more like Americans, the British, the Australians, the Canadians or any other English speakers in order to lay claim on the language.

2. ... It isn't even necessary to appreciate the culture of a country whose principal language is English in order to use it effectively.
3. Just because the other person doesn't speak English the way we do, doesn't mean he/she is wrong or speaking incorrectly.
4. (Speakers) maintain their own non-verbal cues...

Then, they discuss attitudes toward English in India. Japanese teachers and students are often impressed that in India, students want to learn "the kind of English used by educated Indians," rather than American English or British English. When they study the reasons why Indian students want to learn English, Japanese teachers and students are surprised that Indians are not learning English in order to study American or British culture as much as the Japanese are taught to. (See Figure 4 in the Appendix.)

During discussions, participants are informed of the fact that in much of Asia, English is no longer a colonial import. Throughout the region, English is the language of culture, politics, and above all, business. English-speaking Asians claim English as their own language. "The English language is now ours," said Filipino poet Gemino Abad. "We have colonized it, too."

At this stage, they are led to examine some grammatical features of Colloquial Singapore English to see that Asian Englishes are diverse, with different social roles attached to the adopted language. Likewise, it is important to comprehend that each country, whether ESL or EFL, has used the language in its traditional cultural and linguistic contexts, thereby producing a distinct variety characterized by unique structural and functional features. Proficiency levels also are different with English-as-an-intranational-language countries producing more skillful speakers than English-as-an-international-language counterparts.

Finally, participants debate the pros and cons of Japanese English in terms of feasibility and desirability. It is easy to understand that Japanese English is more obtainable than American English, but it requires information and enlightenment to recognize that Japanese English is more desirable than American English. A clear vision of English as an international language constitutes an essential part of the knowledge that makes it possible to accept Japanese English as a legitimate variety for Japanese users of the language. (See Figure 5 in the Appendix.)

After attending a 3-day seminar, one teacher wrote:

> I was once amazed at Vietnamese students' enthusiasm in trying to communicate in English, and wondered what made the difference. I have now realized that we had a wrong view of English. We will feel more at ease if we know that the important thing is to communicate in Japanese English, and build up and maintain a friendly relationship with different people. Teachers of English are to blame for the stress with which Japanese people speak English, because they are not tolerant toward students' grammatical mistakes and limit their freedom to speak. Such a stress in speaking English will be minimized if teachers appreciate the fact that a student has communicated in English. The first step will be to change teachers' concept of English.

Likewise, as students learn more about the reality of English as a language for international communication, they show positive attitudes toward non-native speaker varieties of English. More often than not, they express agreement with the idea of English as such. Some students told me that that was the most interesting idea that they'd learned in college.

Most remarkably, they told me that they were so confident of the idea that they used it as their answer to the question often asked by recruiters at a job-interview session: what did you study in college? According to reports from graduating students, recruiters invariably express their interest in the idea and interview sessions develop into a prolonged but enlightening exchange of opinions between student applicants and personnel officers about how they should recognize, promote, and use English in their companies. (See Figure 6 in the Appendix.)

A Change in Sight

Other events that are indicative of a change in traditional Japanese attitudes toward English are occurring in the business sections of Japanese society. Blue-chip companies in Japan provide in-service training in English during or after their office hours. Fujitsu, a mammoth electronics firm, requires that every employee learn English and take a national proficiency test to demonstrate his or her achievement.

Participants at company workshops report that knowledge of English as a multinational and multicultural language really helps them understand what they can do with their varieties of English at international settings. It further motivates them to work harder to improve their ability for more effective communication.

Once Japanese business people recognize the legitimacy of Asian varieties of English, they become interested to learn why Asian people speak English the way they do. To meet these demands for linguistic and cultural information, reinforced by an ever-increasing number of inquisitive Japanese tourists visiting Asian cities, the Sanseido publishing company is now compiling a Japanese dictionary of Asian Englishes. If English is to be an Asian language, informal, colloquial, and basilectal forms of English that are emerging in many parts of Asia should be correctly understood.

On the scholarly front, young intellectuals are exploring and developing new important research fields. Hirano (1998), for example, applies marketing strategies to promote the idea of Japanese English as a useful variety. By so doing, she creates a new domain of sociolinguistic inquiry called language marketing.

Thus, the stigma put on indigenized Englishes and other EFL learners' varieties is wearing itself out in some important sections of Japanese society. Most likely, these changing attitudes can give impetus to proposed initiatives for reorientation and improvement in Japan's English-language instruction practice.

Truly, a series of significant educational breakthroughs have already been registered in many localities. For instance, the City of Yokohama, Japan's second largest city (pop. 3.2 million) that forms an important part of the Greater Tokyo Metroplex (pop. 30 million), decided to employ foreign residents as assistant teachers whose job it is to introduce their countries in English to the city's elementary school children.

The Yokohama Board of Education took these measures in an attempt to utilize magnificent human resources available in this international port city and to strengthen international understanding education at the elementary school level. Temporary assistant teachers from such countries as Bangladesh, Sri Lanka, India, Malaysia, or Singapore, where English is not considered as a native language, have taught classes in the language for wider communication.

Conclusion

Diffusion presupposes diversification. Specifically, a common language has to be a diverse language. This principle is essential to recognize English as an international language. Japanese students can contribute to this cause by using the language as Japanese English. And all of us, who know more about English as such, should devise effective ways to explain the idea so that our students can have a better understanding of the language they are learning as well as creating.

References

Bautista, Maria Lourdes S. (ed.) 1997. *English is an Asian Language.* Sydney: The Macquarie Library Pty Ltd.

Honna, Nobuyuki. 1995. English in Japanese Society: Language within Language. *Journal of Multilingual and Multicultural Development,* 16(1-2).

Honna, Nobuyuki & Takeshita, Yuko. 1998. Teaching English as an International Language: A Japanese Perspective. *Asian Englishes,* 1(1).

Hirano, Junko. 1998. Marketing Strategies for 'Japanese English' as a Means of International Communication. An MA thesis presented to the Graduate School of International Politics, Economics, and Business, Aoyama Gakuin University. (In Japanese)

Matsuoka, Noboru. 1998. English for International Communication and English Tests for College Entrance Examinations. An MA thesis presented to the Graduate School of International Politics, Economics, and Business, Aoyama Gakuin University. (In Japanese)

Ogose, Hideko. 1998. On the Recognition of English as a Language for International Communication in Elementary Education. *International Communication Studies* 2 a journal published by Aoyama Gakuin University's Graduate School of International Politics, Economics and Business. (In Japanese)

Parasher, S.V. 1991. *Indian English: Functions and Form*. Bombay: Bahri Publications.

Smith, Larry (ed.) 1983. *Readings in English as an International Language*. Oxford: Pergamon Press.

Suzuki, Takao. 1985. *Language as a Weapon*. Tokyo: Shinchosha. (In Japanese)

Appendix

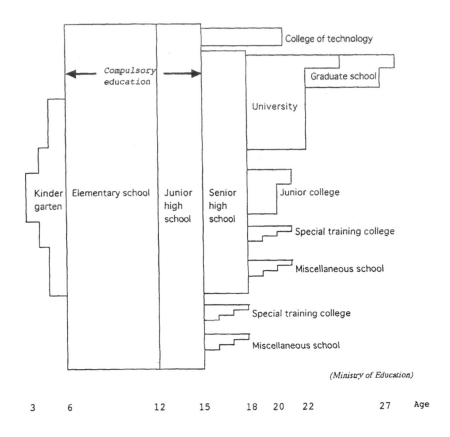

Figure 1: The Japanese Education System

English as an Anglo/American Language

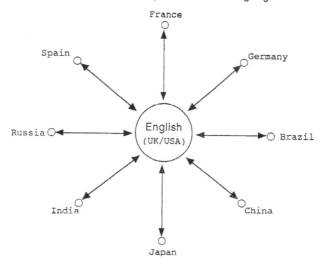

English as an International Language

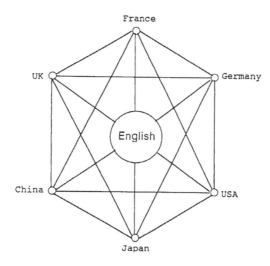

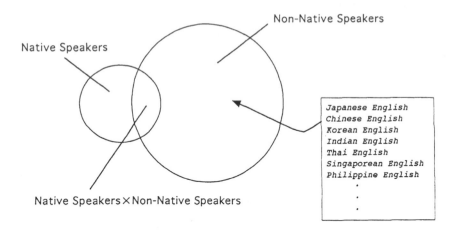

Figure 3: English as a Multinational /Multicultural Language

Varieties of English Suitable for Teaching	Percentage (%)
American English	4.0
British English	33.5
The kind of English used by educated Indians	60.8
Any other	1.7

(Parasher, 1991)

The Reasons Why Indian Students Want to Learn English

*1. To get current information in the fields of science and technology.

*2. For international communication.

*3. As a link language among people whose mother tongues are different.

*4. As the language of higher education and learning.

*5. To get information about the rest of the world.

*6. To maintain high standards of education.

*7. For inter-state communication.

*8. As one of the official languages of the Union of India.

*9. To run our own social, political, and economic activities smoothly.

10. To popularize our religion, philosophy, literature, and culture abroad.

11. To study the culture of English-speaking people.

The asterisk indicates an item pointed out by more than half of the students surveyed. *(Parasher, 1991)*

Figure 4: The variety of English Students Want Taught in India

Input	Program	Output Expectation

Japanese Students ⟶ American English ⟶ American English Speakers
or
Japanese English Speakers

Evaluation Criteria of the Model:
Is this model feasible?
Is this model desirable?

Present Unrealistic Understanding:

	Feasibility	Desirability
AE Speaker Model	No	Yes
JE Speaker Model	Yes	No

! !

Modified Realistic Understanding:

	Feasibility	Desirability
AE Speaker Model	No	No
JE Speaker Model	Yes	Yes

Figure 5: Japanese English – a legitimate variety?

1 = I disagree completely.   5 = I agree a little.
2 = I disagree.   6 = I agree.
3 = I disagree a little.   7 = I agree completely.
4 = I am neutral.

Q. What do you think about the spread of English and its diversification ?

(a) It is desirable for English to be diversified as a result of its global spread.

(b) The diversification of English enriches the language.

(c) The diversification of English as a result of its internationalization is unavoidable.

(d) In spite of English as an international language, its diversification has to be restricted to a minimum level.

(e) The diversification of English is undesirable since it endangers Standard English.

Figure 6: Student Attitudes toward English

Table 1: Basic Facts about Schools in Japan *(Ministry of Education, 1997)*

	No. of schools	National	Public	Private	No. of classes	No. of students	No. of teaching staff	No. of clerical staff
Elementary Schools	24,376	73	24,132	171	282,974	7,855,386	420,897	102,473
Junior high schools	11,257	78	10,518	661	134,963	4,481,483	270,224	40,573
Senior high schools	5,496	17	4,164	1,315	7,418	4,371,349	276,145	62,320
Blind schools	71	1	68	2	...	4,324	3,500	19,774
Deaf schools	107	1	105	1	2,026	6,841	4,816	2,179
Schools for the physically handicapped and	800	43	744	13	20,280	75,280	45,630	12,871
Kindergartens	14,690	49	6,085	8,556	72,715	1,789,457	103,933	20,871
Special vocational schools	6,545	147	220	3,178	...	788,549	37,221	16,742
Miscellaneous schools	2,601	2	51	2,548	...	281,129	14,970	6,415
Technical schools	62	54	5	3	...	56,294	4,384	3,206
Junior colleges	595	29	62	504	...	446,750	19,885	12,447
Universities	586	98	57	431	...	2,638,821	141,785	171,727

LANGUAGE LEARNING STRATEGIES: A MALAYSIAN PERSPECTIVE

Florence G. Kayad

Introduction

Language learning strategies (LLS) have been identified as one of the individual factors that contribute to differential success rates among second language learners (Larsen-Freeman and Long, 1991; Larsen-Freeman, 1991, Ellis, 1994). Comparative studies of LLS and success rates, often measured by proficiency level, have shown that the types of LLS used, and the frequency of use of those strategies are crucial for language learning (Bialystok, 1979; Politzer and McGroarty, 1985; O'Malley et al.; Oxford and Nyikos, 1989; Mangubhai, 1991; Green and Oxford, 1995).

Strategy research using various methods and instruments, such as the Strategy Inventory for Language Learning (SILL, Oxford, 1989, cited in Oxford, 1990) has identified some consistent patterns in the use of different types of strategies among learners with different proficiency levels. In general, all learners, despite their proficiency level, are active strategy users. The present study, while being one of many pieces of strategy research across nations using the SILL, is among the very few correlational studies of LLS and L2 proficiency level among university undergraduates in the Malaysian context. The study investigates the LLS of a sample of university ESL learners at University Malaysia Sarawak (Unimas) in order to answer four primary questions as follows:

1. What types of LLS do proficient (P) and less proficient (LP) ESL learners use to learn English?
2. Are there any significant differences in the frequency of strategy use by the two groups?
3. Are there any significant differences in the choice of strategies used?
4. What is the relationship between strategy use and proficiency level?

Background of the research

Proponents of LLS research have formulated useful typologies of strategies. Studies of the "good language learner" (Stern, 1975; Rubin, 1975; Naiman, Frohlich, Stern, and Todesco, 1978), have identified the prevalent characteristics and behaviors among more successful language learners in order to better understand the learners and their learning processes. Based on that understanding, language teachers can help the less successful learners to improve their learning. Current strategy research has taken a step further from describing and explaining strategies to determining the relationship between LLS and L2 proficiency (Bialystok, 1981; Politzer and McGroarty, 1985; Mangubhai, 1991; Green & Oxford, 1995; Dreyer and Oxford, 1996; Wen & Johnson, 1997). Studies of the effect of strategy use have also been carried out across cultures (Tinkham, 1989; Rosna Awang Hashim and Sharifah Azizah Syed Sahil, 1994; Bedell and Oxford, 1996; Pickard, 1996) and with less successful ESL learners (Vann and Abraham, 1990).

Comparative strategy research across cultures, learning environment and other individual difference variables have concluded that the learners' ability to process information is affected by their knowledge and experience of L2 learning. Nation and McLaughlin's (1986) comparative study of "expert" and "novice" learners' information processing strategies noted that "expert" or good language learners seemed to possess "high-order plans" to organize the linguistic information and used automatic processing to complete the learning task. It was also found that although both successful and less successful learners use the same strategies, how the strategies are used, such as in terms of frequency and appropriateness, affect the success of L2 learning (Vann and Abraham, 1990; Mangubhai, 1991)

Culture is another factor affecting LLS use. Asian learners seemed to use rote learning or memorization strategies more often than their Western counterparts (O'Malley, 1987). In fact, rote learning has been reported to be beneficial and effective, and even enjoyable by sophomore level high school Japanese students compared to their American counterparts. Successful Japanese learners of English at university level reported that memorization is their main LLS (LoCastro, 1994).

Strategy research using summative rating scales such as the Strategy Inventory for Language Learning (SILL), which is one of the most comprehensive and most frequently used strategy scales around the world today (Oxford and Burry-Stock, 1995), has shown certain patterns in strategy use among L2 learners. The SILL consists of fifty LLS which are distributed under six broad strategy categories, namely, memory, cognitive, compensation, metacognitive, affective and social strategies. Among other things, correlational studies of LLS and proficiency level using the SILL among Asian ESL learners have shown that although proficiency and overall strategy use were not significantly correlated, certain strategy categories were (Mullins, 1992, cited in Oxford and Burry-Stock, 1995; Bedell, 1993, cited in Bedell and Oxford, 1996, Green and Oxford, 1995). It was reported that almost all strategy categories were used at a high level, with compensation, cognitive and metacognitive consistently in the top three. Green and Oxford (1995) noted that there was a greater use of LLS among the more successful learners and that some strategies showed significant variation by proficiency level.

The current study

The current study compares the proficient and less proficient ESL learners in the Malaysian context in terms of their choice and frequency of strategy use. It is a survey of LLS using the adapted Strategy Inventory for Language Learning (SILL) version 7.0 for ESL/EFL learners (Oxford, 1989, taken from Oxford, 1990). The questionnaire consists of two parts: students' background information and the SILL. The SILL comprises fifty items (strategies) in the form of self-report statements such as "I do such and such when learning English". Students self-rate their frequency of use of those strategies on a five-point Likert scale from 1 for "never or almost never true of me" to 5 for "always or almost always true of me". The fifty items are distributed across six strategy categories, namely, memory (9 items), cognitive (14 items), compensation (6 items), metacognitive (9 items), affective (6 items), and social (6 items) strategies.

The participants in this study were selected from the top and bottom quartile of the population of first year undergraduates across all programs at the university. Selection was made based on the performance in the university English placement test. Thus, the definition of proficiency is restricted to the context of the study in which proficient learners comprise the top quartile and the less proficient learners the bottom quartile.

A total of 181 students, 98 in the top quartile and 83 in the bottom quartile, were selected and given the questionnaire but only 84 returned the completed questionnaire. The findings and conclusions of the study are based on the completed and returned questionnaires. Table 1 shows the distribution of participants according to their respective programs of study.

Table 1: Distribution of Participants by Programs of Study

Program	No of students		Total	%
	LP	P		(N=84)
1. Engineering	2	12	14	16.7
2. Cognitive Science & Human Development	5	3	8	9.5
3. Social Sciences	11	2	13	15.4
4. Resource Science and Technology	3	12	15	17.9
5. Applied and Creative Arts	6	4	10	11.9
6. Information Technology	9	6	15	17.9
7. Language and Communication Studies	0	5	5	5.9
8. Economics and Business	4	0	4	4.8
Total	40	44	84	100

All students who participated in the study have had eleven years of learning English throughout their primary and secondary school education, and have sat for the English exam at the Sijil Pelajaran Malaysia (SPM) level at the end of their secondary school education. At the university level, all students have taken at least one generic English course based on their placement test result as required by the university.

Data collection and analysis

One-way ANOVA was used to investigate the differences between the means of the two samples (proficient and less proficient groups). The t-test was used to determine the significant differences in the use of individual strategies by proficiency level. The strength of the relationship between proficiency level and LLS were determined by the correlation coefficient. Reliability analysis of the adapted version of the SILL, written in English, with the 84 respondents was relatively high at .89. The survey was conducted via correspondence.

The results

Types of strategies used

All the six types (categories) of strategies on the SILL, namely memory, cognitive, compensation, metacognitive, affective and social strategies, were used by both proficient and less proficient students. However, descriptive statistics such as frequencies and percentages of strategy use at the individual strategy level showed that not all the fifty strategies were used. This was indicated by the number of students who rated a particular strategy on the score of 1 for "never or almost never true of me". On the basis of frequency count of individual strategy use, there are four main groups of strategy use as follows:

1. strategies used by all (both proficient and less proficient learners)
2. strategies used by all proficient learners only
3. strategies used by all less proficient learners only
4. strategies not used by both proficiency groups

Table 2 shows the distribution of individual strategies used.

Table 2: Strategy groups according to their use by proficient and less proficient learners

	Strategy use group	Strategy no*	Total	%(N=50)
1.	used by all proficient and less proficient learners	1,13,16,20,25,30,31,32,36,38,49	11	22
2.	used by all proficient learners only	2,10,15,17,29,37	6	12
3.	used by all less proficient learners only	4, 12, 18, 19, 21, 24, 33, 35, 39, 40, 41, 42, 45, 46, 47, 48, 50	17	34
4.	not used by both proficient and less proficient learners	3, 5, 6, 7, 8, 9, 11, 14, 22, 23, 26, 27, 28, 34, 43, 44	16	32
Total			50	100

*Refer to Appendix 1 for a summary of the strategies

225

Differences in the choice and frequency of strategy use by proficiency level

In this study, LLS is analyzed in terms of its frequency of use based on Oxford's classification of the SILL average analysis (Oxford, 1989, cited in 1990) as follows:

Classification	Frequency of use	Average score
High	Always or almost always true of me	4.5 to 5.0
	Usually used	3.5 to 4.4
Medium	Sometimes used	2.5 to 3.4
	Generally not used	1.5 to 2.4
Low	Never or almost never used	1.0 to 1.4

There seemed to be no significant differences [t (82) = .38 p < .719] in strategy use by both proficient and less proficient learners at the overall strategy level. Based on the classification of strategy use in the table above, both proficient and less proficient learners are medium strategy users with the overall strategy mean of 3.4. However, the one-way ANOVA test results found significant differences in the mean use of the six types (strategy categories) of strategies listed on the SILL, as shown in Table 3.

Table 3: One-way ANOVA results showing differences in the use of the six strategy categories by proficiency level

Dependent variable (SILL category)	*Less proficient (LP)*		*Proficient (P)*		*F[1,82] and significance level*
	Mean	*S.D.*	*Mean*	*S.D.*	
1. Memory	28.48	4.41	26.84	6.15	1.9245 p <.1691
2. Cognitive	45.68	5.24	51.25	6.38	18.9023 p < .0000
3. Compensation	20.73	3.08	20.86	3.49	.0370 p < .8480
4. Metacognitive	33.35	4.31	33.64	5.59	.0682 p < .7947
5. Affective	20.38	3.08	15.14	4.32	40.2802 p < .0000
6. Social	20.08	3.12	20.09	4.07	.7896 p < .3768

From the table above, proficiency level seemed to have a significant effect on the strategy use of cognitive (F [1,82] 18.9023 p < .0000) and affective (F [1,82] 40.2802 p < .0000) strategies.

The following table shows the mean use of each strategy category by learners in the two groups.

Table 4: The mean use of each strategy category by proficiency level

Strategy category	Less proficient learners LP	Proficient learners P
1. Memory	3.16	2.98
2. Cognitive	3.26	3.66
3. Compensation	3.46	3.48
4. Metacognitive	3.71	3.74
5. Affective	3.40	2.52
6. Social	3.47	3.35

At the individual strategy level, the t-test results showed significant differences in the use of 14 out of 50 strategies in the SILL. Those strategies are listed in Table 5.

Table 5: t-test results showing significant differences in the use of individual strategies by proficiency level

Strategy* No/Category	Less Proficient learners Mean	S.D.	Proficient learners Mean	S.D.	df 82 t value	2-tail significance
6. Memory	2.40	1.03	1.66	.99	3.36	.001
7. Memory	3.00	.99	2.09	1.16	3.85	.000
15. Cognitive	3.88	1.02	4.68	.56	- 4.55	.000
16. Cognitive	3.18	.84	4.34	.81	- 6.48	.000
17. Cognitive	2.68	.89	4.07	1.02	- 6.64	.000
20. Cognitive	3.05	.75	3.73	.95	- 3.61	.001
29. Compensation	3.73	.78	4.23	.71	- 3.08	.003
39. Affective	3.90	.78	3.16	1.38	2.99	.004
41. Affective	3.45	1.01	2.57	1.23	3.57	.001
42. Affective	3.48	.72	2.05	1.08	7.09	.000
43. Affective	2.28	1.11	1.50	.73	3.81	.000
44. Affective	3.30	1.04	2.20	1.13	4.60	.000
46. Social	3.45	.93	2.82	1.11	2.82	.006
49. Social	2.90	.63	3.98	.82	- 6.69	.000

*Refer Appendix 1 for summary of the strategies

From the table above, it seems that proficiency level had a significant effect on the learners' use of some of the strategies. Those strategies were found across all strategy types (categories) except metacognitive strategies.

Some strategies were used more often by proficient learners while others were used more often by less proficient learners. The strategies used more often or with a high level of frequency (3.5 to 5.0) by proficient learners are listed in Table 6.

Table 6: Strategies used more often by proficient learners and their means and standard deviation

Category/No.	Strategy	Mean	S.D
	Summary		
MEM1	Associate new material with already known	3.84	.89
MEM2	Use new English word in sentence	3.61	.90
MEM4	Connect word to mental picture or situation	3.57	1.27
COG12	Practice sounds of English	3.53	.85
COG13	Use unknown words in different ways	3.57	.73
COG14	Start conversations in English	3.77	1.16
COG15	Watch TV. or movie in English	4.68	.56
COG16	Read for pleasure in English	4.34	.81
COG17	Write notes, etc. in English	4.07	1.02
COG18	Skim then read carefully	3.84	1.14
COG20	Try to find patterns	3.73	.95
COG22	Try not translate word for word	3.73	1.07
COM24	Guess meaning of unfamiliar words	4.05	.97
COM29	Use circumlocution or synonyms	4.23	.73
COM30	Seek many ways to use English	3.91	.98
MET31	Notice my mistakes/Try to do better	4.27	.69
MET32	Pay attention when someone is speaking	4.27	.62
MET36	Seek opportunities to speak in English	3.98	.79
MET37	Have clear goals for improving skills	3.59	.90
SOC49	Ask question in English	3.98	.82

From the table above, cognitive strategies seemed to be used more often by proficient learners. Most of these strategies require the functional use of English. Less proficient learners on the other hand, seemed to use some other strategies more often than the proficient ones. The strategies used more often by less proficient learners are listed in Table 7.

Table 7: Strategies used more often by less proficient learners and their means and standard deviation

Category/No.	Strategy	Mean	S.D.
COG21	Find meanings dividing words into parts	3.65	.77
COM25	Use gestures when stuck for word	3.50	1.04
COM28	Try to guess what other people would say	3.58	.75
MET33	Try to find out about language learning	4.23	.62
MET38	Think about my progress in learning	3.73	.68
AFF39	Try to relax when I feel afraid	3.90	.78
AFF40	Encourage self to speak when afraid	3.98	.62
AFF41	Give self reward for doing well	3.45	1.01
AFF42	Noticing when I'm tense or nervous	3.48	.72
SOC45	Ask other person to slow down or repeat	4.05	.85
SOC46	Ask to be corrected when talking	3.45	.93
SOC47	Practice English with other students	3.58	.81
SOC48	Ask for help from English speakers	3.80	.82

The relationship between strategy use and proficiency level

The magnitude of relationship between strategy use and proficiency level is based on Guildford's index for the interpretation of correlational values in the table below.

Table 8: Guildford's suggested value of r

Correlation coefficient (r)	Suggested value of r
< .2	almost negligible
.2 to .4	low correlation; definite but small
.4 to .7	moderate/substantial
.7 to .9	high correlation; marked relationship
.9 to 1.0	very high; very dependable

The results of the correlational test are presented in Table 9 below.

Table 9: The relationship between proficiency level and strategy use at the strategy category level using Pearson's Product-Moment Correlation Coefficient

Strategy category	Group (Proficiency level) N = 84	
Memory	- .1514	p = .169
Cognitive	.4328	p = .000
Compensation	.0212	p = .000
Metacognitive	.0288	p = .795
Affective	- .5739	p = .000
Social	- .0977	p = .377

From the table above, it is evident that only cognitive strategies seemed to be positively correlated with proficiency level. This suggests that proficient students use this type of strategy more often than the less proficient ones. Affective strategies on the other hand seemed to be used more often by less proficient learners as indicated by the negative correlation found.

Discussion

The study is concerned with the choice and frequency of strategy use in relation to L2 proficiency. In terms of the amount and frequency of strategy use, both proficient and less proficient learners seem to be equally active strategy users in that both groups fell in the medium (mean use of 3.4) strategy user category according to Oxford's (1989) classification. However, the existence of a pattern in the types of strategies used suggests that L2 proficiency level seems to affect the use of some strategies to a certain extent.

Two categories/types of strategies that show significant differences in their choice and frequency of use by proficient and less proficient learners are cognitive and affective strategies (F [1,82] 18.9023 p < .0000 and 40.2802 p < .0000 respectively). Proficient learners reported using more cognitive strategies more often than less proficient learners. The cognitive strategies used at a high level of frequency by the proficient learners include using English for listening (COG15 Watching TV or movies in English), reading (COG16. Read for pleasure in English) and writing (COG17 Write notes, etc. in English). These strategies require the active use of English for functional use in naturalistic situations. In addition, these strategies (for example, reading for pleasure, writing notes, etc. in English) are voluntary in nature. This suggests that the proficient learners must possess adequate mastery of the English language as well as the motivation and confidence to choose to use the language in informal, out-of-class contexts. Green and Oxford's (1995) factor analysis of the strategies on the SILL used by the ESL learners in their study found that the use of strategies for "active, naturalistic" use of English was one of the factors most strongly related to proficiency level. In the present study, cognitive strategies were the only strategies that had a substantial or moderate positive correlation with proficiency (.4328 p = .000) which further suggests that L2 proficiency affects the use of some strategies to a certain extent.

Affective strategies, on the other hand, seem to be used more often by less proficient learners than proficient learners (mean strategy use of 3.40 to 2.52). Out of the six affective strategies listed, four are used significantly more often by most of the less proficient learners. These strategies involve managing fears and anxiety in learning English such as by trying to relax, giving self-reward and noticing tension and nervousness. This suggest that the less proficient learners are aware of their fear and anxiety in learning English and thus use affective strategies to help manage their feelings and overcome their fears in learning English. Gardner and MacIntyre's model of SLA (1993) includes language anxiety as one of the most important affective factors that affect learners' participation and performance in second language learning. Language anxiety tends to have a negative effect on course grades, and motivation. Language anxiety leads to low motivation, which in turn leads to less participation in the learning. In this study, affective strategies seem to have a substantial negative correlation (- .5739 p = .000) with proficiency level.

In addition to the strategies discussed above, the pattern of strategy use related to L2 proficiency level can be seen in the use of the other types of strategies which are used more often by learners in the different proficiency groups. For example, the metacognitive strategies used more often by the proficient learners include self-correcting (MET 31) and seeking opportunities to read in English (MET36), the social strategy of asking questions in English (AFF 49), and the compensation strategies such as guessing (COM24) and using circumlocution (COM29). These strategies represent the characteristics of the "good language learner" who, among other things, is willing to take risks (by guessing) and participates actively (asking questions in English, seeking opportunities for more practice using the language).

Less proficient learners, on the other hand, use other strategies (beside affective strategies) that seem to reflect further their anxiety in language learning. For example, the metacognitive strategies used more often by less proficient learners include thinking about their progress in language learning (MET38). Other strategies used more often by less proficient learners include the compensation strategy of using gestures when stuck for words (COM25) and asking their interlocutors to slow down or repeat (SOC45). These strategies are not low level strategies in themselves but in comparison with the other strategies used by the proficient learners, these strategies seem less challenging in that they do not require as much linguistic knowledge as do the ones used more often by the proficient learners. It may be concluded that some strategies that might be useful in supporting learning, such as the affective strategies, do not actually contribute directly to learning. On the other hand, cognitive strategies which were found to be positively correlated with proficiency level, may be contributing directly to the learning process (see Rubin, 1981).

The pattern of strategy use in relation to L2 proficiency level discussed above brings us to the crucial question of why a particular strategy is used. Do the learners use the particular strategies because they have the ability (proficiency) to do so or because the use of those strategies will develop their proficiency? In other words, which one comes first: proficiency or strategy use? This question can be addressed by looking at the two strategy types that are moderately correlated with L2 proficiency, namely cognitive strategies and affective strategies. Cognitive strategies are rule-related practice strategies (Oxford, 1989). It may be argued that the proficient learners used more of these strategies at a high frequency level because they have a better mastery of English to be able to speak, read and write in it compared to the less proficient learners. However, it is also possible that by using these strategies more often, the proficient learners can improve their knowledge and skills of English. The possibility of such a bi-directional effect of proficiency on language strategy use has also been noted in similar studies (Green and Oxford, 1995). The bi-directional effect of proficiency on language use is not as clear in the use of affective strategies by less proficient learners. For instance, the lack of knowledge and skills in English is likely the cause of language anxiety among less proficient learners. Therefore, affective strategies for emotions management are used more often by less proficient learners. In this case, the low level of proficiency is more likely to account for the choice and frequency of strategies used rather than the use of those strategies leading to low level of proficiency. Nevertheless, it may be argued that if the less proficient learners emphasise the use of those strategies without attempting the other more functional and practical strategies as found in the cognitive strategies type, they might not have the opportunity and practice to improve their proficiency in English. As correlation does not imply a cause and effect relationship, the findings of the study regarding strategy use and proficiency level is more appropriate for determining the characteristics of the learners in terms of strategy use. There needs to be a further investigation in this area, using other appropriate research methods in order to determine the strength of the bi-directionality, if any. Consequently, the strategies identified as contributing directly to the second language learning should be tested before they can be taught to the learners through strategy instruction or training.

Although there is no significant difference in the frequency of use of the other four types of strategies, namely, memory, compensation, metacognitive and social strategies, the pattern discussed earlier is quite consistent. For instance, proficient learners choose metacognitive strategies that are related to cognitive strategies in that the plans about language learning are carried out in naturalistic situations. It is recommended that future studies adopt a contextual approach to determine the effectiveness of the strategies used.

Implications and suggestions

This present study serves as a starting point in the investigation of language learning strategies in relation to language proficiency. The data analysis reveals a pattern in the choice and frequency of strategies used by learners in different proficiency groups. The findings have some implications for the learning and teaching of English, especially in a non-native context. Firstly, it is an awareness-raising experience for both the teacher and the learner. The language teacher can be made more aware of the language learning strategies that their learners use. This awareness will help the teachers to better understand their learners' learning behaviour and needs, and will, thus, be useful as a guideline for planning ways to help the students improve their language learning. In participating in this kind of study, the learners can be made more aware of the many different types of strategies which they can use for language learning. The fact that some strategies listed in the SILL were not used by the learners indicates that there needs to be a further investigation of strategy types and use.

Secondly, the possibility of the bi-directional effect of strategy use and proficiency level suggests that some strategies are more effective and useful for improving second language proficiency. For example, the cognitive strategies, which were used significantly more often by the more proficient learners, have been noted as strategies that are directly related to learning as they involve the use of the target language to process language input. Hence, such strategies may be more effective for language learning and these can be taught to the learners.

The third implication of this study concerns the planning and implementation of strategy training. Having identified the strategies that might have a bi-directional effect on language learning, the questions of how, when and why such strategies can be taught must be considered. Based on the findings of the present study, the answer to how a type of strategies can be taught will have to consider the proficiency level of the learners involved. Before the less proficient learners can be trained to use cognitive strategies, they need, first, to be prepared with linguistic knowledge and, secondly, to overcome their language anxiety. A more supportive environment in which the teacher is more sensitive to the needs and the problems of the less proficient learners might facilitate and motivate language learning.

While learners self-rate their frequency of strategy use, the strategies are restricted to the fifty strategies listed on the SILL. There is a need for further investigation of other possible strategies, apart from the ones listed, that the learners might have used. The next stage in this kind of study should look into the possible correlation between teaching and learning strategies. This is possible by investigating the teaching strategies of the language teachers themselves.

References

Bedell, D. and Oxford, R. L. 1996. Cross-cultural comparisons of language learning strategies in the People's Republic of China and other countries. *Language learning strategies around the world: Cross-cultural perspectives.* (Technical report no. 13) ed. by R.L. Oxford (pp. 47-60) Honolulu: University of Hawaii Second Language Teaching and Curriculum Center.

Bialystok, E. 1979. The role of conscious strategies in second language proficiency. *The Canadian Modern Language Review* 35. 372-394.

Bialystok, E. 1981. The role of conscious strategies in second language proficiency. *Modern Language Journal* 65(1). 24-35.

Dreyer, C. and Oxford, R. L. 1996. Learning strategies and other predictors of ESL proficiency among Afrikaan speakers in South Africa. *Language learning strategies around the world: Cross cultural perspectives.* (Technical Report no. 13) ed. by Rebecca L. Oxford (pp. 61-74). Honolulu: University of Hawaii Second Language Teaching and Curriculum Center.

Ellis, R. 1994. *The study of second language acquisition.* New York: Oxford University Press.

Gardner, R. C. and MacIntyre, P. D. 1992. A student's contribution to second language learning. Part II: Cognitive strategies. *Language Teaching* 25(4). 211-220.

Gardner, R. C. and MacIntyre, P. D. 1993. A student's contribution to second language learning. Part II: Affective variables. *Language Teaching* 26. 1-11.

Green, J. M. and Oxford, R. L. 1995. A closer look at learning strategy, L2 proficiency, and gender. *TESOL Quarterly* 29(2). 261-297.

Larsen-Freeman, D. 1991. Second language acquisition research: Staking out the territory. *TESOL Quarterly* 25. 315-350.

Larsen-Freeman, D. and Long, M. 1991. *An introduction to second language acquisition research.* London: Longman.

LoCastro, V. 1994. Learning strategies and learning environments. *TESOL Quarterly* 28(2). 409-414.

MacIntyre, P. D. 1994. Toward a social psychological model of strategy use. *Foreign Language Annals* 27(2). 185-194.

Mangubhai, F. 1991. The processing behaviours of adult second language learners and their relationship to second language proficiency. *Applied Linguistics* 12(3). 268-298. Oxford University Press.

Mullins, P. 1992. *Successful English language learning strategies of students enrolled in the Faculty of Arts, Chulalongkorn University, Bangkok, Thailand.* Unpublished doctoral dissertation, United States International University, San Diego, CA.

Naiman, N., Frohlich, M., Stern, H. and Todesco, A. 1978. The good language learner *Research in Education Series No. 7.* Toronto: Ontario Institute for Studies in Education.

Nation, R. and McLaughlin, B. 1986. Novice and experts: An information-processing approach to the "good language learner" problem. *Applied Psycholinguistics* 7. 41-56.

O'Malley, J. M. 1987. The effects of training in the use of learning strategies on acquiring English as a second language. *Learner strategies in language learning* ed. by Anita L. Wenden and Joan Rubin 134-144. New Jersey: Prentice-Hall.

O'Malley, J. M., Chamot, A. U., Stewner-Manzanares, G., Russo, R. P. and Kupper, L. 1985. Learning strategy applications with students of English as a second language. *TESOL Quarterly* 19. 557-584.

Oxford, R. L. 1990. *Language learning strategies: What every teacher should know.* New York: Newbury House/Harper & Row.

Oxford, R. L. and Burry-Stock, J. A. 1995. Assessing the use of language learning strategies worldwide with the ESL/EFL version of the Strategy Inventory for Language Learning. *System* 23(2). 153-175.

Oxford, R. L. and Nyikos, M. 1989. Variables affecting choice of language learning strategies by university students. *Modern Language Journal* 73. 291-300.

Pickard, N. 1996. Out-of-class language learning strategies. *ELT Journal* 50(2). 150-158 Oxford University Press.

Politzer, R. L. and McGroarty, M. 1985. An exploratory study of learning behaviors and their relationship to gains in linguistic and communicative competence. *TESOL Quarterly* 19. 103-123.

Rosna Awang Hashim and Sharifah Azizah Syed Sahil 1994. Examining learners' language learning strategies. *RELC Journal* 25(2). 1-20.

Rubin, J. 1975. What the "good language learner" can teach us. *TESOL Quarterly* 9. 41-51.

Rubin, J. 1981. Study of cognitive processes in second language learning. *Applied Linguistics* 11(2). 118-131.

Stern, H. H. 1975. What can we learn from the good language learner? *The Canadian Modern Language Review* 34. 304-318.

Stern, H. H. 1983. *Fundamental concepts in language teaching.* Oxford: Oxford University Press.

Tinkham, T. 1989. Rote-learning, attitudes, and abilities: A comparison of Japanese and American students. *TESOL Quarterly* 23(4) 695-698.

Vann, R. and Abraham, R. 1990. Strategies of unsuccessful language learners. *TESOL Quarterly* 24(2). 177-198.

Wen, Q. and Johnson, K. 1997. L2 learner variables and English achievement: A study of tertiary level English majors in China. *Applied Linguistics* 18(1). 27-48.

Appendix 1: List of SILL items and their summary

MEMORY
1. Associate new material with already known
2. Use new English words in sentence
3. Connect word sound with image or picture
4. Connect word to mental picture or situation
5. Use rhymes to remember new words
6. Use flashcards to remember new words
7. Physically act out new words
8. Review English lessons often
9. Connect words and location

COGNITIVE
10. Say or write new words several times
11. Try to talk like native English speakers
12. Practice sounds of English
13. Use unknown words in different ways
14. Start conversation in English
15. Watch TV or movies in English
16. Read for pleasure in English
17. Write notes, etc. in English
18. Skim then read carefully
19. Seek L1 words similar to L2 words
20. Try to find patterns
21. Find meanings by dividing words into parts
22. Try not to translate word for word
23. Make summaries of information

COMPENSATION
24. Guess meaning of unfamiliar words
25. Use gestures when stuck for a word
26. Make up new words when stuck
27. Read without looking up new words
28. Try to guess what other people will say
29. Use circumlocutions or synonyms

METACOGNITIVE
30. Seek many ways to use English
31. Notice my mistakes/try to do better
32. Pay attention when someone else is speaking

33. Try to find out about language learning
34. Plan schedule to have enough time
35. Look for people to talk to in English
36. Seek opportunities to read in English
37. Have clear goals for improving skills
38. Think about my progress in learning

AFFECTIVE

39. Try to relax when I feel afraid
40. Encourage self to speak when afraid
41. Give self-reward for doing well
42. Notice when I'm tense or nervous
43. Record feelings in learning diary
44. Talk to someone about feeling

SOCIAL

45. Ask other person to slow down or repeat
46. Ask to be corrected when talking
47. Practice English with other students
48. Ask for help from English speakers
49. Ask questions in English
50. Try to develop cultural understanding

(from Green and Oxford, 1995, pp. 280-281)

LEARNER AUTONOMY AND THE LANGUAGE TEACHER

David Crabbe

Introduction

In the past 10 years, in many countries, there have been extraordinary changes in the way education is resourced, in the demand for accountability, in the potential modes of delivering education using electronic media. Whether we like it or not, the old orders are being challenged. New roles are being imposed on educational institutions and, with them, new role relationships between the stakeholders, not only between students and teachers, but also between teachers and education managers.

There are frequent references to these changes in a wide range of contemporary publications. Dennett (1997) refers to them in a passing analogy between body/mind dualism and the running of Oxford University:

> It used to be that the dons were in charge, and the bursars and other bureaucrats, right up to the vice chancellor, acted under their guidance and at their behest. Nowadays, the dons, like their counterparts on American university faculties, are more clearly in the role of employees hired by a central administration.

The same change at university level was recently emphasised by the retiring vice chancellor (or Chief Executive Officer) at my own university, in parrying a criticism made by an emeritus professor,

> I am surprised that anyone still believes that the community of scholars and scientists can just be left to 'organise themselves to do teaching and research'. This belief was prevalent in

Oxford and Cambridge until recently, but even they are now moving to accept that they have not been doing it well.[1]

Students are also being asked in many places to pay more for their education on the grounds that the state cannot afford full subsidy and that students should be expected to contribute to their education and in that way, become more committed to succeeding in it. The uncomfortable corollary of that is that the student as a customer can be given the right by society to sue when the service provided is not considered to be what it claims to be. This opinion was put forward in the *New Zealand Education Review* by two lawyers specialising in dispute resolution:

> Tertiary institutions need to be aware that they are selling an education product, with students as their customers...

> The Education Act gives institutes academic freedom subject to the demands of accountability. Therefore where accountability at law exists, academic freedom will end.

> (Connor and Price, 1997)

And in case you think change is always completely new, the incoming vice-chancellor at my university, in a newspaper article even more recently published, was reported as saying

> The dynamics of universities have changed. Students now regard themselves as paying customers. It's not a bad thing, either, because it creates a much healthier environment.

The article goes on:

> Things have come almost full circle, he says, because that's how universities began in Italy. Students hired and fired the tutors who taught them, and Cambridge started when some

---

[1] Prof. L. Holborow – letter to *The Evening Post* newspaper. Wellington, 1 April 1998.

Oxford scholars were dissatisfied and wanted to hire some new teachers.[2]

At the same time as these changes to educational management and learner-teacher relationships have been taking place, the movement to promote learner autonomy has grown, even though the movement's roots are in a time when there was a different approach to public policy. It is not my purpose here to explore the relationships between these public policy changes and the growing interest in autonomy, and whether they are, or can be, in harmony or in opposition. Political thought from both sides of centre can take any one concept and make it their own and any one concept can probably absorb flavours from both sides. It is useful, however, to reflect on the underlying meanings of the notion of 'learner autonomy' in the 1990s. There is no denying that it has a strong link to Western liberal strands of thought that emphasise the rights of individual learners to determine their future and to develop the capacity to do so. Holec, in his pioneering monograph on learner autonomy, quotes Janne:

> [adult education] ... becomes an instrument for arousing an increasing sense of awareness and liberation in man, and, in some cases, an instrument for changing the environment itself. From the idea of man 'product of his society' one moves to the idea of man 'producer of his society'. (cited in Holec, 1981: 1)

Since Holec's publication the concept of autonomy has been embraced by a larger number of mainstream teachers. As the concept has become more popular, it has, I believe, become less political and used more to refer to the effectiveness and efficiency of learning. This is a cognitive rather than a social focus, although the development and exercise of autonomy inevitably involves a social domain – even if only the social domain of the classroom. It is also a more utilitarian viewpoint – it is the learning of language efficiently (in resources) and effectively (in results) that is the end, not the balance of power between students and teachers and the social implications of that balance. As such it is, perhaps, in tune with our times.

---

[2] Article in *The Dominion* newspaper. Wellington, 18 April 1998

In the first part of this paper, I want to locate the notion of autonomy within a schema of language learning and teaching in order to highlight its relevance to language teachers from whatever background. Then I would like to review the possibilities for action that language teachers can take to foster autonomy. I shall conclude with the theme of the Seminar and attempt to summarise the insights for the language teacher.

What is the relevance of learner autonomy to the English language teacher?

What does it mean to say that a language learner is autonomous?

Table 1 attempts to represent personal learning on the one hand and the social organisation designed to encourage personal learning on the other. The left-hand side lists the ingredients that might be considered important for individual acquisition to take place. The right hand side lists some of the features of a teacher-organised class – a social arrangement for individual learning.

Table 1: Individual Learning and Social organisation for learning

Second Language learning	
Factors in knowledge and skill acquisition by individuals	**Features of social organisation for learning**
Cognitive in nature Universal Personal	Social in nature Culturally specific Public
Motivation Beliefs and Attitudes Goal clarity and commitment Language use (input and interaction) Language rehearsal Language awareness	Social events, usually a teacher-managed class in an institutional setting Role relationships Discourse about language Discourse about organisation of group

244

Second Language learning	
Problem-solving about language	activity
Language learning awareness	Discourse about learning
Problem-solving about language	
learning	Public accreditation outcome

It is generally agreed that a learner who can self-manage the components of language learning, such as those listed on the left hand side, would be considered autonomous. That is to say, autonomy is a cognitive phenomenon, a mental ability to manage the learning in a way that implicit or explicit goals are achieved. One would expect the ability to be found in varying degrees in individuals, but not confined to any particular group of societies – a universal capacity. Holec (1981) usefully distinguishes autonomy – this capacity to manage one's own learning, from self-direction to actually using the capacity in any one situation. The capacity is likely to be exercised in different ways in different contexts. The point is that, whatever the context, an autonomous learner is able to benefit optimally from the opportunities for language learning, whether those opportunities are within a class or in the wider community.

Is autonomy a good thing?

Is autonomy defined in this way a good thing? Taking the utilitarian viewpoint, does it lead to more effective and more efficient learning? We can attempt to answer this question deductively and inductively. We can deduce that a learner who can effectively solve the learning problem of achieving new knowledge and new skill, using perhaps a generic knowledge or awareness of language and language learning, is likely to be effective and efficient. This argument in propositional form would be something like this:

1. Language learning is a problem of getting from proficiency state A to proficiency state B, assuming the resources and opportunities available are sufficient for that purpose.

2. A learner who is a 'good' problem-solver in language learning will be able to solve this problem and any associated problems that arise on the way.
3. Finding the solution to the problem will lead to appropriate action and effective learning.

Of course, there is a lack of meaning in this argument – a good problem solver will solve a problem well. We would have to say what we meant by good problem-solver and what counts as sufficient resources but with that in mind, it seems a reasonable deduction. It is possible of course to see solutions and not apply them. Sherlock Holme's brother, Mycroft, comes to mind as a fictional character who has what we would now call brilliant lateral thinking, but lacks the energy of his famous brother to apply the solutions. This is to do with motivation rather than problem solving. (See Dickinson, 1995 for a review of motivation in relation to autonomy.)

An inductive answer is harder to find at this stage. There are studies showing effective autonomous learning (Dam and Legenhausen, 1996 for example). As in all studies that attempt to ascribe progress to specific variables, it is a challenge to take account of all the intervening contextual variables and many more case studies are needed. Pending further positive inductive work, both by researchers and practising teachers, I propose that we accept at this stage the deduction that, all other things being equal, a learner who has good problem solving skills in language and language learning and good motivation, is likely to have higher success than others.

What is the role of an institutional language curriculum for learner autonomy?

For most of those who work in the area of learner autonomy, the answer to this question is quite simple: an institutional language curriculum should incorporate autonomy as a specific goal. This is not to say that every learner must achieve autonomy. This is an unrealistic outcome and, besides, it is somewhat contradictory to impose autonomy as a mode of learning. Rather the goal is a process goal – a goal to set up processes and conditions in the classroom that are expected to foster autonomy.

Accepting the fostering of autonomy as a process goal in language curricula means that teachers aim not only at providing conditions for language acquisition but also at demonstrating how to manage the acquisition. For the learners who are already autonomous, the goal will be recognised and easily responded to. For the learners who have limited degrees of autonomy, the classroom is the place where they develop greater control over the learning process by engaging in it consciously. The next section of this paper will explore *how* autonomy might be addressed as a curricular goal. There are, however, three points that need to be dealt with first.

The first is that autonomy is a mental capacity, and independent of whether we are learning as a member of a group. This point was made by Holec (1981) and many others after him but it needs repeating. Autonomy does not mean studying alone. Learners, whether autonomous or not, attend classes for a number of reasons. If they are in compulsory education, they have little choice. If they wish to be accredited in some way, again they have little choice. But apart from those pragmatic reasons, it is reasonable to believe that participating in classroom learning can *enhance* an autonomous learner's efficiency. This is a point made some time ago by Breen and Candlin (1980:100):

> A communicative methodology is characterised by making this negotiative role – this learning how to learn – a public as well as a private undertaking...

> Quite simply, in order to learn to communicate ... the learner must be encouraged to communicate – to communicate about the learning process, and to communicate about the changing object of learning on the basis of accepting that 'learning how to learn' is a problem shared, and solved, by other learners.

Classrooms, then, can provide, shared problem-solving about learning, social encouragement, feedback, controlled input, practice opportunity, all of which are grist to an autonomous language learner's mill.

The second point is that there are likely to be significant cultural differences in classrooms as social events and in their capacity to work towards autonomy as a goal. As social events, classrooms have a life of their own, a life that draws breath from cultural patterns of behaviour and role relationships that define and are defined by classroom discourse and the society at large. Some evidence of this is offered in a paper by Coleman (1996), in which he likened an Indonesian tertiary English classroom to a shadow puppet (*wayang kulit*) performance. He observed that there was a ritualistic aspect to classrooms and moreover that the real learning took place outside the classroom. (See also Huang and van Naerrsen 1987 for this last point). The question of cultural dimension of encouraging autonomy will be dealt with separately in the next section.

The third point is that individual learners participating in any one event are likely to be working independently at the same time as cooperatively. Dick Allwright noted this some years ago in relation to autonomy (1988).

> Each lesson is a different lesson for each learner, and, as teachers know very well already, different learners take away quite different things from the same lesson...

> ... if learners somehow individualise what they learn, it may be interesting to look into what happens in classrooms that makes such idiosyncrasy of 'uptake' possible. Perhaps the learners are already 'autonomously individualising' their classroom experiences.

Thus, however structured a class is and however much the teacher is controlling the sequence of activity, within the activities themselves, learners will be operating as independent minds that are following their own agenda of learning. The result of this will not always be enlightenment but we need to allow individual agendas to emerge and be satisfied, as Allwright's article suggests.

What is the cultural dimension of encouraging autonomy?

Table 1 separates autonomy as a mental capacity to manage one's language learning, a human universal that anyone can potentially develop, from the social context of organised learning – the classroom.

The variation between classrooms is to be found in the way in which learner autonomy is recognised and given scope, and in the way in which the teacher's functions are performed. In some classrooms autonomy is explicitly valued and teachers make an attempt to foster it. In other classrooms, it is not referred to at all – the performance of the classroom event takes no account of it. Culture will play a part in this although the diversity within any one culture needs to be remembered: the mix of individuals is an equally important factor.

Whatever the means of achieving it, the importance of learner management of learning is, I suggest, on the list of new insights for language teachers. Teachers need to help learners to harness this universal potential to problem-solve and develop it for language learning. They will no doubt do this in ways appropriate to the culture of which they are members.

I have heard a fear expressed that autonomy is a challenge to the traditional role of the teacher in many cultures. It is worth spending a minute or two discussing that particular issue. (See Little 1998 for a parallel treatment of this issue). Firstly, it needs to be repeated that autonomy does not mean working alone – it is rather an internal ability to manage one's learning processes. There is no reason to see this leading to a tendency to challenge teachers in institutional contexts. Autonomous learners are members of a society and are just as likely to respect conventions of cooperation as anyone else. The respect for teachers is based on factors such as superior knowledge, social status, and age. This respect is unlikely to change because a capacity to problem-solve is fostered; one would think rather that it would be enhanced.

Secondly, the traditional functions of a teacher should remain fairly intact. These traditional teacher functions include modelling, presenting (information about the language), explaining, encouraging, setting standards, assessing performance against those standards. The added element is that the teacher is not only doing this in relation to language but also in relation to language learning with a view to making novice learners more expert.

I suspect that the social constraints in fostering autonomy are in fact found everywhere and are more to do with the willingness of human members of a social group to change. The sort of changes required is addressed in the next section.

How do curricula foster autonomy?

How is autonomy as a process goal to be worked towards? The core of autonomy, as I have defined it, is good problem solving about language and language learning. In a recent interview with a learner about his learning I attempted to address the nature of the problem by asking him to describe his difficulties in using English. The learner, whom we can call Vittorio, is an Italian student who is studying at university level in New Zealand. His English proficiency is functional for his purposes: he can speak fluently on a range of ideas with non-intrusive hesitation. His writing is well organised and with a good degree of accuracy. However, he does experience some difficulties in using English.

Vittorio's first concern was that he wanted to improve his listening and the goal that he identified was to increase his vocabulary:

> First of all I think that for me it's ... to improve my capacity to understand what the others say...

> ... and also my vocabulary because yesterday we spoke about my vocabulary and I know that my vocabulary my passive vocabulary is bigger than the active one ... and probably I think that the second step is to improve my grammar ... my grammar in particular because there are a lot of difference between Italian and English about the use of some verbal form for example and so ... and then to be able to write good English ... but I think it's a consequence of the grammar. If the grammar is good and then I will be able to write a better English ... I hope [laugh]

Already here Vittorio is linking a communication problem (listening and writing) to a learning goal (vocabulary and grammar).

On being prompted to talk about the listening problem further, he made the following observation:

> Talking with friends I think it's very difficult to talk with the person of my ages ... and I think it's difficult because ... use not common or slang word they new words

He contrasted this difficulty in talking to young New Zealanders with talking with people who have lived abroad and are used to talking with people from different language backgrounds. He suggested also that he is more used to an American accent. He then commented on listening to lectures:

> Sometimes I have difficulties with some teacher because they speak very fast ... very ( ) or else for example I am attending a ( ) and class is very crowded we are I think to a hundred or more and it's not easy to understand my teacher...

He pointed out a difference between an Italian and a New Zealand university system:

> The teacher in university or at secondary school they speak slow because we need to take notes and so I think that also for a foreign student is easier ... in fact the different here with with your school system is that in Italy we have a lot of lectures and we take a lot of notes and the teacher try to makes summaries of all the books and make some examples and you have to write (it) sometimes is enough if you study what is [in] the book ( ) but also is sometime is enough the notes.

These short extracts show to what extent the learner had analysed a communication difficulty. There are external factors in the problem – the quality of what has to be listened to and the different role of lectures in the two university systems – and internal factors, vocabulary knowledge and familiarity with accent.

How does this representation lead to a solution? The learner himself suggested talking with someone and using a cassette tape...

> first of all with text and then maybe without text or trying to write what I listen ... what I heard and then look at the real text ... compare my words and so probably but I think that the fastest way is to speak with someone with a person very kind person ... and with a person that er could repeat you what I said er and er and try to [laughs] understand what you are trying to say.

It seems to me that this is a learner who is able to represent the problem in a fairly sophisticated way and is able to suggest action that could be taken to solve the problem. The question for teachers is: how do we encourage and support learners in this reflection on communication experience and in taking appropriate action when there are a class full of them? From my experience of working with English teachers, this is not the sort of question they typically ask. There is an obvious reason for this: the pressing need for a teacher is to manage the classroom event as a recognisably professional occasion and it is probably fair to say that reflection by individuals about learning is still on the fringe of mainstream professional activity.

There is no universal, technical answer to the question of how to foster thinking about the language learning process. Classrooms are essentially dynamic, social places in which role relationships are derived from the cultural background and from the interplay of the personalities of the individuals involved. A teacher trying to achieve a process goal of encouraging autonomy needs to have a set of possibilities to explore in relation to his or her own teaching and to adopt and adapt for their own teaching context.

Table 2 lists a set of such possibilities, taking the same factors in individual language acquisition as are listed in Table 1. Examples of standards of process that teachers should be providing in order to foster autonomy are listed in the second column and in the third, associated teacher knowledge and skill. The standards represent targets for teachers to achieve in their classrooms but, again, it should be emphasised that these are only starting points for reflection in any one context.

Table 2: Possibilities for teacher action to foster problem solving about learning by individuals in classes

Acquisition factor in which learners can develop self-management.	Examples of process standards for teachers to reach	Associated teacher knowledge or skill
Motivation Attitudes and beliefs	Provide opportunity for learners to explore purposes for learning language and to create scenarios of use related to that purpose Make explicit links between learning tasks and communication goals	Knowledge of strategies to deal with specific difficulties Ability to analyse communication in pedagogically useful ways
Goal clarity and commitment	Regular clarification with learners of goals at all levels (curricular, personal, long term and short term) Regular exploration of diversity of means to reach those goals	Ability to analyse communication in pedagogically useful ways Ability to set realistic and productive goals. Knowledge of diversity of strategies to achieve those goals.
Language use and language rehearsal	Elicit ways of getting practice in using the language outside the classroom. Explore and model ways of rehearsing language use related to need.	Knowledge of resources available in the community to use the language. Knowledge of range of strategies to rehearse language.

Acquisition factor in which learners can develop self-management.	Examples of process standards for teachers to reach	Associated teacher knowledge or skill
Language awareness and problem-solving about language	Provide open-ended problems in relation to language and language use for learners to solve cooperatively or independently.	Ability to describe language pedagogically, knowledge of language in use.
Language learning awareness and problem-solving about language learning	Provide for regular discourse about the learning of language. Provide opportunity for learners to explore difficulties experienced in actual communication and to reflect on strategies to deal with them Provide cooperative work on problem solving about how to reach given goals in language learning.	Ability to represent the complexity of language learning problems, to explore possible causes of problems. Knowledge of a range of strategies to apply to particular problems

Effecting change

Such a table does not offer a solution to the problem of fostering autonomy. The neat structure of a table belies the raggedness of real life in the classroom. The table offers a set of parameters and suggestions for conceptualising and managing a complex task involving groups of individuals and change.

Underlying change are the beliefs of those making and affected by the change. Underlying the commitment to the goal of fostering language learning are teacher beliefs about language learning. Underlying the way in which the goal is worked towards are teacher perceptions of the class as an event and their role in that event. Given a particular perception, how does learning how to learn by individuals fit into it? Peter Voller identifies the danger of simply replacing one knowledge transmitted by a teacher with another knowledge:

> ... instead of transmitting a body of facts about the target language, the teacher's role is now to transmit a body of facts about the most efficient ways (according to expert linguists) to learn a language.

> Voller
> (1997:107)

This is clearly not at all useful. Voller suggests that teachers who are committed to autonomy tend not to adopt a transmission mode but a more 'interpretative' mode of learning in which teachers play a facilitative, resource person role. The fact that some teachers prefer a transmission mode compounds the problem. If we are looking at fostering autonomy in learners who are not autonomous, there is little point in setting an autonomy fostering goal for teachers who are themselves operating with beliefs that do not facilitate autonomy in learners. Teachers with positive attitudes and constructive beliefs about the language and language learning, together with a framework of classroom activity that is focussed on individuals achieving their goals provide a healthy starting point for fostering autonomy.

Insights for teachers: a summary

In summary, I would like to return to the theme of this Seminar and list the insights for teaching that arise from work on learner autonomy. Some – or perhaps all – of these insights are not new – insights occur and re-occur over the history of humankind. Insights always need to be renewed in any one culture and period. Until they are embodied in our collective actions and discourse about actions, they remain just flashes of light with no lasting illumination.

1. Autonomy is a universal mental capacity to solve the problem of language learning and is relevant to all cultural

contexts. Successful learners will already work autonomously; others might be helped to do the same.

2. Fostering autonomy should therefore be adopted as a process goal in all classroom contexts because it is fundamental to successful education

3. Teacher commitment to the process goal of fostering autonomy is a necessary first step followed by an active approach to seeking ways of meeting that goal in relation to individuals working as members of a group. The adoption of a goal leads to strategies to achieve it.

4. Possible teacher actions to foster autonomy are listed below. These actions are integrated into established classroom functions of providing encouragement, feedback, appropriate input.

   - to emphasise goal-directed behaviour over unanalysed, customary behaviour. Clarity of goals, which are set either externally or by negotiation, is the first step for learners and teachers alike in reflecting on the strategic means to achieve those goals. Very often the immediate goals are related to experience in actual communication, as the interview with Vittorio shows. One could expect that the more personal the goal, the more commitment there would be to it. Offering learners opportunities to self-evaluate their own progress in using the language and thereby set up new goals.

   - to consider the classroom event and what goals it can achieve as an event (as opposed to the goals that learners can achieve).

   - to consider the outside opportunities for classroom practice and the role of the classroom in relation to those outside opportunities.

   - to become good language learning problem-solvers themselves, including being able to represent problems in a sophisticated way and to identify appropriate solutions to them. Teachers should be experts not only in language but also in individual language learning.

References

Allwright, D. 1988. Autonomy and individualisation in whole-class instruction. *Individualisation and Autonomy in Language Learning* ed. by Brookes and Grundy. ELT Documents 131. Modern English Publications/British Council.

Breen, M. & Candlin, C. 1980. The essentials of a communicative curriculum. *Applied Linguistics* 1:2. 89-112

Coleman, H. 1996. Shadow puppets and language lessons: interpreting classroom behaviour in its cultural context. *Society and the Language Classroom* ed. by H. Coleman. Cambridge: Cambridge University Press.

Connor, D. and S. Price, 1997. A product not a privilege. *The New Zealand Education Review*, Feb 5, 1997.

Dam, L. & Legenhausen, L. 1996. The acquisition of vocabulary in an autonomous learning environment – the first months of beginning English. *Taking Control: Autonomy in Language Learning.* ed. by R. Pemberton, E. Li, W. Or & H. Pierson. Hong Kong: Hong Kong University Press.

Dennet, D. 1997. *Kinds of Minds: Towards an Understanding of Consciousness.* London: Phoenix.

Dickinson, L. 1995. Autonomy and motivation: a literature review. *System.* 23(2).

Holec, H. 1981. *Autonomy and Foreign Language Learning.* Oxford: Pergamon Press

Huang, X. & van Naerssen, M. 1987. Learning strategies for oral communication. *Applied Linguistics.* 8(3), 287-307

Little, D. 1998. The construct of autonomy. *Language Learner Autonomy: Defining the Field and Effecting Change.* ed. by S. Cotterall and D.Crabbe. Bochum University Press (forthcoming).

Voller, P. 1997. Does the teacher have a role in autonomous language learning? *Autonomy and Independence in Language Learning.* ed. by P. Benson and P. Voller. London: Longman.

TEXT AND TASK: AUTHENTICITY IN LANGUAGE LEARNING

Andrea H Peñaflorida

Introduction

"As unto the cord the bow is, so unto man is woman – useless each without the other." This famous quotation penned by one of America's great poets, Henry Wadsworth Longfellow, reveals the inseverability of the chain that binds man and woman together which, if I may say, is also true with words, objects, things and other entities.

I consider *text* and *task* in language learning as two words that collocate, that is, words that often occur together. This pair of words is inseparable just like *man* and *woman* in Longfellow's Hiawatha.

What is *text* without *task?* Similarly, what is *task* without *text?* My paper introduces *text* and *task* as necessary components of language learning with *authenticity* as the pivotal point upon which both components revolve.

Text, Task and Authenticity: Realities in Language Learning

Simply put, text provides the point of departure for the task. In this framework, *task* is seen as having only two components, *input* and *output.*

Input is any language material, verbal or non-verbal, which a learner receives from which he can learn, whereas *output* is any language material, verbal or non-verbal, which the learner produces. From the task evolves the strategies for communicative language teaching such as problem solving, negotiation of meaning, information transfer, or information gap activities.

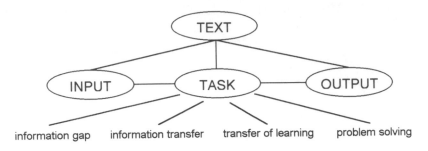

Later, I will expand this framework into one where other task components are added.

This next framework shows that for *text* and *task* to lend reality to language learning, there must be *authenticity*.

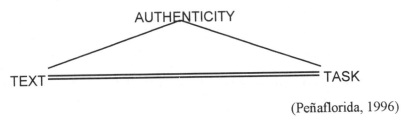

(Peñaflorida, 1996)

Authenticity is a basic ELT term which refers to the degree to which language teaching materials have the qualities of natural speech or writing. Nunan (1989) describes two types of authenticity: (1) authenticity of the texts which are used as the basis of materials development, and (2) authenticity of the tasks which learners perform in connection with the texts. Texts and tasks are authentic if they were designed for purposes other than language teaching.

Texts which are taken from newspapers, magazines, brochures, leaflets, radio broadcasts, news broadcasts are called authentic materials. These were originally used in real situations and were not designed for use in language teaching. But why do we now use these authentic materials or texts in the classroom? Principally because learners should be exposed to language in real use.

Wajnryb (1988) defines a sound English text as:

- one which is grammatical
- one which is textually cohesive, i.e., it should not be a random collection of unrelated sentences, but a tightly-linked, textually connected semantic whole
- a text which makes sense in terms of the real world, i.e., a meaningful text.

The last definition refers to text authenticity.

On the other hand, authentic tasks are responses to written or spoken materials which would be natural to real participants in a real situation. For example, learners in a classroom who read a text such as an advertisement telling them that a sale is going on at National Book Store decide among themselves which books to purchase then go to the store to buy the book. The task is authentic. As Taschner (1996) says, "authentic texts require authentic tasks." (p. 5). Students need to know that what they do in the language classroom applies to their language needs outside the classroom. It is therefore imperative to encourage them to apply their developing language skills to the world beyond the classroom.

Authenticity of text in order to use real-life material is just as important as the authenticity of response of the student to the text.

> Whenever we read, listen to, or watch 'texts' in real life, we have reactions or responses to them; we may be interested, indifferent, excited, or disgusted. The response may be intellectually emotional, or aesthetic, it may involve cognitive or affective factors – but it is there. Nobody ever reads or listens to anything without some reaction to it, and it is this reaction which we feel is the essence of communication, for this is what the text has truly communicated. (Morrow and Schocker, 1987. p. 251)

When using authentic materials in teaching grammar for example, the teacher must proceed from text to language rather than from language to text. Nunan (1989) believes that the teacher can present learners with more realistic texts if he/she derives language exercises from the texts rather than decide on the grammatical points and then construct texts to exemplify these.

Morrow and Schocker (1987, p. 248) state that "A key element in communicative language learning lies not only on the emphasis of giving students practice in both the forms of language and the processes of using them but also in using texts which encourage more student talk than teacher talk." The text is the initial teacher's input which generates exercises intended to illustrate real-life language use in the classroom and its use is "based on the conviction that practising doing things with language will be more fruitful than practicing language forms out of context." (p. 248)

This means that students learn by doing which subsumes language forms, and not learning language forms in a vacuum. Grammar is not learned as grammar per se; rather, as part of a whole. This then necessitates the choice of text. Morrow and Schocker say that:

> The rationale for the choice of texts has to do not with uses to which it can be put, but with the subject matter involved. The hope is that by choosing texts that are inherently interesting, the teacher will motivate students to involve themselves in work in a particular topic area, and that the foreign language will be naturally used as the medium in which this work or task will be carried out. (p. 219)

Going back to our first framework, we can see that there are only two components of tasks given: input and output. When expanded, the framework will look like this:

The majority of learning tasks have just three components: goals, input, activities (or output) and these three in turn imply certain roles as we see at the right side of the framework.

Goals are the general intentions behind any given task. Input and output or activities have been explained earlier on. Teacher role is that of facilitator, learner role is that of active participant in the activities, and setting refers to classroom organization such as the use of pair work, group work, and so on.

At this point, let me show you an example of *text* and *task* specified in real-world terms. Look carefully at this questionnaire. Make sure you understand all the questions in it.

Look carefully at this questionnaire, then do the following:

1. Read it individually
2. Pair off with your seatmate, then interview the other using this questionnaire
3. Change roles.

WHAT ARE YOUR STUDY HABITS?

A short questionnaire to discover your study habits.

1. How much time do you spend in studying your lessons?
   (a) 30 minutes a day
   (b) one hour a day
   (c) two or more hours a day

2. While studying do you
   (a) turn on the TV
   (b) listen to music
   (c) eat junk food

3. Before you go to bed do you
   (a) fix your things for school
   (b) review your lessons
   (c) call up your friend

---

4. If you have trouble doing your homework-assignment, do you
   (a) call up a friend and/or classmate
   (b) ask a member of the family to help you
   (c) just stop doing it

5. If you wake up in the middle of the night and suddenly remember the appropriate word or sentence to include in your writing assignment, do you
   (a) get up and write it
   (b) simply ignore it
   (c) go back to sleep

6. Do other people complain about your study habits?
   (a) never
   (b) frequently
   (c) sometimes

7. When an examination is scheduled, do you
   (a) study well ahead of time?
   (b) study the day/night before the exam?
   (c) study immediately before the exam? (an hour or so)

8. Do you review for your exam
   (a) alone
   (b) with a classmate
   (c) with a group of classmates

Adapted from Maley and Moulding
(1981) in Nunan, 1989, p. 11

In the example just given, the questionnaire is the *text,* and the *task* is the response to the questionnaire.

Applying Nunan's framework on task components, we see a complete task as follows:

Goal: Exchanging personal information
Input: Questionnaire on study habits

Activity: 1. Reading questionnaire
                   2. Asking and answering questions about study habits
Teacher role: Monitor and facilitator
Learner role: Conversational partner
Setting: Classroom/pair work

The approach is task-based because the learners are *actively involved,* and *they make decisions* that they need to take in the classrooms.

The beauty of using this type of material is that it makes teaching less painful and learning less boring, more interactive and communicative.

With this approach gone is the overloaded, overworked, overtaxed, overburdened teacher and, hopefully, gone too is the underpaid, underestimated, underrated, and undervalued teacher.

It is not enough to come up with interesting texts. It is equally important to know how to design tasks out of texts.

Let us look at another model which gives the principles of task design. This model or framework was given by Nunan (1996) in his talk at the International Conference of Teachers held in Penang, Malaysia.

THE LANGUAGE   THE PEDAGOGICAL PROCEDURES

authenticity of data   task dependency
transparency of form and function   from reproductive to creative
                                    from declarative to procedural
                                    self-evaluative

TASK

THE LEARNING PROCESS   THE LEARNERS

transparency of goals   space to contribute
explicit strategies   active roles
experimental/learning through doing opportunities to make choices
inductive learning

Tasks can be used as building blocks in developing lessons and units of work. In the design of tasks, four major principles, as shown in the model may be considered:

1. The language

   The language should contain authenticity of data and transparency of form and function. A learner cannot develop facility or skill without a knowledge of grammar. For example, the choice of tenses shows one's attitude to research if, as Nunan says, research is still alive today. Now the question is: Why is a great deal of grammar teaching unsuccessful? This question is for language teachers to answer. In terms of form and function, it is neither one or the other but both. Language instruction is more effective if there is harmony between form and function.

2. The pedagogical procedures

   Four principles are listed under pedagogical procedures: the principle of task dependency, from reproductive to creative, from declarative to procedural, and self-evaluative. In my examples, I will emphasize the principle of *task dependency*.

3. The learning process

   The features of the learning process are: transparency of goals, explicit strategies, experiential/learning through doing, and inductive learning. Learning can be more effective if every strategy can be made more effective.

4. The learners

   Here, Nunan gives three features: (1) space to contribute, (2) active roles and (3) opportunities to make choices. Learners have to be given space to contribute in various ways – ways of bringing their own experience, their own background to the learning process. Learners should be provided with active and creative roles. Learners should be given the opportunity to make choices.

Let us now go back to the principle of task dependency which is all about building sequences or dependency of tasks. For instance, if there are three or more tasks based on one or two texts, the first task – Task 1 – is the easiest. Task 2 will depend on Task 1 for its completion, Task 3 on Task 2, Task 4 on Task 3, and so on down the line.

Here is an example of a lesson on building sequences or task dependency:

Lesson:	Analyzing an Authentic Medical Case
Title of Case:	The Case of a 14-Year Old Comatose Boy
Text:	

A 14-year-old lay comatose on a respirator after suffering severe carbon monoxide poisoning in a household fire. His mother and father requested that the device be turned off so that he could be allowed to die and his organs used for transplantation. The hospital burn specialist called in a doctor who determined that the child showed brain-wave activity. "It wasn't yet possible to declare his brain dead," recalls the physician ethicist. "It would have undermined the basic principles of medical ethics, which is respect for the person who is still a living, breathing human being." A few days later, after a neurologist confirmed the boy's irreversible condition, the respirator was turned off but by that time it was too late to use his organs.

Task 1. Group Work: Analyzing a Case

    (a) Form groups of four and study the case of the comatose boy.
    (b) Brainstorm about the case following the steps in the sample case analysis you have just studied.
    (c) Analyze the case according to the steps you have just brainstormed about.

Task 2. Writing a Case Analysis Report

    Write a complete report of the case you analyzed in Task 1.

Task 3. Giving an Oral Report

> Give a 10-minute oral report of "The Case of a 14-Year Old
> Comatose Boy."

Nunan's principles of task design have been applied in the preceding
exercise as follows:

- The language used is authentic.
- The learning process especially for grammar is a process of
  discovery (inductive).
- The pedagogical procedure shows there is task dependency.
- The learners contribute ideas, perform active roles and
  enjoy the opportunity to make choices in the use of
  language.

Conclusion

Text and *task* authenticity in language learning offers varied
possibilities for classroom activities. Students learn to use "real world"
language. The language used is natural and spontaneous, not artificial and
contrived. The classroom is always a hub-hub of interesting activities with
the students at the center. One of the benefits of using authentic materials is
that the teacher who teaches in far-flung places where there is a dearth of
instructional materials can design her own lessons using authentic sources.

Based on the discussion of *text* and *task,* allow me to summarize their
characteristics to serve as guidelines for teachers who want to design their
own tasks.

Characteristics of Texts

1. Texts explore tasks; texts illustrate task types.
2. Texts serve as models of language in action.
3. Texts are used for presentation purposes.
4. Texts communicate and therefore elicit reaction to them.
5. Texts involve students in terms of their responses.
6. Authentic texts make students realize that the foreign
   language has a reality outside the classroom.

7. Texts empower students to become creative agents of change and transformation.

Characteristics of Tasks

1. Tasks are text based.
2. Tasks are student-centered.
3. Tasks are interactive.
4. Tasks are learner-centered.
5. Tasks are a step towards learning autonomy.
6. Tasks "animate" texts.

Implications for Classroom Practice

A teacher can maximize the students' chances of success on a given task by presenting it in the most helpful conditions. Students perform most effectively when given texts and tasks that are within their schema, and this can be done most successfully through the use of authentic materials.

Students, on the other hand, when given texts and tasks that are interesting and challenging and are within their understanding, will surely enjoy coming to their English language classes because they are given the choice to learn by doing which is a step towards autonomy in language learning.

We have just seen how two terminological distinctions in language learning as well as materials design, text and task, integrate and merge just like man and woman in Longfellow's Hiawatha. I started my paper with Longfellow's lines from Hiawatha as "As unto the cord bow is, so unto man is woman." This time, I would like to end with this paraphrase: "As unto the text, the task is, so unto authenticity is real life language learning."

References

Maley, A. & Moulding, S. 1981. *Learning to listen*. Cambridge: Cambridge University Press.

Morrow, Keith & Schocker, Marita. 1987. Using texts in a communicative approach. *ELT Journal* 41(4) 248-251.

Nunan, David. 1987. *Designing tasks for the communicative classroom.* Cambridge: Cambridge University Press.

Nunan, David. 1996. *Principles of task design.* Lecture given at the International Conference for English Teachers in Penang, Malaysia, May 1996.

Peñaflorida, Andrea H., Fortez, E. & Gonzalez A. 1991. *English for specific purposes: medicine.* Manila: De La Salle University Press.

Taschner, Jeff. 1992. *Text and tasks.* Manila: Linguistic Society of the Philippines.

Wajnryb, Ruth. 1988. The dictogloss method of language teaching: a text-based, communicative approach to grammar. *English Teaching Forum* XXVI (3).

EDUCATIONAL INNOVATIONS IN THE THAI NATIONAL ENGLISH TEXTBOOKS FOR PRIMARY SCHOOLS: "ON THE SPRINGBOARD"

Chaleosri Pibulchol

On Educational Innovations

Educational innovations are here taken to mean changes made in education. Educational change is a dynamic process involving interacting variables. Starting with the classroom, changes probably occur in curriculum materials, teaching practices, and beliefs or understanding about both the curriculum and learning practice (Husen and Postlethwaite, 1994).

In the case of the Thai national textbook series "On the Springboard", changes are introduced both in learning and teaching practices. The books are written to serve the new Primary English curriculum which emphasizes the use of communication on the ground that learners are individuals with unique characteristics and interests; they are naturally curious and responsible for learning. Thus, the emphasis is on both subject matter, and the needs and interests of learners. The subject matter is geared at developing the learner's intellectual process and self-actualization. The textbook series has also targeted teachers for change. Since most English teachers in primary schools in Thailand are not English majors and know little or nothing at all about methodology, the book is designed as a teaching innovation for them. The teachers are exposed to teaching techniques which will in turn help them develop from being teacher-centred to learner-centred.

The Development of the Learners' Intellectual Process

To develop the learners' intellectual process, cognitive strategies are employed through the patterns of the P-P-P model (presentation, practice and production), and task-based activities. The content which focuses on functions of the English language demonstrates learning situations that enable learners to practice thinking, analytical and problem-solving skills, and use of the language. In every unit, the learners are made to apply thinking skills to bridge the content and the context. They discover, analyze, hypothesize and finally learn. For example in Lesson 1 (Book 2, Unit 11) the language focus of the lesson is 'Be careful! Don't...'. The instruction *Look, discuss and repeat* requires the learners to look at pictures illustrating accidents that usually occur at work (cut your finger, burn your arm) and at play (hurt your head, break your leg); then they discuss the possible language their mothers may say in such situations. By this means, the language becomes meaningful to the learners since they have experience with the language of their choosing. Also, they are free to make mistakes. To comprehend the language (vocabulary and structures), the learners have to work out the meaning of the words or hypothesize about the grammatical rules (e.g., what types of words are used with Be... and Don't...) by analyzing the language and the context illustrated. Through discussion, they have a chance to interact with both content and context and see how both influence the function of the language used.

To enable the use of language, task-based activities mostly in the form of games are demonstrated in both practice and production stages. The instructions such as *Game, Game in pairs* and *Game in groups* specify the nature of interaction the learners will be involved with. Under the mask of fun and motivating games, the learners are required to use language creatively and purposefully. Cooperative learning plays a part in their learning since most of the time they have to work in pairs or groups to reach the goal set. In each activity, a goal is specified, but the method of reaching it is not. The learners have to seek their own way, using the language being learnt, to reach the goal. Thus, they learn to manage their learning, making it systematic and efficient (Sowell, 1996). For example, in Lesson 1 (Book 2, Unit 11), the learners practice the language being presented through a game that demands team work to act out an accident in front of the class. Their friends try to guess the situation and give a warning. Competition is used to create motivation. The team with the highest score wins the game.

Various kinds of task-based activities at the production stage offer the learners opportunities to use language integrated under the instructions *Look, listen and speak; Look, read and speak; Read and write in your workbook; Listen and write in your workbook;* etc. To accomplish the tasks, the learners are made to get involved in thinking (inferring, speculating, deducting, analyzing) and problem-solving processes which serve as a means to an end. For example, in Lesson 3 (Book 4, Unit 18), the learners look at a series of pictures and rearrange them to form a story. They then compare and discuss their versions with their friends before checking the answers. Another reading task in Lesson 1 (Book 2, Unit 11) encourages the learners to read the story and identify the persons, using the information as clues. The whole process of rearranging, comparing, discussing and checking in the former activity and problem-solving in the latter involves the learners in comprehending, analyzing and applying knowledge (Sowell, 1996).

Learner's Self-actualization

Self-actualization is obviously promoted. With the emphasis on learner-centredness, the tasks and especially the project work lead towards learner autonomy and growth. They enable the individual learners to develop to their fullest potential. The goals are explicitly specified in the work assigned and the learners seek ways to complete the goal-setting. For example, in Lesson 3 (Book 4, Unit 21), the learners work in pairs, taking turn giving directions to identify the specific places on the map. Through the task, the learners have a chance to evaluate how successful they have been. Also, the project work at the end of each unit encourages the learners to develop themselves through direct experience. For example, in Project Work (Book 2, Unit 13), the first project gets the learners involved in an experiment – a Magic Balloon. They have to read the instructions and work out the result. The other project (Book 2, Unit 13) asks the learners to fill in the price list for the topic "At the Market" in their "My Picture Dictionary". The learners are made to go to the local shops and survey the prices to fulfill their work. Thus, the project gives the learners opportunity to take more responsibility for their own learning as well as make the real world a part of their learning.

In addition, the activities "Can you read?" and "How to learn" in each Revision Unit offer a supporting role to help individual learners discover their strengths and weaknesses in their own learning. For example, in Revision Unit II (Book 1), the "Can you read?" activity instructs the learners to take turns checking their ability to recognize active vocabulary learnt in the three previous units. The "How to learn" activity, on the other hand, demands the learners to work in groups. In Part I "What do you think?", the learners discuss the value of English in Thai society, especially in their local situation. Part II "Can you do it?" requires the learners to evaluate their success in learning – how much they have learnt. The process involves the learners in gathering information systematically and encourages them to express their views and learn effective learning strategies from each other. The final part "Do you know?" concentrates on sharing learning strategies among the learners.

Changing the Change-agent – the Teacher

While the curriculum demands teachers to set up a learner-centered mode of teaching (Ministry of Education, 1997), most English teachers in primary school have no background in teaching methodology, especially the communicative approach. Only a small number have a chance to participate in in-service training courses or seminars. The rest depend solely on the textbooks they use (Ministry of Education, 1994). With this realization, the textbook series 'On the Springboard' is designed to support the teachers in the country, especially the ones with little background in developing their teaching abilities, or working with class materials.

To familiarize the teachers with the methodology, the Presentation-Practice-Production model combined with an atmosphere of learner involvement is employed in each lesson. The teachers are made to realize that their roles are being changed from the knowers to the informants, the conductors and the facilitators, and that the classroom interaction is not directive as it used to be, but a more collaborative mode of interaction with the learners. For example, in lesson 2, (Book 1, Unit 3), Instruction 2 *Look, Listen and answer* instructs the teachers to elicit from the students the context and the language (in Thai) from the illustrations (the playing of shadows – a dog, an elephant, a bird, and a bear), and play the tape to model the language. Then, the teachers are asked to elicit from the students the meaning of the language focus: What's that? It's a (dog). before moving to the repetition after the tape and the expansion of the sentences. This suggests to the teachers a guideline for the presenting of a structure: 'meaning' – through a situation where the real language is used, followed by 'sound' – the pronunciation, stress and intonation of the language presented and last, 'form' – the highlighting of the language patterns by the teacher and the students. Instruction 3 *Game* demonstrates to the teachers a game-like activity with full instructions to offer them a method to deal with the practice stage in a way that allows students to use the language differently from traditional drills. The teachers see themselves as the conductors managing the activity in which students work in teams, taking turns to make a shadow for their friends to guess. Instruction 5 *Game* gives the teachers the opportunity of being the facilitators and monitors when observing the students freely use the language through a game-like activity in groups of four, guessing the animals from jigsaw pieces.

As mentioned earlier, most primary school English teachers in Thailand are not English-majors and have no confidence in using English. To encourage more use of the classroom language, a note on the language to be used during the lesson e.g. ○**Team A, ask. Team B, guess.** is given at the bottom of the page. Also, a note on grammatical rules or pronunciation of the problem sounds is provided e.g. ☆**elephant** ☆**What's that? = What's that?** Here the word 'elephant' with the mark of the stress is given since it is always wrongly pronounced.

In addition, the teachers are given a variety of activity types and modes of learning to broaden their vision of what communicative activities look like. The concept of pre-task, task, and post-task is introduced to highlight learner involvement at all times – before, during and after the activity. For example, in Exercise 2 (Book 4, Unit 24), a pre-reading activity with a set of instructions is given so that the teachers can manage the lesson in a way that involves students in sharing their experience of the game played locally, reading the text to see how it is played in a foreign country, and doing the comparison as a follow-up activity.

The teachers are also given the opportunity to evaluate their teaching. The 'How to Learn' section in the Revision Unit under the topics **'What do you think?' 'Can you do it?'** and **'Do you know?'** provides rich data of learners' problems, learning styles, attitudes and expectations. This will serve as feedback on their teaching and help them see more of what they have done and, hopefully, lead them to self-evaluated professional development.

Conclusion

To a certain extent, the textbook series 'On the Springboard' aims for a change in both teachers and students. However, for any change to take place, it has to be accepted by the teachers and the students who will realize it (Tudor, 1996). It is a matter of developing teachers and students who can live comfortably with the demands that are placed on them, especially in Thailand's English teaching-learning situation where teacher-centeredness has long been employed. It is hoped, however, if a change takes place in the role of learners, then a parallel change in the role of the teacher is inevitable.

References

Husen, T. & Postlethwaite, N. (eds.) 1994. *International encyclopædia of education*. England: Elsevier Science Ltd.

Ministry of Education. 1997. *The 1996 English Curriculum*. Bangkok: Suksaaphan.

Ministry of Education. 1996. *On the Springboard Book 1*. Bangkok: Suksaaphan.

Ministry of Education. 1996. *On the Springboard Book 2*. Bangkok: Suksaaphan.

Ministry of Education. 1996. *On the Springboard Book 3*. Bangkok: Suksaaphan.

Ministry of Education. 1996. *On the Springboard Book 4*. Bangkok: Suksaaphan.

Ministry of Education. 1994. *The Teaching-Learning Development*. Bangkok: Teaching-Learning Development Centre.

Sowell, E. V. 1996. *Curriculum: An Integrative Introduction*. New Jersey: Prentice Hall, Inc.

Tudor, Ian. 1996. *Learner-Centredness as language Education*. Cambridge: Cambridge University Press.

Section III: Computers and Language Learning

Computer-Assisted Language Learning: What Teachers Need to Know
Michael Levy

Computer-Imaginative Tools for the Design of Digital Learning Environments
Martin A. Siegel

COMPUTER-ASSISTED LANGUAGE LEARNING: WHAT TEACHERS NEED TO KNOW

Michael Levy

When it comes to technology and computers everyone seems to be for or against. People seem to be either terribly enthusiastic about the use of computers in education, or strongly against the whole idea: they do not want anything to do with computers, they prefer people to machines. These strong reactions to computers, and technology more generally, can provide a useful point of departure for thinking about CALL and what language teachers need to know. You see, to answer the question, "What do language teachers need to know?" we need to understand some of the ways in which technology impacts on us as individuals and on society as a whole. We also need to try and reach beyond all the media hype, the extreme views positive or negative, and search for understanding, and then make a calm and thoughtful assessment of what role we want the computer to play in language teaching and learning.

So I would like to begin by making some observations about our relationship with technology and to suggest some reasons why people can get so passionate about it, for or against. I will describe how the role of the computer and beliefs about how students learn, both help to determine the teacher's role in CALL. I will argue that the role of the teacher in CALL is crucial, but the whole enterprise will only be successful if the language teacher is properly prepared and supported.

Why is it that so often people seem to be for or against when it comes to technology? This idea is picked up by Sherry Turkle (1996) in her book, *Life on to Screen*, which describes the new communities and cultures established through email and the Internet. Turkle characterizes writers who comment on the societal impact of new technologies as 'utopian', 'utilitarian' or 'apocalyptic'. I will discuss the utopian and apocalyptic views now, and come back to the middle path, the utilitarian view, a little later.

Books in the 'utopian' category, and here *Being Digital* by Nicholas Negroponte (1996) is a good example, suggest that technology is to be welcomed with open arms. According to Turkle it is "a field for the flowering of participating democracy and a medium for the transformation of education" (1996: 231). Technology is going to take us to a new world that is fairer and more just, where we collaborate and share our ideas, and where an improved education is accessible to all. If one reads *Being Digital* one senses a tremendous excitement at all the positive changes that are going to occur – that will in various ways better our lives and our educational systems. These changes are presented as inevitable: catch the wave as the bold move forward, or be left behind. Of course being left behind, or being accused of not having the latest technology, is an accusation that educational institutions take very seriously in the closing years of the twentieth century, and no doubt this will continue into the twenty-first. According to Turkle, books of the utopian kind have dominated the field so far.

But not all agree that technology is set to deliver us into this wonderful new world. In direct opposition to the utopian view is the apocalyptic vision, and here the *Gutenberg Elegies* by Sven Birkerts (1994) is a good illustration. (I note that Claire Kramsch in her address at the RELC conference in 1996 recommended this book to the audience.) Writers such as Birkerts urge us to guard against "increasing social and personal fragmentation, more widespread surveillance, and loss of direct knowledge of the world" as new technologies increasingly make their presence felt in our lives, the workplace and education. Birkerts warns us about the dangers of technology.

So we have two very different views of technology being presented, one very positive, the other exactly the opposite. Why are some commentators so strongly in favour, while others are so strongly against?

Well, I am certainly not the first to claim that technology is a catalyst for change. Neil Postman refers to the kind of change that technology precipitates as ecological: one thing does not change with the introduction of technology, everything does. To bring it closer to home for a moment, if we think about the language learning curriculum, for example, the introduction of technology does not simply add a new, extra component, it has the potential to sweep through the curriculum and change it throughout. Ready access to up-to-date authentic materials via the Internet can radically alter the content of the curriculum, as can access and interaction with native speakers of the target language.

It is the potential for change – positive or negative – that engages the hopes and fears of writers on technology and society. The introduction of new technologies in society, in education, in CALL is about change. The strong positions taken by commentators reflecting on the effects of technology on society also show that we are dealing with two kinds of potential: one positive, one negative. With the introduction of technology there is the potential for gain, as there is the potential for loss. (Technology itself is quite neutral. What matters are the human decision-making systems, collectively and individually, that must understand the nature of technology and direct the course of its introduction wisely.)

Let me digress for a moment to talk a little more about technology and its capacity to instigate change. I would like to make two key points here.

Firstly – though it may not appear this way with the relatively recent introduction of new computing technologies – humans have always had technological tools, and they have always faced new challenges as a result of the inevitable changes that they bring forth. But the predominant function of these technological tools has changed over time. In earlier days such tools were essential for our survival. We needed them to make shelter, to catch food and to protect ourselves from wild animals. In later times technological tools have been used to amplify our limited physical capacities: telescopes or microscopes so we could see further, earth moving machines, or machines for transportation so we could travel faster over land, sea or air. But of most relevance today are the developments in communication technologies that enable us to communicate through speech and the written word to those distant from us, and the capacity to create virtual worlds that simulate real world environments.

In considering our relationship to technology, then, we have moved – at least in the developed world – from using technology primarily to ensure our survival to using technology to extend our sensory capabilities and to communicate with the world beyond where we are physically located.

Let me give you a very simple example. I have a colleague at the University of Queensland, Michael Harrington, whose office is two doors down the corridor from my own. Quite regularly when I need to communicate with him, I am faced with a dilemma: should I email my message so as not to interrupt his work – he may not be in his office anyway – or should I walk ten metres, knock on his door and talk to him face to face. As a matter of fact I consciously try to do both, even though occasionally I may be interrupting him – because I believe something fundamentally human is lost when the contact is only ever through email. Email is in fact being encouraged in language teaching at the moment – for lots of good reasons such as increasing student participation in language classrooms around the globe. However, if we as language teachers were to push this idea too far, then we would be doing our students a great disservice. Also interaction over the Internet is currently and predominantly text-based – you have to type. We should not forget that the majority of students are learning a language so that they may confidently speak to others: face to face; in the same physical space; and in the same time. (You never used to have to add all those extra qualifications!)

My second point is this: when you use a technology to complete a task, three interconnected agencies undergo change. Technological tools not only change and shape the world, they change and shape us too, and more often than not the nature of the task as well. Technology mediates our relationship with the world and instigates change on many levels.

This point is exemplified nicely by considering the relationship between technology and writing. Any kind of writing has always intrinsically involved technology, a point well made and developed in Christina Haas's (1996) book, *The Materiality of Literacy*. The inevitable impact of technology on writing – and reading for that matter – and the ways in which it shapes writing are, surprisingly, often not accounted for. Writing has always required a tool to make the mark and a surface on which to store it. Markers have evolved from the finger, the stick, the quill, and chalk to the keyboard. The storage medium has moved from sand through to stone, clay, paper, to the floppy disk and beyond. The technological tools one employs to write inevitably and fundamentally affect the process and the product of writing. Should it be surprising that we view the word processor as liberating when we consider the limitations of the previous technologies we had available to us for writing: imagine writing an essay with a hammer, chisel and stone? It would be almost inconceivable because of the technology then available. Writing an essay requires a writing technology that is up to the job; we are now seeing the same principle occurring with hypertext, where the conventional book technology is not up to the job. Nonetheless, books as a technology are still important, especially for text that is in the form of a narrative. The point is that all technologies, including the more recent ones, enable us to see, imagine and create the world in different ways.

So, from the discussion so far then, what do language teachers need to know?

Firstly, the introduction of technology instigates change: there is always a potential for loss, as there is a potential for gain.

Secondly, technology has the potential to isolate the individual – the student from the teacher perhaps, or from other students. The cliché that we are able to talk to someone the other side of the world, but not to our neighbour, contains a vital message for the humanistic language teacher who is keen on technology. Whatever the ultimate use of technology, human-human contact must remain central. We know that students can accumulate a great deal of knowledge about language, yet still not be able to use it confidently with others in real-time interactions.

Thirdly, technological tools are inseparably involved in many of the things that we do, such as reading and writing. We cannot read and write without technology of some kind. Technology therefore is not simply an optional adjunct, something we simply remove or avoid. So it might be wise to try to understand its impact and effects.

In the discussion so far, we can see that understanding the role of technology in society (and in education) is more complex than it would at first seem. This situation is made more difficult at a time where a fascination with technology holds many in its grasp, where overly extravagant claims are made about its capabilities, and where so many institutional leaders believe that the introduction of new technologies is somehow automatically going to improve our educational systems in the future. These are dangerous ideas. Technology will not take us where we want to go without timely and appropriate intervention on our part. There are significant dangers as well as benefits. To chart a path forward we need to appreciate clearly what computers or technology can and cannot do and, in parallel, we need to establish an appropriate role for the language teacher and provide the proper support.

The role of the computer and the teacher is a question I explored at length in my book (1997). In particular I make the distinction between two principal roles for the computer: the computer tutor, which evaluates, and the computer tool, which does not.

This distinction is illustrated well in the typical word processor. Here we have a program that is fundamentally a tool (which does not evaluate), but which is accompanied by a number of tutor-like programs (that do evaluate) – the grammar checker, for example. In observing non-native speakers using a grammar checker to assist them in their work, it is depressing to see the advice they are given and their response to it. On many occasions, on the advice of the checker, the student alters something that is correct to something that is not – or the checker does not pick up an important error that the student has made. My own work shows that only about 20% of the rules in grammar checkers work reliably with non-native speakers of English. Of course, grammar checkers have been designed for native speakers, and that is the context in which they work best – though native speakers would, I think, question their value also. (At least the native speaker user has a more complete knowledge of the language available to fall back on when the program's advice is presented.)

But of course, the point I want to make here is that we have to be especially careful when computers are used to evaluate learner input, that is when they are employed as tutors rather than tools. Their feedback has to be timely and accurate. In the role of tutor, the teacher, and the student have to 'trust' the computer to do its job properly. Control is delegated to the computer to manage the learning, and as such students will rely on its judgements. The student's default setting, so to speak, is that the computer knows what it is doing and that the feedback is correct. If the computer cannot be relied upon, it should probably not be allowed this relationship with the learner.

Yet at the same time, computer tutors offer the promise of greatly extending and enriching the language learning opportunities available to students, in the self-access centre, or in the student's own home. They can therefore liberate the student – for certain aspects of language learning (vocabulary, grammar, listening comprehension, rehearsal and practice and so on) – so students are not limited to learning a language solely with a teacher, in the classroom.

Computer tools, on the other hand, are fundamentally different. They do not evaluate; instead they provide a way of managing information, or communicating with others. In CALL, computer tools include email, conferencing programs (written and spoken), different kinds of dictionaries, concordancing programs, language archives (spoken as well as written material), and, of course, word-processing programs. Here the computer is a kind of enabling device, providing a means of completing a particular task more efficiently, more effectively, or more conveniently. Unlike the tutor, in the role of the tool the computer does not set the task: this has to be done by the learner, individually, or collaboratively with the teacher or with other learners.

These two roles for the computer imply very different roles for the teacher. The teacher may have a minimal role if the CALL materials have been conceived as a self-contained, tutorial package; alternatively, the teacher may play a pivotal role in creating suitable tasks for computer tools.

In the tutorial tradition, there is a separateness between CALL and non-CALL work – separate in terms of placing computers in a language laboratory for example, or in setting aside a specific parcel of work that the students complete at the computer without the teacher present. Here the use of the computer to 'free' the teacher from the 'more tiresome labours' of language teaching arises, a point first made by Skinner in 1954 and repeated many times since by many writers on CALL. A division of labour is implicit here, with the computer or technology looking after certain aspects of language learning, vocabulary extension for example, while the human teacher caters for other aspects, perhaps those that necessitate human interaction and involvement.

In contrast, the computer tool role is likely to place greater demands on the teacher in task setting and learner training. For instance, for the effective use of email, Warschauer (1995) suggests the language teacher needs to:

- choose the appropriate software
- learn how to use the email system confidently
- train students
- organize access to computers
- prepare handouts, including basic easy-to-read instructions
- organize assistance for students in the early stages of use
- prepare suitable task-based learning projects

- monitor progress, and provide guidance on an on-going basis

Though extra assistance may be available, usually all of these tasks will fall to the language teacher. For computing tools, such as the email, considerable effort has to be put into creating suitable language learning tasks, and in creating a suitable working environment within which the tools can be used effectively.

Thus, to bring the strands of the discussion together, we have a technology – a rather unpredictable beast – that can extend and enrich our student's language learning experience if used wisely, but which can also distract or mislead if we are not keenly aware of its limitations also. In thinking about the role of the computer in CALL – in the tutor and the tool roles – we have seen there are strong implications for and demands on the language teacher. But beyond that, how the computer is designed, or how the computer tool is used, will depend upon the language teachers' beliefs about how students learn. By way of example, I would like to look at two rather different conceptions of learning, and see how they might affect both the role of the computer and the role of the teacher in language learning.

The role of the computer and the teacher will depend very much on your conception of how students learn. In contemporary CALL, a broad division may be made between learning approaches that focus on the individual learner, and those that emphasize social factors.

These two positions are well represented by the work of Piaget (1980) and Vygotsky (1978). Piaget has already exerted a strong influence on theory and practice in education and software design, and the indications are that Vygotsky and his followers are currently exerting a comparable influence. Piaget and Vygotsky represent fundamental positions on teaching as well as learning and are most helpful in distinguishing key differences in perspective, particularly in the ways in which the roles of the teacher and the computer are perceived. Further they are both regarded as constructivist, and as this orientation currently represents the dominant approach in educational multimedia design, their views are of special interest.

Both Piaget and Vygotsky are concerned with how the individual learner learns and constructs knowledge. They are both seen as constructivist because of their emphasis on the ways in which the learner constructs his or her own understanding and makes sense of the surrounding environment. However, beyond this area of agreement, Piaget and Vygotsky differ considerably in how they see a learner's cognitive mechanisms working.

Piaget, generally regarded as the founder of constructivism, typically sees the learner as a lone, inventive scientist trying to make sense of the world. He stresses the fact the learner is both mentally and physically active in adapting to the complexities of the world. His conception of the learner is highly individualistic and pays little attention to social processes.

According to Piaget, people grow through play and constructive activity by alternately changing themselves and the world around them. Where computers have potential in this context is in extending our ability to transform and manipulate the world through simulation. We can learn and practice on our own in a simulated world before having to deal with an unpredictable real-world environment. A well-known implementation of this concept is seen in the work of Seymour Papert, who was once a student of Piaget.

Papert developed a microworld called *Mathland* which was designed in such a way that certain kinds of mathematical thinking could be facilitated (Papert, 1982). Papert describes the microworld as "a 'place' ... where certain kinds of ... thinking could hatch and grow with particular ease" and "a 'growing place' for a specific species of powerful ideas or intellectual structures" (Papert, 1982: 125).

The microworld concept has also been explored in the field of language learning, in CALL and in Intelligent CALL, and a number of programs have been created. In a recent interpretation of the microworld idea, Hamburger (1995) describes a second language tutoring system called FLUENT (Foreign Language Understanding Engendered by Naturalistic Techniques). One graphical presentation of a microworld in FLUENT is called Kitchen World. Here the learner manipulates a human figure with a moveable hand which is employed to manipulate objects in the kitchen. Activities require learners to produce words, phrases, and sentences to achieve simple goals, and the system responds appropriately at each stage. The microworld idea is also evident in virtual worlds created in cyberspace, where users, and potentially language learners, can engage in exploring and making sense of a simulated environment.

Beyond the microworld concept in particular, most Intelligent CALL systems (ICALL) involve a single human learner and a computer tutor. Typically, these systems feature a student model to guide the sequencing and manner of the material presented, and utilize a parser to enable natural language to be processed. They contrast with traditional CALL programs which tend to avoid dealing with student input and evaluation beyond the word level.

In contrast, Vygotsky suggests that such a view of learning is inadequate, and, as Bruner says, that social transaction, not solo performance, is the fundamental vehicle of education. Vygotsky and his followers emphasize the social factors that influence learning. Vygotsky did not consider that learning arose out of acting on and adapting to some impersonal world, as did Piaget, but rather that it resulted from engagement with others.

In CALL, an appeal to Vygotsky's work has been made to support: cooperative or collaborative learning; teachers working with students on purposeful activity; learning in social groups; and a communicative, culturally oriented conception of language learning. Of course, numerous other projects use a collaborative approach or cooperative learning techniques, or encourage learning in a social context without making explicit reference to Vygotsky.

A learning environment that embodies many of these ideas is the goal-oriented framework described by Barson and Debski. They describe a Global Learning Environment (GLEn) which is fundamentally collaborative in nature and "models the system of access to resources and the necessary links between users of the system, thus providing a mental construct and a plan of action" (Barson & Debski, 1996: 62). Learning is defined as "managed action", and the motivation derives from project goals and activities negotiated between students, or students and the teacher.

As far as CALL is concerned, a Vygotskian or sociocultural view of learning has been given a boost by recent advances in networking technology. Now collaboration is not limited to the classroom and the same physical space, but may be extended to include collaboration at a distance. In essence, collaborative work involving computers may occur in at least three different ways, each of which involves social processes:

1. students may collaborate and interact by working together at a computer;
2. students may interact through the machine by networking, conferencing or using electronic mail, for example; or
3. the computer may act as a partner in some way in an ICALL program.

As with the tutor–tool framework described earlier, these two conceptions of learning imply very different roles for the language teacher. Within the Piagetian view, the student is seen to be working alone. The teacher's role is to provide 'rich learning environments' within which learners may make discoveries for themselves. The teacher's role within the Piagetian conception of learning lies firmly in the background.

On the other hand, within the Vygotskian view, the teacher is an active, communicative participant in the learning process. The teacher acts as a support to help the student until the time comes when he or she is able to operate independently. As Bruner (1985) puts it, the teacher functions as "a vicarious form of consciousness". From a Vygotskian perspective, Debski (1997: 48) describes the teacher as a "facilitator, an inseminator of ideas, and a force maintaining the proper level of motivation of students"; and, again, for Barson and Debski (1996: 50), the role of the teacher is to "trigger and support student enterprise as it manifests itself, often in unexpected ways, what they describe as the contingency principle)." In combination, these descriptions of the teacher's role see the teacher as an involved, adaptive individual guiding and motivating student-directed work.

In this discussion of CALL, then, when thinking about the role of the computer, or our beliefs about how language is learnt, we keep coming back to the critical role of the language teacher. It is the teacher who creates meaningful tasks – perhaps collaboratively with learners – so that the computer resources are used to best effect. It is the language teacher who sets up collaborative learning projects that ensure that time on the Internet is not wasted. And it is the language teacher who has the responsibility to ensure that the proper balance is maintained between time spent on the computer – in collaborative projects or computer-mediated tasks – and time spent interacting face to face in the traditional way.

For this to happen, the teacher needs support, and a knowledge base for dealing with computers and technology effectively. Let us see how language teachers stand in this regard.

To help make my case, I will draw upon the results of a CALL Survey I conducted in 1991/2. 213 questionnaires were distributed and 104 (48.8%) usable responses were returned. The questionnaire was sent to 23 different countries and 'key practitioners' in CALL from 18 countries replied. The key practitioners were chosen on the basis of having written programs or published in the field of CALL. The vast majority of respondents (i.e. CALL authors) were practising language teachers (97.1%).

One of the goals of the CALL Survey was to try to establish the key factors for success in CALL. Of the four factors predicted to influence success in CALL, the teacher was found to be the most important – followed by software, management and hardware factors in that order.

Teacher-related factors were the most important in determining the success of CALL materials development. From the literature, Farrington (1989) and Sussex (1991) assert that language teachers must be involved in CALL if it is to flourish in the future. It is language teachers who exert ultimate control over what materials are chosen and subsequently used by students in the classroom. Even if the CALL materials are designed to be standalone, as with a computer tutor perhaps, in the long term students are only likely to make use of the materials if encouraged to do so by their teacher. Moreover, given that few would argue that a computer can look after all of a language learner's needs, the teacher is going to continue to be involved in some way or another. On the other hand, if the computer is used as a tool, the teacher is intimately involved in setting tasks and in guiding students in the optimal use of the computer in their work.

Of the many factors affecting success in CALL as far as the teacher is concerned, time for staff education and materials development was the factor most often recorded. Powerful software authoring tools – easy to use – and a clear framework or paradigm for development were also recurring responses in a number of related questions.

The degree of support that CALL authors gain from their institutions also plays a significant part in determining the success of CALL materials development projects. Here we see time allocation sitting in the top spot again; followed by provision of the appropriate facilities and the level of interest of key personnel. The time factor was again highlighted in looking at what CALL practitioners perceived to be the blocks to successful development. Where more detail was given, release time for staff education and materials development purposes were the most frequently cited.

Though the materials-writing role of the language teacher in CALL has been advocated in the CALL literature for many years – as it has elsewhere – institutions have been slow to formally acknowledge this role by allocating the time such tasks deserve. Time allocation is especially critical for CALL materials writing because authors have to become familiar with the computer and the authoring tool before materials writing can commence; this contrasts strongly with materials prepared using pen and paper, which can proceed immediately. But with language teachers becoming increasingly sensitive to the specific needs of their students and the learning context, it is imperative that the teacher be given time to write language learning materials on and for the computer.

Another point that emerged strongly from the CALL Survey was the need for institutional decision-makers – as well as language teachers – to be convinced of the value of CALL. Only then will the necessary support be forthcoming, especially in terms of staff release time for educational and materials development purposes. Unfortunately, at the moment, when the institutional power brokers support the use of technology in learning, it tends to be for the wrong reasons: to save money on teachers, or to provide a less costly educational service. What we need management to understand is why CALL is valid for the right reasons: that the computer is not a replacement for the teacher, but an additional learning resource that can vastly enrich and extend language learning opportunities. A clear message needs to be sent from language teachers to ensure that the importance of the teacher's role in CALL is acknowledged.

So often, I find, after language teachers have attended a CALL workshop full of enthusiasm and newly acquired skills, that they return to their home institution only to find there is little support or interest: often expressed in terms of poor access to resources or no time allowance for developing skills or materials.

So often institutions seem to believe that the act of simply purchasing a room full of the latest computers is enough – the beginning and the end of educational innovation when it comes to technology. Computers are visible and can proudly be shown to visitors, parents, etc. whereas teacher time, expressed in the form of a computer-literate teaching profession and well-designed learning tasks and materials, cannot.

Of the teacher-related factors that were considered to contribute most to the successful development of CALL, the three most significant factors were found to be the teacher's general level of confidence and competence with computers, the teacher's considered opinion on the validity of CALL, and the teacher's ability to understand what the computer can and cannot do. As for skills, clearly being a good teacher is the most important: you need to be a good teacher without a computer to be a good teacher with one.

And so to teacher education. At the time of the CALL Survey, most teachers were self-taught, or taught informally by colleagues. The number of courses was low. The situation is steadily improving, I believe, with the number of formal CALL courses growing. More recently, interchange via email and the Internet has expanded opportunities for interaction and exchange of ideas and materials among teachers. An excellent example here is the TeleNex project from Hong Kong described in the *ELT Journal* in October 1996. TeleNex stands for Teachers of English Language Education Nexus and provides a computer-based teacher support network with a teaching resources database. Such teacher networks have the potential to be enormously beneficial. But, even so, I still believe that many language teachers are without easy access to the help they need, especially non-technical help, for example on CALL methodology. And when help is available often language teachers do not have the time to make use of it.

In the CALL Survey, I asked key practitioners for comment on the progress of CALL thus far. These comments, though gathered some years ago still, I believe, have contemporary significance. More importantly, for today, I think they help point toward what needs to be done to give CALL the best possible chance of success in the future.

The areas that need to be addressed are: time allocation, technical support, teacher education, long term planning and bridge building.

Time for staff education and materials development is crucial. With rapid technological innovation and change in education generally, and in language teaching and learning in particular, language teachers must be given the proper support to learn and prepare materials for student use. Institutions that simply install new technology expecting it to be used effectively by students are seriously misguided – they will also waste a lot of money. Provision must be made to educate staff and then to allow them to create learning tasks and materials to meet the needs of their students. Obviously, technical support needs to be made available also. Teacher education needs to occur, not only at the more obvious technical level in learning how to operate an authoring tool or the Internet, but also at higher levels in conceptualising language learning with the computer. Teachers need to develop a good understanding of the relationship between technology and society, and within that education, and how views of learning might impact on the role of the teacher. In this regard, longer term planning can help combat the waste inherent in the technology cycle where computers are endlessly being replaced or updated with the latest model. 3-year or 5-year plans can be very helpful here. Finally, we need to continue to build bridges between those who work in CALL, so that we may avoid unnecessary duplication, and make the most of insights and developments that are made.

At the beginning of this paper, I mentioned there was a middle path – what Sherry Turkle describes as the utilitarian option, that is utilizing technology and computers to produce the greatest benefit for the greatest number of people. An example of a book along these lines is *Digital Literacy* by Paul Gilster (1997) which takes a balanced and pragmatic view that I believe is most helpful. We need to reach beyond the hype and the extravagant claims on the one hand and the prophets of doom on the other, to reflect upon what technology really has to offer us for improving the language learning experience of our students. The final outcome will depend on such factors as the role of the computer, beliefs about language learning, the learning context and the goals of the learners themselves.

Those recommending CALL to language teachers, while proclaiming the benefits of the new technological options, often overlook the implications for language teachers, especially when the computer is cast in the role of tool rather than tutor. Computer tools, worthy as they are, do require time, effort and commitment on the part of language teachers. For CALL materials development to be successful and to make significant in-roads into mainstream language teaching practice, substantial support must be given to the language teacher, who must be acknowledged as a key contributing factor that will undoubtedly influence the success of CALL in the future.

References

Barson, J. & Debski, R. 1996. Calling Back CALL: Technology in the Service of Foreign Language Learning Based on Creativity, Contingency, and Goal-Oriented Activity. *Telecollaboration in Foreign Language Learning*. ed. by M. Warschauer (ed.), Hawaii: Second Language Teaching & Curriculum Centre.

Birkerts, S. 1994. *Gutenberg Elegies: The fate of reading in an electronic age*. London: Faber & Faber.

Bruner, J. S. 1985. Vygotsky: a historical and conceptual perspective. *Culture, communication and cognition: Vygotskian perspectives.* ed. by Wertsch, J. V., Cambridge: Cambridge University Press. 1-32.

Debski, R. Gassin, J. & Smith, M. 1997. *Language Learning Through Social Computing*. Occasional Papers Number 16. Melbourne: ALAA and the Horwood Language Centre.

Farrington, B. 1989. AI: 'Grandeur' or 'Servitude'?. *Computer-Assisted Language Learning: Program structure and principles* ed. by K. Cameron. Oxford: Intellect Books. 67-80

Gilster, P. 1997. *Digital Literacy*. New York: John Wiley & Sons.

Haas, C. 1996. *Writing technology: studies on the materiality of literacy*. Mahwah, NJ: Lawrence Erlbaum.

Hamburger, H. 1995. Tutorial tools for language learning by two-medium dialogue. *Intelligent Language Tutors: Theory Shaping Technology*. ed. by V.M. Holland, J.D. Kaplan & M.R. Sands, Mahwah, NJ: Lawrence Erlbaum.

Levy, M. 1997. *CALL: Context and Conceptualization*. Oxford: Clarendon Press.

Negroponte, N. 1996. *Being Digital*. Rydalmere, NSW: Hodder & Stoughton.

Papert, S. 1980. *Mindstorms*. London: Harvester Press.

Piaget, J. 1980. The psychogenesis of knowledge and its epistemological significance. *Language and Learning*. ed. by Piattelli-Palmarini, M., Cambridge, MA: Harvard University Press.

Postman, N. 1992. *Technopoly*. New York: Vintage Books.

Sengupta, S. & Nicholson, S. 1996. On-line and ongoing: teacher development through TeleTeach. *ELT Journal* 50:4. 290-302.

Skinner, B. F. 1954. The science of learning and the art of teaching. *Harvard Educational Review* 24. 86-97.

Sussex, R. D. 1991. Author languages, authoring systems and their relation to the changing focus of Computer-Aided Language Learning. *System* 19:1. 15-27.

Taylor, R. 1980. (ed.) *The Computer in the School: Tutor, Tool, Tutee*. New York: Teacher's College Press.

Turkle, S. 1996. *Life on to Screen*. London: Weidenfeld & Nicolson.

Vygotsky, L. S. 1978. *Mind in Society*. Cambridge, Mass: Harvard University Press.

Warschauer, M. 1995. *Email for English Teaching*. Alexandria, VA: TESOL Inc.

COMPUTER-IMAGINATIVE TOOLS FOR THE DESIGN OF DIGITAL LEARNING ENVIRONMENTS

Martin A. Siegel

Introduction

Today, most Web interactions involve "pointing and clicking" as users navigate through hypermedia text and graphics. While this can be an interesting experience in an ever-expanding, ever-changing environment, we question its ultimate value as a learning tool for the delivery of quality distance education. What are needed are new tools that create powerful instructional interactions that lead to deep conceptual insights as well as the development of sophisticated problem-solving skills. A new paradigm is required to change the focus from content-centered to authentic, cooperative, problem-centered learning. We call this paradigm the "Digital Learning Environment."

A Paradigm Shift

A central assumption of didactic or traditional schooling is that students' mastery of content will transfer to their ability to process diverse information and solve problems of the everyday world. We now know that this assumption is largely false (Bruer, 1993).

Even the most able students find it difficult to make appropriate connections between what they learn in school (the content of biology and government, for example) and understanding the nature of problems and their solutions outside of school (making recommendations about a city's air pollution, for example). These real-world or everyday problems are different from the well-structured, single-solution textbook problems students solve in school (Sternberg, 1985):

Characteristics of Real-world Problems	Characteristics of Classroom Problems
In the everyday world, the first and sometimes most difficult step in problem solving is recognition that a problem exists	The instructor or textbook signals that a problem exists
In everyday problem solving, it is often harder to figure out just what the problem is than to figure out how to solve it	The instructor or textbook provides the problem
Everyday problems tend to be ill-structured	The instructor or textbook defines the problem
In everyday problem solving, it is not usually clear just what information will be needed to solve a given problem, nor is it always clear where the information can be found	Needed information to solve classroom or text-based problems is found in the associated chapter or lecture; often parallel problems (examples) are solved for the student
The solutions to everyday problems depend on and interact with the contexts in which the problems occur	Classroom or text-based problems are self-contained; little or no context is provided
Everyday problems generally have no one right solution, and even the criteria for what constitutes a best solution are often not clear	Classroom or textbook-based problems have one right solution; textbook solutions are found in the back of the book
Solutions to important everyday problems have consequences that matter	Solutions to classroom or textbook-based problems have no consequences other than a grade or school advancement
Everyday problem solving often occurs in groups	Classroom or textbook-based problem solving often occurs alone
Everyday problems can be complicated, messy, and stubbornly persistent	Classroom or textbook-based problems are clear, well-defined, and easily forgotten

Digital Learning Environment

A new paradigm, consistent with emerging models of Web-based instruction, is required to change the focus from content-centered to problem-centered learning. This paradigm – the Digital Learning Environment (DLE) – incorporates the following features:

- a learner-centered and problem-based (rather than content-centered) instructional support system, in which learning is based upon analysis of a series of complex, real-world issues rather than upon memorization of facts and principles (Brown, Collins & Duguid, 1989; Duffy & Jonassen, 1992)

- safe settings for learning, in which making mistakes becomes as powerful a learning tool as employing successful problem-solving strategies in real-world contexts (Schank, 1994)
- a blurring of instructor and student roles, such that instructors model and demonstrate learning in problem-based settings, while students facilitate and manage their own learning environments (Duffy & Cunningham, 1996)
- access to an integrated package of navigational, productivity, communication, collaboration, and knowledge/ wisdom creation tools (Edelson, Pea & Gomez, 1996; Harasim, Hiltz, Teles & Turoff, 1995; Soloway, Guzdial and Hay, 1994)
- management tools that facilitate the development of student goals and activities as a collaboration between students and instructors, of which key components are alternative and traditional assessment practices (Farr & Tone, 1994; Reeves & Okey, 1996)
- independence of any particular hardware or delivery system configuration (Siegel & Sousa, 1994)
- an open, ever-changing, and ever-expanding information architecture, which has access to a global information network like the Internet (or the school's Intranet), in contrast to a closed information architecture (e.g., book, diskette, video disk, or a CD-ROM), which is finite and frozen in time (Siegel & Sousa, 1994)

Taken together, these features are designed to facilitate big concept, multi-disciplinary learning, and the development of authentic, cooperative problem-solving strategies. Learning how to learn in a domain is as important as accumulating facts and decontextualized information (Oshima, Bereiter & Scardamalia, 1995; Riel, 1994). Moreover, direct training and collaboration embedded in tools that foster self-awareness and the development of a community of learners promote changes in instructor and student behavior. Each person – instructor and student – becomes a coach and a learner.

TimeWeb™

At Indiana University's Center for Excellence in Education <http://cee.indiana.edu>, we are creating new Web tools (we call them Wisdom Tools™) to facilitate the goals of the Digital Learning Environment. Our first effort – the TimeWeb™ tool – was designed to be a computer imaginative Web tool, exploiting the strengths of the Web-based environment for instruction. In creating this tool, we considered whether it would be possible to portray, and more importantly, to construct information so that it contributes to deeper student insight and understanding of the content. How could we exploit the strengths of the Web medium to move beyond the "point and click" model of the browser or the hierarchical structure of bookmarks?

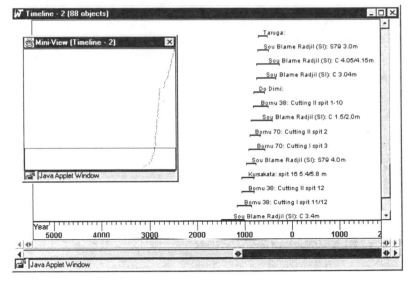

Figure 1

TimeWeb™ allows users:

- to query complex relational databases and display the search results chronologically;
- to shift the time scale, quickly zooming in and out of time; and

- to examine data from several perspectives and resolutions, which are called *forest*, *tree*, and *leaf.*

The first use of TimeWeb™ involves a project funded by the National Endowment for the Humanities (NEH). The project, called "Prehistoric Puzzles", is a collaborative effort of Professor Jeanne Sept from the Department of Anthropology at Indiana University and the Wisdom Tools Group. TimeWeb™ accesses a Sybase relational database containing about 2,000 African prehistory sites and tens of thousands of artifacts and site-specific data (location, climate, dating methods, excavation date, and so on). Students choose selection criteria for each query from a menu of variables. For example, a student can create a query that will display sites with Carbon-14 dates from Western and Central Africa that contain ceramics, microlithic stone tools, iron tools, or domestic animals.

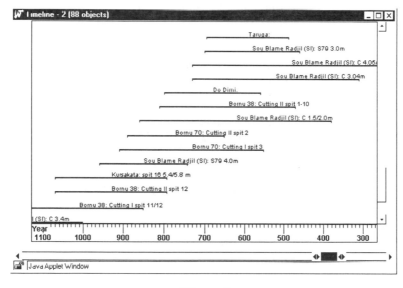

Figure 2

Figure 1 shows the results of such a query. It spans a 7,000-year timeline. The mini view window shows the "forest" view (the overall shape and density of the archaeological site data), and the larger window shows a "tree" view (archaeological site labels and time duration bars). In Figure 2, we see the same data displayed over an 800-year timeline. The student shortened the slider bar, causing the time scale to "open up," dynamically changing from thousands to hundreds of years. The display dynamically changes as well, "stretching" site duration bars over the new time scale. The student now can view the duration for each of the archaeological sites clearly, and can see that, in fact, the sites did not exist at the same time.

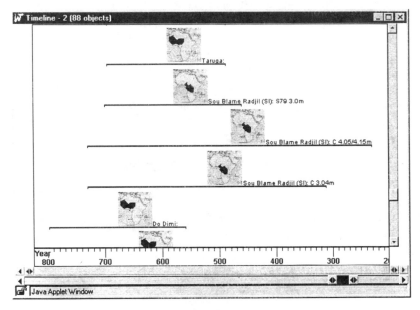

Figure 3

Finally, in Figure 3, the student switches to a "leaf" view (labels, duration bars, and icons). Clicking on a site icon provides access to detailed data, opening a small window containing an index of data associated with that site. Students can select categories of data from this list to produce a custom Web page "on demand" which contains links to detailed information about their chosen site (including text descriptions, maps, pictures, and URL links). The TimeWeb™ visualization tool leads students to a deeper understanding of the content and methods of the archaeologist.

Applications to language education

How might such a tool be used in language education? Imagine a cultural, geographical, and historical timeline of the world, entirely created by students from every nation, written in the native language of each student. Instead of viewing information in the usual hypermedia format, the same information could be plotted on TimeWeb's two-dimensional grid. Categories such as history, politics, literature, theater; religion, philosophy, visual arts, music, science, technology, and daily life are plotted on the vertical-axis and time (in centuries, decades, years, months, etc.) is plotted on the horizontal-axis. Not only could students navigate through this timeline, comparing information found in one category with another, but they could construct their own timelines as well (cultural histories of their own city or town, descriptions of their local geography, etc). Web sites, individual pages, local files, graphics, animations, and sounds would be represented as icons on the two-dimensional time grid; clicking on an icon would take the student directly to that information. By manipulating the time scale and viewing time from varied resolutions (say, zooming into days or moving out to millennia), students would gain additional insights by noting changing patterns and relationships. Students from a school in one country could link with a school from another, agreeing to create parallel cultural histories of their respective regions. Such a problem-based, world-wide activity would provide the motivation and encouragement to study another people's language and culture. The often-cited "global village" concept would become real for these students.

WorldBoard™

James Spohrer, Distinguished Scientist at Apple Computer's Learning Communities Group, and the Wisdom Tools Group at Indiana University are investigating "next generation" Internet applications. Spohrer calls the concept "WorldBoard", a proposed planetary augmented reality system that facilitates innovative ways of associating information with places. "Short-term the goal is to allow users to post messages on any of the six faces of every cubic meter (a hundred billion billion cubic meters) of space humans might go on this planet (see personal web pages when you look at someone's office door; label interesting plants and rocks on nature trails). Long-term WorldBoard allows users to experience any information in any place, co-registered with reality." (Spohrer, 1997)

How would such a system be created?

- Imagine wearing special eyewear (or goggles) that allow you to see computer-generated images floating in front of you. Such eyewear exists today, the most common use existing with high-end video games.

- Now imagine that the generated images seen through your eyewear come from computer servers in a wireless environment. Today's game eyewear are connected to the computer by cable, but it's not too difficult to imagine these same images being transmitted via local wireless servers.

- Today, all Web-based information is associated with an address, specifying the exact location where that information can be found. For example, the address, <http://www.wisdomtools.com> is really equivalent to a numerical address made up of domains and subdomains that identifies a server located within the Center for Excellence in Education at Indiana University in Bloomington, Indiana. The specific information is found on a file directory on this computer server. Once found, the information is transmitted to any computer on the planet linked via the Internet. That is the magic of the Internet!

- But now imagine that many addresses also contain precise readings of latitude, longitude, and altitude. This would pinpoint the location of the information. The information – text, graphic, sound, video, animation, etc – would continue to reside on the server, but the positioning information would tell some detection device that you only view the information at a certain position on the planet. If the wireless eyewear can read its latitude, longitude, and altitude, then it can inquire of the local server, "do you have any information for me at this location?" If the answer is "yes," then the information is displayed through the eyewear. The eyewear's "context sense" and head/eye tracking capabilities allow information to appear fixed and co-registered with reality. This is how a virtual post-it note is seen floating next to a specified object. The note (or really the text, graphic, sound, video, animation, etc) co-exists with the real object. It augments the real object's reality.

- Now suppose that many information objects are located at the same location. This would create a bit of clutter – information pollution! To address this problem, imagine that information resides on channels. For example, ecological information may reside on the eco channel, whereas historic land markers may reside on the tourism channel. By "tuning in" to a different channel you can experience different kinds of information.

- As electronic miniaturization advances, bulky video game-like goggles will give way to normal eyewear. But this will not be the only way to receive geographically based information. The input may be audio through an earpiece or images and sound on a hand-held device (like an Apple Newton).

- Until now, we have described humans moving toward information found at a given location and co-registered with reality. It is also possible for information to follow objects. For example, the person might be the object that is being tracked (via geo-positioning satellites orbiting the Earth). In this way, it will be possible for people to wear their Web pages or people can keep track of their pets.

Within the next decade, we will view the mid-1990s as the start of a World Wide Web that was viewed through workstations. By 2005, reality will become our web! Virtual reality and actual reality will be merged in unique and innovative ways. To provide a simple example, it should be possible for a student to walk through a real forest, point to a tree and "post" a virtual note on the tree asking for information about it. A future hiker through the same forest, wearing special eyewear (similar in size and weight to normal glasses), will see the virtual note, respond to it, and her response will be automatically v-mailed (video mailed) to the first person.

In another example, imagine a group of students in a farm field near a river wearing their virtual eyewear. Standing with them in virtual space is an environmental specialist (who is really 500 miles away at the university). Working with the expert, the students plan various possible landscapes to reclaim the land and attract different animals. Through realistic animations, the students watch the plants and animals at various stages of development over the next 20 years and physically walk through the virtual landscape looking at real objects such as the river and associated virtual objects. After trying out several different experiments, the students select the best landscape and embark on a yearlong project to plant the field and provide shelter for the wildlife they want to attract.

Applications to language education

While this above activity would occur traditionally in a science course, the power of WorldBoard is that the entire experience could be conducted in a different language. If all signs are virtual labels, then the labels could appear theoretically in any language. Language instruction, therefore, transforms into a natural and contextualized learning environment.

Conclusion

Such computing will impact every aspect of how we learn and how we communicate. For the development of distributed language education, we will need to focus less on the latest Web wizardry and more on how the new tools impact our ability to think and learn. In the end, creating the Digital Learning Environment will be a human rather than technological challenge.

> We all live on the great, dynamic web of change. It links us to one another and, in some ways, to everything in the past. And in the way that each of us influences the course of events, it also links us to the future we are all busy making, every second... Each one of us has an effect, somewhere, somewhen.

>   – James Burke

References

Brown, J. S., Collins, A. & Duguid, P. 1989. Situated cognition and the culture of learning. *Educational Researcher.* 18(1), 32-41.

Bruer, John T. 1993. *Schools for thought: A science of learning in the classroom.* Cambridge, MA: The MIT Press.

Burke, James. 1997. *The Pinball Effect: How Renaissance water gardens made the carburetor possible and other journeys through knowledge.* New York: Little Brown & Co.

Duffy, T. M. & Cunningham, D. J. 1996. Constructivism: Implications for the design and delivery of instruction. *Handbook of research on educational communications and technology.* ed. by Jonassen, D. H. New York: Scholastic.

Duffy, T. M. & Jonassen, D. H. (eds.) 1992. *Constructivism and the technology of instruction: a conversation.* Hillsdale, NJ: Lawrence Erlbaum Associates.

Edelson, D. C., Pea, R. D. & Gomez, L. M. 1996. Constructivism in the Collaboratory. *Constructivist learning environments: Case studies in instructional design.* ed. by Wilson, B. G. Englewood Cliffs, NJ: Educational Technology Publications.

Farr, R. & Tone, B. 1994. *Portfolio and performance assessment: Helping students evaluate their progress as readers and writers.* Fort Worth, TX: Harcourt Brace College Publishers.

Harasim, L., Hiltz, S. R., Teles, L. & Turoff, M. 1995. *Learning networks: A field guide to teaching and learning online.* Cambridge, MA: MIT Press.

Oshima, J., Bereiter, C. & Scardamalia, M. 1995. Information-access characteristics for high conceptual progress in a computer-networked learning environment. *Proceedings of CSCL '95: The first international conference on computer support for collaborative learning.* ed. by Schnase, J. L. & Cunnis, E. L. (pp 259-267). Mahwah, NJ: Lawrence Erlbaum Associates.

Reeves, T. C. & Okey, J. R. 1996. Alternative assessment for constructivist learning environments. *Constructivist learning environments: Case studies in instructional design.* ed. by Wilson, B. G. Englewood Cliffs, NJ: Educational Technology Publications.

Riel, M. 1994. Educational change in a technology-rich environment. *Journal of Research on Computing.* 26(4), 452-474.

Schank, R. C. 1994. Why hitchhikers on the Information Highway are going to have to wait a long time for a ride. *The Aspen Institute Quarterly.* 6(2), 28-58.

Siegel, M. A. & Sousa, G. A. 1994. Inventing the virtual textbook: Changing the nature of schooling. *Educational Technology.* 34(7), 49-54.

Soloway, E., Guzdial, M. & Hay, K. 1994. Learner-centered design: The challenge for HCI in the 21st century. *Interactions.* 1(2), 36-48.

Spohrer, J. 1997. "WorldBoard" [Internet site]. http://trp.research. apple.com/events/ISITalk062097/Parts/WorldBoard/default.html

Sternberg, R. J. 1985. Teaching critical thinking, part 1: Are we making critical mistakes? *Phi Delta Kappa.* 67. 194-198.

LIST OF CONTRIBUTORS

David Crabbe
School of Linguistics and
Applied Language Studies
Victoria University of
Wellington
P.O. Box 600,
Wellington
New Zealand

Nobuyuki Honna
Aoyama Gakuin University
1-9-3 Honda
Kokubunji-shi
Tokyo 185
Japan

Donald Freeman
School for International Training
PO Box 676
Brattleboro, Vermont 05302
United States of America

Florence G. Kayad
Lecturer
ESL
Universiti Malaysia Sarawak
390 Lorong 35 Taman BDC
Kuching, Sarawak
Malaysia

S. Gopinathan
School of Education
NTU/NIE
469 Bukit Timah Road
Singapore 259756

Michael John Levy
Centre for Language Teaching &
Research
University of Queensland
Brisbane, Queensland 4072
Australia

Asim Gunarwan
DLSU
c.o. Sekretariat Negara
Gedung Utama, Lantai 2
Jalan Veteran 17
Jakarta 10110
Indonesia

John Joseph Moran
No 7 Simpang 589
Kampong Lambak 'A'
Jalan Pasir Berakas
Berakas
Brunei Darussalam

H. Joan Morley
English Language Institute
University of Michigan
Ann Arbor, Michigan 48109
United States of America

Andrea Peñaflorida
Director
Centre for Language Learning
De La Salle University
2401 Taft Avenue
Manila
Philippines

Chaleosri Pibulchol
Head
Linguistics Department
Faculty of Humanities
Srinakharinwirot University
Sukhumvit 23
Bangkok 10110
Thailand

N. S. Prabhu
302 Sovereign Park
56 K.R. Road, Basavanagudi
Bangalore 560 004
India

Martin A. Siegel
Center for Excellence in
Education
Indiana University
501 N Morton, Suite 224
Bloomington, Indiana 417404
United States of America

Merrill Swain
Modern Language Centre
Ontario Institute for Studies in
Education
252 Bloor Street West
Toronto, Ontario M55 IV6
Canada

Jenny A. Thomas
Linguistics Dept.
School of English & Linguistics
University of Wales
Bangor
Gwynedd
LL57 2DG
United Kingdom

Geoffrey Williams
Dept of English (A20)
University of Sydney
2006
Australia